D0105689

ROME

HAS SPOKEN

T34

ROME
HAS SPOKEN

**A Guide to Forgotten Papal Statements,
and How They Have Changed Through the Centuries**

Maureen Fiedler and Linda Rabben, Editors

SHANAHAN LIBRARY
MARYMOUNT MANHATTAN COLLEGE
221 EAST 71 STREET
NEW YORK, NY 10021

A *Crossroad Book*
The Crossroad Publishing Company
New York

OCLC# 39256298

BX
1747.5
·R66
1998

The Crossroad Publishing Company
370 Lexington Avenue, New York, NY 10017

Copyright © 1998 by The Quixote Center/Catholics Speak Out

All rights reserved. No part of this book may be reproduced, stored in a retrieval system, or transmitted, in any form or by any means, electronic, mechanical, photocopying, recording, or otherwise, without the written permission of The Crossroad Publishing Company.

Printed in the United States of America

Library of Congress Cataloging-in-Publication Data

Rome has spoken : a guide to forgotten papal statements, and how they
   have changed through the centuries / Maureen Fiedler and Linda
   Rabben, editors.
      p.   cm.
   ISBN 0-8245-1774-1 (pbk.)
   1. Catholic Church – Doctrines – Papal documents. 2. Catholic
Church – Doctrines – History. 3. Church and social problems – Catholic
Church – Papal doctrines.   I. Fiedler, Maureen. II. Rabben, Linda,
1947- .
BX1747.5.R66 1998
262.9'1 – dc21   98-19447

2   3   4   5   6   7   8   9   10   02   01   00   99

*To all those
who speak out,
act from conscience,
and struggle for justice*

CONTENTS

ACKNOWLEDGMENTS

Many people helped create this book. It started when our good friend, Charles N. Davis, whom we know as "Charlie," shared a new inspiration with us at a board meeting of Catholics Speak Out.* "Why not put together a small booklet," he suggested one evening, "showing how the church changed its mind over time? Change is not a wild idea; it's church history." He predicted it would be a slim volume, not much work, just quotations, a handy pocket guide on a few key issues. So much for predictions!

Once we began collecting quotations, Charlie's "small project" expanded into an eighteen-month endeavor that has been both fascinating and enlightening. The issues grew to eighteen, the quotations multiplied into the hundreds, and seventeen scholars joined us in the project to give it context, meaning, and depth.

The rest of the board of Catholics Speak Out (Bill Callahan, Maureen Connors, Bill D'Antonio, Dolly Pomerleau, Audrey Smith Rogers, Fred Ruof, and, more recently, Anna Aldave and Bridget Mary Meehan) encouraged us often with new ideas and friendly critique. Dolly played the special role for which she is famous at the Quixote Center, persistently questioning the project itself, calling us to answer hard questions and sharpen our focus.

Finding the quotations for this book would have been impossible without the knowledgeable and friendly assistance of R. Bruce Miller, coordinator of the Religious Studies, Philosophy, and Humanities Library at Catholic University of America. He guided coeditor Linda Rabben to many a long-buried tome, some apparently untouched for decades. Professor Dean Hoge of Catholic University kindly facilitated her entrée to the library.

As we began collecting quotations on various topics, we realized that changes in papal attitudes, and the reasons for them, would not be obvious to the average reader without guidance from an expert in each field. Thus, we owe special thanks to our commentators, who perused our quotations, sometimes made suggestions for additions or deletions, and wrote the essays that show how the official church found ways to change centuries-old positions.

Special thanks also go to the North American General Leadership of the Institute of the Blessed Virgin Mary, headquartered in Toronto, Canada, as

---

*Catholics Speak Out encourages Catholics to take adult responsibility for the life of the church. It is a project of the Quixote Center, an international justice and peace center (see below p. 237).

well as other institutional and individual members of Catholics Speak Out who supported the research. To Michael Leach of the Crossroad Publishing Company go our special thanks for encouraging the project and for suggesting names of commentators.

Finally, the entire staff of the Quixote Center deserves our appreciation for their encouragement and long suffering. They listened to our laments over an ever-expanding workload, worried with us about funding, rejoiced with us as we added highly qualified commentators and celebrated the final product. Thanks to Tony Banout, Bill Callahan, Jane Henderson, Ellen Lynch, Dolly Pomerleau, Walter Winfield, Betty Moyler, Joe Dearborn, Mark Buckley, and Joe Byrne. Special gratitude goes to Mark Buckley for help with some translations from Latin.

This book would still be an "impossible dream" if it weren't for these great folks, in the finest Quixote tradition, who helped us make it a reality.

MAUREEN FIEDLER AND LINDA RABBEN, *Editors*

INCLUSIVE LANGUAGE

We believe that contemporary use of the English language should be inclusive — that is, not sexist, racist, homophobic, or demeaning to people in any way. Consequently, we have striven to ensure that all the parts of this book written and edited by contemporary authors are fully inclusive and offensive to no one.

We are especially conscious of gender-inclusive terminology. "Men" today means males; it is not generic. The same is true with God language. All language about God is imagery, and no image can presume to limit God to one gender, lest we engage in linguistic idolatry. God is not only Father, but Mother, Friend, Spirit, Creator, and so forth.

Even ancient texts such as the Bible, used in our own time, need to be translated into inclusive language to be accessible to contemporary women and men. In fact, Priests for Equality, one of the projects of the Quixote Center, translates and publishes the Scriptures in inclusive language. Their work on the *Inclusive New Testament* and the *Inclusive Psalms* has been highly acclaimed.

The language in the historical quotations from popes, councils, and church fathers is sometimes shocking, and initially we struggled with it. Many of them use language that not only is male and patriarchal, but often demeans other groups of people.

We decided, however, to preserve the original language, since the quotations are not for contemporary devotion or inspiration, as are the Scriptures, but for historical documentation. The original language shows the thinking of church leadership in a given age, and that is what it *must* show for the purposes of this book.

Consequently, with the exception of the documents of Vatican II (which have already been translated using inclusive language), we have left the words of popes and councils as they wrote them. For most Scripture passages, we have used the translations by Priests for Equality. But in the chapter "Women in the Church," we had to quote older translations of Scriptures, as well as other documents that helped mold and justify sexist thinking and practice for centuries. In that chapter, we offer the translations of Priests for Equality in an editors' note, so readers may compare the older versions to new translations that are valid and inclusive.

MAUREEN FIEDLER AND LINDA RABBEN, *Editors*

ROME
HAS SPOKEN

INTRODUCTION

When I'm on the road or the radio discussing church positions on contraception, the ordination of women, or clerical celibacy, someone inevitably admonishes me, "How can you talk about change? Rome has spoken on the issue, and the teaching is God's law. Catholics should be obedient and accept it." The implication? Change is impossible. Keep your mouth shut. Dialogue is next to heresy. The case is closed — for all time.

Church conservatives aren't the only ones who think teachings are etched in stone. I've met many Catholics, brought up on Vatican II theology, who won't participate in church reform efforts because, they say, "What's the use? The church will never change anyway. Why should I waste my time?" The implication? If change hasn't occurred after a decade or so of trying, it probably won't happen.

The Current Climate in the Church

These attitudes have been reinforced during the papacy of John Paul II. Prominent theologians and others who have developed new ideas or advocated dialogue on contentious issues have sometimes felt the heavy hand of sanctions, ranging from loss of official status to silencing or even excommunication. Hans Küng, Leonardo Boff, Charles Curran, Tissa Balasuriya of Sri Lanka, William R. Callahan, Sr. Carmel McEnroy, RSM, the nuns who signed the 1984 *New York Times* ad, Sr. Ivone Gebara, members of Call to Action of Nebraska, and countless others have suffered reprisals for challenging "changeless" church teachings. In this climate, archconservative Catholics take their cue from the Vatican, proclaiming papal utterances as gospel truth. They often interpret papal statements as the sole measure of orthodoxy and use them to attack those who raise questions about the pope's position on any issue. They promote a kind of "creeping infallibility" that covers topics well beyond official dogma.

Other Catholics, who disagree with papal statements on birth control, the role of women, or gay/lesbian relationships, often feel alienated or baffled by absolutist positions. They see themselves as adults with the right to exercise good conscience. They are confused about the importance and weight they should give to papal statements. Often they have little knowledge of the history of papal pronouncements or the evolution of Catholic dogma. They want change but often think it impossible. Many move to the margins of church life, lose interest, or leave the church altogether.

The Reason for This Book

All of these attitudes deny history; they are the reason for this book. Roman Catholicism may change slowly, but it has changed and it *does* change. Church teachings, policies, pastoral practices, and structures have evolved, and *even turned around completely,* in the past two thousand years.

Those who witnessed the Second Vatican Council remember monumental changes in liturgy, ecumenical dialogue, and teaching on religious freedom, to name only three issues. But younger Catholics have no memory of that experience. And even the Vatican II generation may forget that change is a fact of church life and history, especially when it doesn't happen as quickly as it did in the 1960s.

Many of us can rattle off a laundry list of issues where we know that the church changed dramatically: usury, slavery, anti-Semitism. But many issues are not on that popular list. Few people know, for instance, that some popes in the first millennium favored the election of bishops and a married clergy. Or that church teaching once permitted remarriage after divorce in certain circumstances.

Not all change, of course, has been progressive or unidirectional. Church officials marginalized women after the first three centuries of Christianity. Celibate priests replaced the traditional married clergy. Teachings on theological dissent ebbed and flowed over the centuries.

But the point here is not that all ecclesial change is moving us closer to a progressive nirvana. It is simply this: change has taken place — good, bad, or indifferent. Those who claim change is impossible need to reacquaint themselves with church history.

Finding information on such changes is not easy. Much of it is buried in dusty tomes in research libraries. In this book we seek to remedy that situation by providing a ready reference to eighteen major issues where change has been significant. For the first time, one volume presents evidence that change, even when it is called "continuity," has been a hallmark of the Roman Catholic Church during two millennia. This book shows that Rome may have spoken, but the case is not closed.

The Ever Changing Church

Popes and councils have shown a surprising flexibility on teachings and policies of great significance. Popes have changed their minds, reversed their predecessors' positions, or quietly buried or blurred old views that had become irrelevant or embarrassing. Church institutions and practices have altered subtly — or, in some cases, not so subtly — under the influence of structures and values of the world of which the church has been part: the

Roman Empire, the monarchies of Europe, the capitalist economic system, the institutions of patriarchy.

But change is not always easy to spot. Patterns vary. They do not always move in a straight line from liberal to conservative or conservative to liberal. Sometimes change comes in waves. At other times the Vatican recognizes "special circumstances." Sometimes change is unacknowledged or silent.

When change does take place, the Vatican rarely trumpets the fact because of its deep concern about the appearance of continuity. Church officials often claim that a new position is the one that has held sway for centuries.

The Importance of Papal and Conciliar Positions

"How many legions does the pope have?" Stalin once asked, suggesting that any leader who has only the power of statements and moral suasion cannot have much impact on the world.

Stalin was naïve. Papal and conciliar teachings and policies have had enormous influence throughout history. For many inside and outside the church, the institution of the papacy is a worldwide symbol of rectitude, morality, and guidance. For others, it is a stumbling block, a bulwark against progress or even an enemy. But for almost no one is it unimportant. When the pope travels, cameras follow. When the pope speaks, the media reports it and the world listens. And since the pope has a huge constituency, powerful political allies, and influence, the world often heeds him.

The significance of papal pronouncements becomes clear when we imagine what the world might have been like if the Vatican had taken different positions. Imagine the history of the Jews in Europe, had popes unequivocally condemned anti-Semitism from the beginning. Might different teaching have deprived Hitler of the support that permitted the Holocaust to happen? Imagine how different the history of the Western Hemisphere might have been, and how the lives of millions of people might have been spared, if popes had condemned slavery unequivocally before the nineteenth century. Imagine what the church would be like if we still elected bishops, or had married clergy, as Catholics did in the first millennium.

When the Vatican takes a position on an issue, it signals its adherents about right and wrong, good directions and bad. In opening the doors to ecumenical dialogue, for example, Vatican II released energy and goodwill in millions of people who yearn for Christian unity. When the Vatican condemned nuclear war, it may not have eliminated the bomb, but it led many Catholics and others to challenge the morality of nuclear deterrence. On the other hand, in refusing to ordain women, the Vatican lends support to every other form of gender discrimination in the world.

John Paul II has reinforced the significance of papal statements by putting his unmistakable imprint on the history of the late twentieth century, inside and outside the church. His political statements and actions in eastern Europe clearly assisted the downfall of communism. His stand on the dignity of human life, especially his strong opposition to the death penalty, raised awareness worldwide. But his relations with Latin America muted much of liberation theology and his statements and actions in countries like Nicaragua denied high-level church support to movements of the poor in Central America in the 1980s. He attempted to move the church's "option for the poor" toward works of charity and away from ministries that challenge unjust political and economic structures.

Within the church, his doctrinal orthodoxy and repression of dissent have threatened free theological development. His centralization of church authority has undermined the collegial policies envisioned by Vatican II. But his openings to the Jewish community have greatly improved interfaith relations, and his reversal of Galileo's condemnation has revealed a church capable of admitting error, albeit hundreds of years after the fact.

Theological Significance of the Topics

The topics covered in this book are at various levels of theological significance. Some deal with solemn magisterial teachings such as infallibility, religious freedom, and (some would say) the ordination of women. Others focus on significant moral teachings that are part of the ordinary magisterium, such as those on contraception, slavery, relations with the Jewish people, usury, divorce and remarriage, war and peace. Still others deal with fundamental issues that underlie moral teaching, such as the role of conscience and attitudes toward sexual intimacy and pleasure.

Changes in scriptural interpretation are especially important because Scripture is a major source of revelation. The changing approach to Scripture played an important role in shifting other positions, such as those on evolution, Copernican theory, and the case of Galileo.

Several topics deal with *both* solemn church teachings *and* policies for handling dissent and disagreement: ecumenism, religious freedom, primacy of conscience, theological dissent, the relation of the church to the natural and physical sciences (evolution and Copernican theory).

Other chapters deal with matters of church policy, structure, or discipline: democracy in the church, the election of bishops, a married clergy, and the status of women in the church.

Structuring the Topics

Each chapter focuses on one issue. After a brief introduction, a series of quotations provides documentation for changes in teaching, policy, structure, or practice that span church history. We have tried to select key quotations that highlight the most significant official attitudes of an age. We begin with Scripture when it is relevant. In a few cases, we quote church fathers whose views have influenced official institutional opinion. When necessary for understanding a quotation, we include a few lines to explain its historical context. When quotations are relevant to more than one topic, they are cited in more than one chapter.

Following the quotations in each chapter is an essay by a commentator well versed in that field. The commentaries explain key changes over time.

Finally, each chapter concludes with discussion questions, so that readers may initiate dialogue or discussion on the topic.

The Topics

We deal with eighteen topics in a loosely thematic order. These do not exhaust the theological and moral issues that can be analyzed for historical change. We simply raise some of the issues most often discussed in the contemporary church.

In the first chapter, Robert McClory traces the history of infallibility. Christians in early centuries understood infallibility to mean that the community of faith was protected from error in the broad sense over time. It was not until 1870 that the First Vatican Council applied it to the pope as a single individual and proclaimed it as a formal dogma.

In chapter 2, the quotations trace the church's wavering attitude toward claims of individual conscience, when those claims are not in line with the teaching of the magisterium. Commentator Sheila Briggs traces the concept of conscience from its Greco-Roman roots. She shows how official church positions after the Reformation moved from confining conscience within the limits of the magisterium to embracing a true liberty of conscience in the teachings of Vatican II. Pope John Paul II, on the other hand, has reemphasized the role of the magisterium as morally binding for all believers.

In her commentary on scriptural interpretation, Alice Laffey shows how the church has always "interpreted" Scripture, albeit in various ways. She emphasizes that the post-Tridentine church made the Scriptures inaccessible to the faithful for several centuries, until the time of the Second Vatican Council. During the same period, the church moved from a fundamentalist approach (taking the Scriptures literally) to acceptance of critical and historical methodologies in the twentieth century.

The fourth chapter, on religious freedom, documents the sharp change in teaching that occurred in the twentieth century, when popes finally dropped their traditional demands for church-state unity. Vatican II's declaration of religious freedom forbids the state to coerce people into accepting any faith. Charles Curran recounts this remarkable shift.

In chapter 5, the statements demonstrate the church's shift from hostility to dialogue in its relations with other Christian denominations. George Tavard, an ecumenist since before the Second Vatican Council, believes that a genuine movement of the Spirit led to the church's new openness to Orthodox and Protestant Christians. He welcomes the church's new ecumenism but laments the lack of substantive progress toward unity.

The quotations in chapter 6 recount centuries of anti-Semitic attitudes in official church pronouncements. Only in recent times, in the long shadow of the Holocaust, has the church recognized its sin, apologized, and condemned anti-Semitism. Writing from the University of Haifa in Israel, Kenneth Stow explains changes in papal attitudes throughout history and recognizes the significant change that John Paul II has fostered. He suggests, however, that much theological work remains to be done.

The quotations about slavery recount the sordid history of the church's support for this inhuman institution. Diana Hayes discusses the history of slavery and the church's long attempts to justify it under "natural law." The church's position shifted from support to condemnation in the late nineteenth century, only after slavery was legally abolished almost everywhere.

In chapter 8, the quotations show how the early church, which valued broad participation, evolved into an imperial structure in which power still operates from the top down. Commentator Rosemary Radford Ruether argues that democracy is in the church's early tradition and that deification of monarchical structures amounts to idolatry.

The quotations on theological dissent show an ebb and flow in official attitudes over the ages. The church shifted from using the secular arm to imprison, torture, or execute dissenters, to using psychological and ecclesial sanctions to stifle internal disagreement. Richard McCormick, SJ, shows how the church treated dissenters differently at different times, depending on the church's self-definition, the educational status of clergy and laity, the church's mode of exercising authority, interreligious contact and conflict, and church-state relations.

In chapter 10, on women in the church, the quotations reveal ambiguities in the New Testament letters of Paul as well as the misogyny of church fathers and many popes. Women in priestly roles gradually gave way to male dominance with a few exceptions, such as the abbesses of the Middle Ages. In my commentary, I discuss how sharp changes in an antifemale direction occurred in early centuries. Glacially slow changes in our own time may signal an eventual return to the early tradition of gender equality.

The statements on married clergy document church policies that permitted a married clergy until the second millennium; we also provide lists of popes who were married, the sons of popes, or noncelibate. Anthony Padovano explains how attitudes toward women, sexuality, and inheritance of church property led the hierarchy to impose mandatory celibacy on priests. He argues that recent developments presage a return to the practice of earlier times.

Chapter 12 documents the church's long history of negative attitudes toward sexuality. These attitudes have begun to change only in recent times.

Christine Gudorf shows how changes in economic structures and the role of women in the family affected Catholic practice and church teachings.

In chapter 13, the quotations show that early teaching on contraception was influenced heavily by ancient beliefs about sorcery and potions, negative views of sexuality and pleasure, and a strong desire to procreate the human race. Even the "rhythm" method (abstinence during fertile periods) of birth control was condemned. In her commentary, Maggie Hume shows that historical developments and positive modern views of sexuality influenced the church to permit "rhythm," to change its rationale for prohibiting artificial means of contraception, and even to consider reversing the prohibition itself in the 1960s.

The quotations on divorce and remarriage in chapter 14 document a change from moderate permissiveness to absolutist assertions about the indissolubility of marriage. Charles N. Davis argues that the church's imposition of mandatory celibacy on the clergy, which deprived them of the experience of marriage, influenced the development of church laws that made remarriage all but impossible. He suggests that the earlier tradition may be reviving.

In the chapter on Copernican theory and Galileo, the quotations focus on the life and work of Galileo, who embodied the church's struggle with the natural sciences. James Orgren recounts the tragic story of how Galileo's sun-centered theory of the universe led the church to condemn him for heresy in the seventeenth century. The Vatican reversed this judgment only in our own time. Orgren shows how stifling open discussion retarded scientific and technological development in Catholic Europe, and he suggests parallels between this issue and others in the church today.

The quotations in chapter 16 show how the church has moved from condemning Darwinian theory in the nineteenth century to accepting it in the late twentieth century. John Haught believes that theology would be enriched if more theologians incorporated insights from the natural sciences into their writing.

The quotations on war and peace show that the early pacifist church changed after the Edict of Milan (313) and accepted the theory of "just war," which led to the Crusades on one hand and produced efforts to limit conflict on the other. In recent times, Vatican II condemned nuclear war, and many bishops have questioned the morality of nuclear deterrence. William Slavick discusses the ongoing tensions that continue between those who espouse the church's early nonviolent ethic and those who accept just-war theories.

In chapter 18, the quotations show how the church at first condemned usury unequivocally, then found "exceptions" to the rule, and finally did a silent reversal on the entire subject. Commentator Amata Miller, IHM, recounts how the church changed its views on usury in response to changing economic realities, began to borrow and lend at interest, and finally required that church administrators practice responsible stewardship by investing church funds at interest.

The afterword by coeditor Linda Rabben describes her search for the quotations among hundreds of sources and explains what this project taught her about the Catholic Church's history — and her own.

In each chapter, the commentator is responsible only for her or his essay. The coeditors take full responsibility for the accuracy of the introductions, quotations, and discussion questions. Sources of the quotations, as well as a complete bibliography, are at the back of the book.

Conclusion

Change is a sign of life. Inertia is the mark of fossils. We have documented profound changes here, and many developments indicate that more are in the offing. Fifty years from now, people may well look back on the debates of today and wonder what all the fuss was about. That's hopeful.

This venerable institution called the Roman Catholic Church, now almost two thousand years old, is still alive and growing.

MAUREEN FIEDLER, SL
April 1998

Chapter 1

INFALLIBILITY

In the first millennium, the church understood infallibility in a broad, communal sense — that is, that the Spirit would preserve the community of faith over the long term and bring it into balance when it went astray. With time, as popes strengthened and centralized their authority, they began to assert that they were "without error." This tendency was challenged by the centuries-long conciliar movement, exemplified by the Council of Constance, which decreed that councils were superior to popes. With the continued centralization of papal power, the First Vatican Council defined infallibility as a dogma in 1870. Even now, numerous theologians question the way in which it was declared and how it has been applied. It is likely to remain a hot subject of ecclesial debate.

SCRIPTURE

Matthew 28:18–20:
"Jesus came forward and addressed them in these words:

> All authority has been given me
> > Both in heaven and on earth;
> Go, therefore, and make disciples of all the nations....
> Teach them to carry out
> > Everything I have commanded you.
> And know that I am with you always,
> > Even until the end of the world!"

Matthew 16:17–19:
"Blessed are you, Simon begot of Jonah! No mere mortal has revealed this to you, but my Abba God in heaven. I also tell you this: your name now is 'Rock,' and on bedrock like this I will build my community, and the jaws of death will not prevail against it.

> Here — I'll give you the keys to the reign of heaven:
> > Whatever you declare bound on earth
> > > Will be bound in heaven,
> > And whatever you declare loosed on earth
> > > Will be loosed in heaven."

Luke 22:31–32:

"Simon, Simon! Satan has demanded that you be sifted like wheat. But I've prayed for you, that your faith may not fail. You, in turn, must give strength to your brothers and sisters."

Context: From the thirteenth century on, this text was used to justify papal infallibility.

Galatians 2:11, 14:

"When Peter came to Antioch, however, I opposed him to his face, since he was manifestly in the wrong.... When I saw they weren't respecting the true meaning of the Good News, I said to Peter in front of everyone, 'You're a Jew, yet you live like a gentile and not a Jew. So why do you want to make the gentiles adopt Jewish ways?'"

Context: The New Testament portrays Jesus as promising to be with the church through the Holy Spirit until the end of time. This promise is made to the whole church. Peter is given a special position as strengthener of the body. Yet, as Paul indicates in Galatians, Peter was not regarded as having absolute authority in all matters or an absolute hold on truth.

CHURCH FATHERS

Irenaeus, c. 150:

"All the churches would do well to concur with the church of Rome because of its greater preeminence."

Ambrose, c. 320:

"Where Peter is there is the church."

EARLY CHURCH

Boniface I, c. 420:

"It has never been lawful for what has once been decided by the Apostolic See to be reconsidered."

Editors' Note: This is usually quoted as "Roma locuta est; causa finita est" (Rome has spoken; the case is closed).

Hormisdas, c. 510:

"In Rome the Catholic religion has been preserved intact from the beginning."

Context: Many statements attributed to the church fathers and early popes hold Rome and the papacy in high regard. Unfortunately, it is impossible to determine which statements are authentic, because in the mid-eighth century, forgeries and additions appeared in many early texts in order to enhance Rome's authority. Nor do these affirmations, even if authentic, establish a doctrine of papal infallibility.

Second Council of Constantinople, 553:

The Second Council of Constantinople found the current pope, Vigilius, guilty of heresy and "formally excommunicated from the body of the faithful."

Third Council of Constantinople, 681:

The Third Council of Constantinople ruled that in official declarations, Pope Honorius had "confirmed the impious opinions" of the heretic Sergius and "anathematized" the pope from the church.

Context: Occasionally ecumenical councils chided popes for "false teaching" and even excommunicated several. On none of these occasions did they hesitate to take stern action; nor did they seem to believe that papal teaching was somehow exempt from error.

MEDIEVAL CHURCH

Gregory VII, *Dictatus Papae*, 1074:

"The Roman church has never erred; and according to the testimony of Scripture it never will err."

Decretum, 1140:

- "Where matters of faith are concerned...a general council is greater than a pope."

- "For although the Roman pope has sometimes erred, this does not mean that the Roman church has, which is understood to be not he alone but all the faithful, for the church is the aggregate of the faithful."

- "The first See cannot be judged by anyone except when he is convicted of deviation from the faith."

  Context: The Decretum, *a collection of papal and other authoritative pronouncements compiled by the monk Gratian, is one of the precursors of canon law. Several popes, including Marcellinus (296–304), Vigilius (537–55), Honorius (625–38), and John XXII (1316–34), were accused of heresy.*

Innocent III, c. 1200:

- "The pope is the meeting point between God and man...who can judge all things and be judged by no one."

- "Every cleric must obey the pope, even if he commands what is evil; for no one may judge the pope."

Innocent III, *Etsi Karissimus in Christo,* 1215:

"On behalf of Almighty God, Father, Son and Holy Spirit, and by the authority of SS Peter and Paul his apostles, and by our own authority, acting on the general advice of our brethren, we utterly reject and condemn this settlement [the Magna Carta] and under threat of excommunication we order that the king should not dare to observe it and that the barons and their associates should not require it to be observed: the charter, with all undertakings and guarantees whether confirming it or resulting from it, we declare to be null, and void of all validity for ever. Wherefore, let no man deem it lawful to infringe this document of our annulment and prohibition, or presume to oppose it. If anyone should presume to do so, let him know that he will incur the anger of Almighty God and of SS Peter and Paul his apostles."

Context: King John of England had made himself a vassal of the pope, who thenceforth considered England his fief. This condemnation of the Magna Carta is an example of how medieval popes asserted their absolute authority in profane as well as sacred matters.

Boniface VIII, *Unam Sanctam,* 1302:

"We declare, affirm, and define as a truth necessary for salvation that every human being is subject to the Roman pontiff."

John XXII, *Quia Quorundam,* 1324:

The pope has the right "when he perceives that statutes issued by himself or his predecessors are disadvantageous ... to provide that they no longer be disadvantageous." The theory of irreformability is "pestiferous doctrine ... pernicious audacity."

Context: This theory said that a current pope could not override a predecessor's pronouncements. John XXII condemned it.

Clement VI, c. 1350:

"The pope, as the Vicar of Christ on earth, possesses the same full power of jurisdiction that Christ himself possessed during his human life."

Council of Constance, 1414:

"This synod declares that it has immediate power from Christ, which every state and dignity, even if it be the papal dignity, must obey in what concerns faith, the eradication of schism ... and the reformation of the church."

Context: Confronted with the scandal of three men all claiming to be the one true pope (each with some measure of popular support), the bishops at Constance solemnly proclaimed that an ecumenical council is superior to the pope in matters of faith and governance. Pius II contradicted that declaration forty-six years later.

Pius II, *Execrabilis,* 1460:

"Some imbued with a spirit of rebellion ... suppose they can appeal from the pope, the vicar of Christ ... to a future council.... We condemn appeals of this kind, reject them as erroneous and abominable, and declare them to be of no effect."

MODERN ERA

Pius IX, *Ineffabilis Deus,* 1854:

"The most Blessed Virgin Mary was, from the first moment of her conception ... preserved immune from all stain of original sin.... If anyone shall dare to think ... otherwise than has been defined [here] by us let him know that he certainly has abandoned the divine and Catholic Church."

Context: The proclamation of the Immaculate Conception set a precedent: the pope on his own authority defined a dogma of faith and required acceptance by the universal church.

Pius IX, *Tuas Libenter,* 1863:

"The subjection which must be given to an act of divine faith ... must not be limited to those things which have been defined [by councils or popes] but must also be extended to those things which are handed on by the ordinary magisterium of the church scattered throughout the world."

Context: Some eight years before Vatican I, Pius IX in effect declared that a measure of infallibility extends to all doctrines taught universally and constantly through the centuries.

First Vatican Council, *Pastor Aeternus,* 1870:

"We teach and define ... that the Roman Pontiff, when he speaks *ex cathedra,* that is, when in the exercise of his office as pastor and teacher of all Christians, he defines, by virtue of his supreme apostolic authority, a doctrine of faith or morals to be held by the whole church — is, by reason of the divine assistance promised to him in blessed Peter, possessed of that infallibility with which the Divine Redeemer wished his church to be endowed in defining doctrines of faith and morals; and consequently that such definitions of the Roman Pontiff are irreformable of their own nature, and not by reason of the church's consent."

Context: This is the formal declaration of papal infallibility. The council declared that the pope has "full and supreme jurisdiction of the church in those matters which concern discipline and direction of the church dispersed throughout the world" and based this claim on earlier popes and councils. But the Council of Constance (see above) had said that popes were subject to the councils.

Pius XII, *Munificentissimus Deus*, 1950:

"From the universal consent of the ordinary universal magisterium of the church a certain and firm argument is drawn by which the bodily assumption of the Blessed Virgin Mary into heaven is verified... and therefore to be believed by all the children of the church."

Context: This was the first example of an infallible papal statement made ex cathedra since the 1870 proclamation of the doctrine of papal infallibility.

Second Vatican Council, *Dogmatic Constitution on the Church*, 1964:

- "The faithful... should concur with their bishop's judgment, made in the name of Christ, in matters of faith and morals, and adhere to it with a religious docility of spirit. This religious docility of the will and intellect must be extended in a special way to the authentic teaching authority of the Roman Pontiff, even when he does not speak *ex cathedra....*"

- "Although individual bishops do not enjoy the prerogative of infallibility, they do, however, proclaim infallibly the doctrine of Christ when... they are in agreement that a particular teaching is to be held definitively."

- "Just as, in accordance with the Lord's decree, St. Peter and the other apostles constitute one apostolic college, so in like fashion the Roman Pontiff, Peter's successor, and the bishops, the successors of the apostles, are joined together. Indeed, the collegiate character and structure of the episcopal order is clearly shown by the very ancient discipline whereby the bishops installed throughout the whole world lived in communion with one another and with the Roman Pontiff in a bond of unity, charity, and peace."

- "This infallibility... with which the divine redeemer wished to endow his church in defining doctrine pertaining to faith and morals extends just as far as the deposit of revelation.... The Roman Pontiff, head of the college of bishops, enjoys this infallibility in virtue of his office."

Second Vatican Council, *Pastoral Constitution on the Church in the Modern World*, 1965:

"The body of the faithful as a whole, anointed as they are by the Holy One, cannot err in matters of belief."

Congregation for the Doctrine of the Faith, *Mysterium Ecclesiae*, 1973:

"According to Catholic doctrine, the infallibility of the magisterium of the church extends not only to the deposit of faith, but also to those things without which this deposit cannot be properly safeguarded and explained."

Catechism of the Catholic Church, 1992:

"The church's magisterium exercises the authority it holds from Christ to the fullest extent when it defines dogmas, that is, when it proposes truths contained in divine revelation or having a necessary connection with them, in a form obliging the Christian people to an irrevocable adherence of faith."

Context: This statement baffles theologians, since it seems to say Catholics must not only believe revealed doctrines but must also place an act of faith in so-called "secondary truths" that have some connection with revelation.

John Paul II, *Tertio Millennio Adveniente,* 1994:

"[The church] cannot cross the threshold of the new millennium without encouraging her children to purify themselves, through repentance, of past errors and instances of infidelity, inconsistency, and slowness to act. Acknowledging the weaknesses of the past is an act of honesty and courage which helps us to strengthen our faith, which alerts us to face today's temptations and challenges, and prepares us to meet them."

Congregation for the Doctrine of the Faith, Reply to the *Dubium* [Doubt], 1995:

"*Dubium:* Whether the teaching that the church has no authority whatsoever to confer priestly ordination on women, which is presented in the Apostolic Letter *Ordinatio Sacerdotalis* to be held definitively, is to be understood as belonging to the deposit of the faith.

"*Responsum:* In the affirmative.

"This teaching requires definitive assent, since, founded on the written Word of God, and from the beginning constantly preserved and applied in the Tradition of the church, it has been set forth infallibly by the ordinary and universal magisterium (cf. Second Vatican Council, *Dogmatic Constitution on the Church, Lumen Gentium* 25, 2). Thus, in the present circumstances, the Roman Pontiff, exercising his proper office of confirming the brethren (cf. Luke 22:32), has handed on this same teaching by a formal declaration, explicitly stating what is to be held always, everywhere, and by all, as belonging to the deposit of the faith."

Context: Scholars immediately challenged this attempt to declare "infallible" the policy of ordaining only males, touching off a new debate on infallibility itself.

Congregation for the Doctrine of the Faith, 1996:

The ban on women's ordination belongs to the "second level of religious truths" — that is, truths which, "though not formally revealed," are nevertheless "connected in such a way with Revelation that one destroys the fabric of Revelation itself by denying the content of the second level."

Context: In matters of ambiguity, Catholics may rely on the recommendation of the 1983 Code of Canon Law, 749: "No doctrine is understood to be infallibly defined unless this fact is clearly established."

INFALLIBILITY IN FLUX
Robert McClory

The concept of infallibility (or absolute immunity from error) is closely re-lated to the church's conviction from its earliest days that the Holy Spirit would be with the community of the faithful throughout the ages. This did not mean that every belief carried a divine guarantee or that the church would not make colossal mistakes, but that the Spirit sent by Jesus would over the long term preserve it and bring it back into balance when it went astray.

Though the community was organized around the apostles and later their successors (the bishops), it did not regard these leaders as exclusive spokes-persons and decision makers: the Spirit was in the whole church. Thus, St. Cyprian told his priests and deacons in the second century, "I have made it a rule ever since the beginning of my episcopate to make no decision merely on the strength of my own personal opinion without consulting you and without the approbation of the people."

With the reconciliation between Christianity and the Roman Empire in the fourth century, the official teachers, the hierarchy, began to acquire the trappings, even the titles, of the empire's political leadership. A tendency arose to divide the church into two classes — the teachers (the bishops along with the clergy) and the taught (the laity). What the church thought all too easily became equated with what the bishops thought. That tendency and the tension it produced have been with the church ever since.

Yet bishops who were sensitive to the Spirit's presence in the whole com-munity served the church well during the first thousand years of its existence. They were particularly important when rancorous disputes threatened to tear the body of Christ apart. Almost miraculously, the gathering of bishops at the great ecumenical councils — at Nicea, Ephesus, Chalcedon, and Con-stantinople, for example — served to settle disputes and articulate the faith in formulas that the whole church (eventually) accepted. The first known use of the term "infallibility" came from Bishop Abu Quarra in the ninth century and referred exclusively to the definitive teachings of ecumenical councils. Though highly regarded (at least in the West), the popes did not attend any of the first seven councils, and in some cases the councils rejected papal positions (and even popes themselves).

Papal power grew from the tenth century on, and the notion of the pope as both the spiritual and political leader of Christendom became popular. Still, it was not until the thirteenth century that anyone seriously proposed infallibility as a papal attribute. Pietro Olivi, a Franciscan friar, feared that future popes might withdraw their favor from the Franciscans and saw infallibility as a way of restricting the papal office. The next pope, John XXII, rejected his ideas, but the notion of an infallible leader exercised continuing appeal.

Between the thirteenth and sixteenth centuries, papal authority rose and fell and rose again. Perhaps its greatest challenge was conciliarism — the belief that ecumenical councils represent the highest level of authority in the church, and to them the pope must be subject. The Council of Constance first defined it in 1414, but Pius II overturned the doctrine forty-six years later. The theory of council over pope persisted, however, especially in France and Germany, well into the nineteenth century.

The upheaval of the Protestant Reformation convinced great numbers of Catholics that the church needed strong, central control — and the popes of that era did much to purge the church of chronic abuses and reestablish its balance. Robert Bellarmine, among others, viewed this kind of leadership as a sign of divine approbation: "When the pope teaches the whole church in things pertaining to faith, he cannot err. Nor can he err in moral precepts prescribed for the whole church."

The Enlightenment of the seventeenth and eighteenth centuries may have weakened the church's hold on the masses, but it proved a genuine boon to papal authority. Old assumptions about heaven and earth collapsed, intellectuals ridiculed simple belief, scientists and artists and political theorists proposed radical new ideas, and the French Revolution brought down ancient regimes, replacing them with tottering republics and fragile democracies. The old church seemed a last bastion of stability in a scary new world. Popularizers like Joseph De Maistre argued that popes had to be infallible by their very nature, and it was time for civilization to rally around these lone oracles of absolute truth.

In those uncertain times Pius IX was elected pope in 1846, and he would remain on the throne for thirty-seven years, the longest reign in papal history. Early on, he became convinced that the time was ripe for an ecumenical council to define papal infallibility, though he did not reveal his purpose when he convened the bishops. The First Vatican Council, which began in 1869 and concluded in mid-1870, was among the most tumultuous in history. Great numbers of the bishops believed the infallibility doctrine was not well founded in the deposit of faith, was unnecessary, and would provoke non-Catholic resentment. Meanwhile, advocates of the doctrine worked for as strong a statement as possible. The volume of argument during the sessions was exceeded only by the behind-the-scenes wheeling and dealing. By the time the council proclaimed the doctrine's final version at St. Peter's (in the midst of a violent thunderstorm), one-third of the bishops had gone home, many in protest.

In the immediate aftermath, the papacy received unprecedented attention, and papal authority became more centralized than ever. Leaders like Archbishop Henry Edward Manning of England viewed the pope as the lone, unquestioned spokesman for Christ in this world. Meanwhile others, notably John Henry Newman, tried to understand the new doctrine in a wider context — to see the papacy (and indeed the entire hierarchy) in relationship to the larger church. Eventually, this more modest interpretation of infallibility gained support and received backing at the Second Vatican Council in the mid-1960s.

Vatican II explicitly elevated the position of bishops by stating that they are not "branch managers" for the pope but teach in their own right and form a "college" with the pope. The council also said in effect that there is only one basic kind of infallibility, which resides in the "body of the faithful," the church as a whole. Yet that infallibility may express itself in three ways: in the universal and constant teaching of all the bishops throughout the world; in the declarations of ecumenical councils; and in the definitions of a pope when he solemnly articulates the faith of the larger church. At the same time Vatican II repeated almost word for word Vatican I's more rigid, pope-centered interpretation of infallibility, leaving observers in an enduring state of confusion.

Since Vatican II, many critics, notably Fr. Hans Küng, have argued that the church needs to discard the whole notion of infallible and irreformable expressions of the faith in favor of the more ancient, less rigid belief in the Spirit's perennial protection of the body of Christ (which Küng calls "indefectibility"). Meanwhile, Pope John Paul II and the Congregation for the Doctrine of the Faith (CDF) have moved back toward the First Vatican Council's more rigid concept of papal authority.

This appears specifically in their handling of women's ordination. John Paul II has repeatedly refused to discuss the question and has ordered the church to follow suit — despite the fact that both the Vatican's own Scripture scholars and experts on tradition contend the matter deserves reconsideration. The CDF's strong statements in 1995 and 1996 further muddied the waters, since the congregation said the ban on women priests is not to be regarded as a matter of divine revelation but only a "secondary truth," which all the faithful must nevertheless hold as infallible.

We very much need clarification of infallibility. What Cardinal Joseph Ratzinger, the CDF prefect, observed in 1969 regarding papal teaching is still true today: "Where there is neither consensus on the part of the universal church nor clear testimony in the sources, no binding decision is possible. If such a decision were formally made, it would lack the necessary conditions and the question of the decision's legitimacy would have to be reexamined."

Discussion Questions
INFALLIBILITY

1. How does the concept of infallibility strike you personally? Has it had any impact on your life?

2. Has your understanding of infallibility changed over the years? If so, how?

3. What values did the First Vatican Council choose to emphasize with the definition of infallibility? What values did it deemphasize or leave aside?

4. Is it possible to doubt, or deny, an infallibly proposed doctrine and still be a loyal Catholic? If so, under what circumstances?

5. Do you accept Mary's Immaculate Conception as an infallible dogma? How about the CDF's proclamation against women's ordination?

6. How do you think the First Vatican Council's definition of infallibility has affected Catholics? How has it affected relations with other religious denominations?

7. How might infallibility be reinterpreted, should a future council choose to do so?

Chapter 2

PRIMACY OF CONSCIENCE

The meaning and use of the concept of conscience have varied widely over time. Since the Reformation, the theological understanding of "primacy" of conscience in moral decision-making has fluctuated significantly. The key question is: can a person make a moral judgment in good conscience if it is not in agreement with the teaching of the magisterium? Official church pronouncements in the eighteenth and nineteenth centuries essentially said no, constraining the exercise of conscience within the confines of church teaching. The Second Vatican Council, however, recognized the freedom and autonomy of conscience in applying moral principles to specific situations. Recent statements by Pope John Paul II, however, have reverted to the earlier emphasis on the predominant role of the magisterium.

For discussions of related topics, see chapter 4, "Religious Freedom," and chapter 9, "Theological Dissent."

SCRIPTURE

Romans 2:14–16:

"When gentiles, who do not possess the law, do instinctively what the law requires, these, though not having the law, are a law to themselves. They show that what the law requires is written on their hearts, to which their own conscience also bears witness; and their conflicting thoughts will accuse or perhaps excuse them on the day when, according to my gospel, God, through Jesus Christ, will judge the secret thoughts of all."

MEDIEVAL CHURCH

Innocent III, c. 1200:

"What is not from faith is sin, and whatever is done contrary to conscience leads to hell."

Thomas Aquinas, *Summa Theologiae*, c. 1270:

- "Conscience is nothing else than the application of knowledge to some action.... If a man were to know that human reason was dictating something contrary to God's commandment, he would not be bound to abide by reason: but then reason would not be entirely erroneous. But when erring reason proposes something as being commanded by God, then to scorn the dictate of reason is to scorn the commandment of God."

- [Citing Augustine] "Now all men know the truth to a certain extent, at least as to the common principles of the natural law: and as to the others, they partake of the knowledge of truth, some more, some less; and in this respect are more or less cognizant of the eternal law."

- "*Synderesis* is said to be the law of our mind, because it is a habit containing the precepts of the natural law, which are the first principles of human actions."

  Editors' Note: Although not a pope, Aquinas has been more influential than any other theologian in defining conscience.

MODERN ERA

Pius VI, *Quod Aliquantum*, 1791:

Quod Aliquantum condemned "this absolute liberty which not only assures people of the right not to be disturbed about their religious opinions but also gives them this license to think, write, and even have printed with impunity all that the most unruly imagination can suggest about religion.... What could be more senseless than to establish among men equality and this unbridled freedom which seems to quench reason...? What is more contrary to the rights of the creator God who limited human freedom by prohibiting evil?"

Context: The French Revolution was at its height, and its anticlerical measures threatened the church.

Pius IX, *Quanta Cura*, 1864:

Quanta cura condemned "that erroneous opinion which is especially injurious to the Catholic Church and the salvation of souls, called by our predecessor Gregory XVI insane raving, namely, that freedom of conscience and of worship is the proper right of each man, and that this should be proclaimed and asserted in every rightly constituted society."

Context: The famous "Syllabus of Errors" was appended to this encyclical.

Leo XIII, *Libertas Praestantissimum*, 1888:

- "The only way in which the liberty of conscience can be understood is the freedom to follow God's commands and to do one's duty."

- "It is quite unlawful to demand, to defend, or to grant unconditional freedom of thought, of speech, of writing or of worship, as if these were so many rights given by nature to man. For if nature had really granted them, it would be lawful to refuse obedience to God, and there would be no restraint on human liberty. It likewise follows that freedom in these things may be tolerated wherever there is just cause; but only with such moderation as will prevent its degenerating into license and excess."

Pius XII, Mystici Corporis, 1946:

[Quoting canon law] "No one may be forced to accept the Catholic faith against his will.... For faith, without which it is impossible to please God, must be an entirely free homage of the intellect and will. Hence, if it should happen that, contrary to the constant teaching of this Apostolic See, anyone should be brought against his will to embrace the Catholic faith, we cannot do otherwise, in the realization of our duty, than disavow such an action."

John XXIII, Pacem in Terris, 1963:

"Also among humanity's rights is that of being able to worship God in accordance with the right dictates of one's own conscience, and to profess one's religion both in private and in public."

Second Vatican Council, Dogmatic Constitution on the Church, 1964:

"Those who, through no fault of their own, do not know the Gospel of Christ or his church, but who nevertheless seek God with a sincere heart, and, moved by grace, try in their actions to do his will as they know it through the dictates of their conscience — these too may attain eternal salvation."

Second Vatican Council, Pastoral Constitution on the Church in the Modern World, 1965:

- "Deep within their consciences men and women discover a law which they have not laid upon themselves, but which they must obey.... For they have in their hearts a law inscribed by God. Their dignity rests in observing this law, and by it they will be judged."

- "Let [the laity] realize that their pastors will not always be so expert as to have a ready answer to every problem, even every grave problem, that arises; this is not the role of the clergy: it is rather the task of lay people to shoulder their responsibilities under the guidance of Christian wisdom and with careful attention to the teaching authority of the church."

Second Vatican Council, Declaration on Religious Liberty, 1965:

- "The human person sees and recognizes the demands of the divine law through conscience. All are bound to follow their conscience faithfully in every sphere of activity.... Therefore, the individual must not be forced to act against conscience nor be prevented from acting according to conscience, especially in religious matters."

- "The truth cannot impose itself except by virtue of its own truth, as it makes its entrance into the mind at once quietly and with power."

Paul VI, *Populorum Progressio,* 1967:

"It is finally the right of the parents having completely examined the case to make a decision about the number of their children; a responsibility they take upon themselves keeping in sight their duty to God, themselves, the children already born, and the community to which they belong, following the dictates of their conscience instructed about the divine law authentically interpreted and strengthened by confidence in God."

Context: This section of the encyclical is headed "Population Growth." While admitting that authorities may take "appropriate measures" to cope with the problems it creates, the pope emphasizes that the ultimate responsibility for family size lies with families themselves.

PAPACY OF JOHN PAUL II

John Paul II, Audience, 1988:

"Because the church's magisterium has been instituted to enlighten the conscience, any appeal to this conscience in order to contest the truth of what has been taught by the magisterium involves the rejection of the Catholic concept of both the magisterium and the moral conscience."

John Paul II, *Veritatis Splendor,* 1993:

"In proclaiming the commandments of God and the charity of Christ, the church's magisterium also teaches the faithful specific particular precepts and requires that they consider them in conscience as morally binding."

Catechism of the Catholic Church, 1994:

- "Conscience is a judgment of reason by which the human person recognizes the moral quality of a concrete act."

- "A well-formed conscience is upright and truthful. It formulates its judgments according to reason, in conformity with the true good willed by the wisdom of the Creator. Everyone must avail himself of the means to form his conscience."

- "A human being must always obey the certain judgment of his conscience."

- "Conscience can remain in ignorance or make erroneous judgments. Such ignorance and errors are not always free of guilt."

- "The Word of God is a light for our path. We must assimilate it in faith and prayer and put it into practice. This is how moral conscience is formed."

CONSCIENCE AND
THE MAGISTERIUM
Sheila Briggs

Papal pronouncements about conscience have varied over the centuries in reaction to shifts in the meaning of conscience itself. Several distinct conceptual strands emerged over time. These accumulated meanings are only partly compatible and have left us without a single consistent understanding of the meaning of conscience. The roots of the idea of conscience lie in the ancient world, where differences between Greek and Roman conceptions developed.

Conscience as Accuser

The Greek word *syneidesis* denoted a conscience that accuses a person of the wrong he or she has done. Conscience does not reflect; it hurts. This meaning has been preserved in the phrase "pangs of conscience." It is also reflected in the thirty occurrences of *syneidesis* in the New Testament. Thus, for the author of the Letter to the Hebrews, Christ's blood is the only sacrifice that can remove sin and deliver us from the accusations of conscience, leaving us "sprinkled clean from an evil conscience" (Heb. 10:22).

In the New Testament, *syneidesis* appears most often in the letters of Paul and his followers. One instance, in Paul's Letter to the Romans, is especially crucial in the history of conscience:

> When gentiles, who do not possess the law, do instinctively what the law requires, these, though not having the law, are a law to themselves. They show that what the law requires is written on their hearts, to which their own conscience also bears witness; and their conflicting thoughts will accuse or perhaps excuse them on the day when, according to my gospel, God, through Jesus Christ, will judge the secret thoughts of all. (Rom. 2:14–16)

Here, Paul links conscience to an internal moral sense, identical in content with the Jewish law. In the context of Paul's letter, the witness of conscience is fundamentally negative and still accusatory. It makes the gentiles aware that they know what God requires of them and condemns them for not accomplishing this.

Nonetheless, Romans 2:14–16 shows the influence of the Latin concept of *conscientia*, which had a broader scope than the Greek *syneidesis*. *Conscientia* denoted the moral consciousness by which human beings are able to evaluate both their past and future actions. This was akin to the way Roman Stoic philosophers, like Cicero and Seneca, used it. They understood conscience as the exercise of reason, through which people could judge whether their actions conformed to the law governing the universe.

Conscience as Moral Sense

In the late fourth century, Jerome undertook the momentous task of preparing a new translation of the Bible into Latin. The result was the Vulgate, the official version of the Bible of the Catholic Church for centuries. In his translation, Jerome made the fateful decision to render *syneidesis* as the Latin *conscientia*. He also identified conscience with another Greek word, *synderesis* (also spelled *synteresis*), which he called the "spark of conscience" innate in human beings.

The most influential development in the history of conscience in the Catholic Church took place later, in the theology of Thomas Aquinas. He reshaped earlier Christian views in a systematic account of conscience in his *Summa Theologiae*. Thomas defined *synderesis* as the exercise of reason through which human beings can know the first principles of morality (ST Ia–IIae 94, 1). As such, it is knowledge of the highest level, the general principles of the natural law accessible to all human beings (ST Ia–IIae 93, 2). Thomas distinguished *conscientia* from *synderesis* and restricted its meaning to the application of the general principles of natural law to human actions (ST Ia–IIae 19, 5).

In this sense, conscience belongs to reason, and Thomas used the two terms interchangeably. His discussion of conscience focused on whether one is bound to follow a mistaken conscience, and whether following a mistaken conscience excuses one from responsibility for one's error (ST Ia–IIae 19, 5–6). He concluded that a mistaken conscience is binding because "every act against reason, whether in the right or in the wrong, is always bad." So even if one's conscience leads one to deny Christ and the belief necessary for salvation, one is still to follow it. Innocent III, the most powerful and imperious of medieval popes, held the same view as Aquinas. The church's doctrine is true, but only faith leads to its sincere acceptance.

This is literally a "damned if you do and damned if you don't" situation. One cannot escape the consequences of unbelief by violating conscience, but following one's mistaken conscience robs one of salvation. Only *involuntary* ignorance of the moral evil removes culpability for an action willed by a mistaken conscience.

Aquinas seems to restrict involuntary ignorance to a lack of knowledge of facts. In his view, one cannot claim ignorance of the first principles of natural law and their obvious application. Such a person is to be blamed, because he or she should have known them. It is very important to note that in Aquinas's discussion of conscience (as both *synderesis* and *conscientia*), he makes no mention of the teaching office of the church. Conscience belongs purely to the realm of reason and nature. Even without the church's teaching, human beings are expected to know the first principles of morality and to act upon them.

The Teachable Conscience

In his treatment of prudence, Aquinas had already characterized conscience (the application of moral reason to human action) as something that could be taught (ST IIa–IIae 49). In the late sixteenth and seventeenth centuries, after the Reformation led to an age of heightened religious sensitivity, moral theologians sought to aid confessors and spiritual directors who were advising the Catholic laity. It was a period in which education expanded and the educated laity felt the need for a well-informed conscience, as the world became more complex and the application of moral principles more ambiguous.

The Jesuits predominated, both in education and in moral theology's new trend toward casuistry. As these theologians reflected on the moral "cases" they encountered in real life, they became convinced that in some circumstances, the conscientious application of moral principles might allow for more than one right course of action. Out of this insight, the doctrine of probabilism and its various offshoots emerged. Probabilism recognized that there might be several morally justifiable applications of the moral law in a given situation.[1] Its opponents (and eventually the papacy) roundly condemned probabilism insofar as they viewed it as encouraging moral laxity.

Religious Tolerance and the Liberty of Conscience

The idea at the root of probabilism — namely, that there could be more than one moral choice in a given circumstance — was not easily vanquished. It was possible to think that conscience might reach divergent conclusions in some instances, not because it was mistaken but because there was a plurality of moral goods. The demand for religious tolerance forced the issue.

Exhaustion after the devastating religious conflicts of the sixteenth and seventeenth centuries certainly led to the call for religious tolerance. This was not the same thing as religious "indifferentism," which considers all religions equally valid. Religious tolerance simply meant giving all religions the freedom to exist. Nonetheless, the notion of tolerance was extremely controversial because most Catholics and Protestants believed that anyone who held a false religion was in danger of hell, and the public expression of false religion could ensnare and ruin others.

The call for religious tolerance fostered a new moral perspective. First, an individual may not only make an internal decision, but also give this decision external expression. Second, universal moral principles remain binding on all, but a plurality of goods fulfills and causes human life to flourish. Third,

---

1. See John Mahoney, *The Making of Moral Theology: A Study of the Roman Catholic Tradition* (Oxford: Oxford University Press, 1987), 135–43. "In moral parlance 'probable' really means 'proveable' or 'arguable,' something for which there is a good argument, or two or more good arguments, irrespective of the merits of any alternative.... The simple probabilist would reply that any action was morally justified for which a good case could be made" (136ff.).

individuals may legitimately choose different goods, according to their circumstances, interests, and desires, as long as they do not violate universal
moral principles.

The Papacy, Modernity, and Conscience

The Reformation did not divide Christians over moral issues. Protestants continued to believe in natural law known to human conscience, but gave it
much less theological importance than Catholics did. In an age of bitter religious conflicts, Protestants accused the Catholic Church of moral laxity and
hypocrisy. Defending Catholic moral authority, Catholic theologians made
the church and the papacy trustworthy interpreters of unquestioned natural
law. Because the church and the pope could not err in matters of morality, they were sure guides for the conscience of believers, and their teachings
should be obeyed. This connection between conscience and the church's and
pope's teaching authority later resulted in the papacy's rejection of much of
modernity. Moral pluralism became a challenge to church and papal authority. Thus, the popes stubbornly resisted the extension of religious freedom, a
clear exercise of conscience, in Catholic countries. They rightly saw that it
accompanied the erosion of their power in the secular realm and the decline
of their control over society.

The papal hostility to modernity and its call for liberty of conscience
reached a climax in the "Syllabus of Errors" of 1864. Here Pius IX anathematized all who demanded that the "Roman Pontiff can and should reconcile
and adapt himself to progress, liberalism, and the modern civilization."

In his 1888 encyclical, *Libertas praestantissimum*, Leo XIII endorsed "civil
liberties without intemperance" but condemned "indiscriminate freedom of
thought, writing, teaching, and...belief." Although the church had insisted
that people follow their conscience, it had not excused them from civil or
ecclesiastical penalties for *acting* on conscience. Leo XIII wished to preserve
the constraint on *behavior* that modern notions of liberty of conscience have
sought to loosen. He opposed the distinction between law and morality that
modern societies have made. For Leo, liberty of conscience was permissible
only if it meant freedom to act according to the dictates of natural reason *as
the church defined them.*

The pontificate of John XXIII and the Second Vatican Council mark a
watershed in the church's relationship with the modern world. For the first
time, the church embraced modernity and the modern understanding of conscience. The Second Vatican Council did not portray conscience as a passive
receptacle of the magisterium. It accepted religious freedom and took a positive view of moral pluralism. It renewed the church's earlier emphasis on the
autonomy of conscience as integral to human dignity and moral reason, with
which God has endowed human beings. Furthermore, the council acknowledged that lay people should not expect their pastors to have ready solutions

for complex practical and moral problems. In expanding the laity's role, both the council and the postconciliar church recognized that lay people often have the expertise necessary to evaluate the church's teaching on concrete moral issues.

During the two decades that John Paul II has governed the church, he has muted this teaching of Vatican II, returning instead to an emphasis on the conformity of right conscience to what the magisterium teaches. This is one of his favorite topics and a dominant concern in the encyclical *Veritatis splendor.* This encyclical assumes that natural law has a fundamental clarity for every age and human culture and implicitly rejects any theory of the historical development of moral consciousness (52–53). The encyclical steps back from the Second Vatican Council's insight that both the church and the world are still historically incomplete in their discovery of God's truth. For John Paul II, conscience is where a person hears the voice of God as instruction in objective moral truth (58–59).

For John Paul II, the magisterium is the individual conscience writ large, with the fundamental exception that it never errs in its moral judgment because it is not vulnerable to the ignorance or subjectivism of the individual conscience (64, 110). Thus, the magisterium is a superconscience, which always apprehends moral truth correctly. The role of the individual conscience is to become a replica of the magisterium.

In *Veritatis splendor,* Pope John Paul II takes his place in the history of conscience. He is unable to return to the premodern world of Paul and Aquinas where moral truth was seen as uniform and unchanging. He also cannot repudiate Vatican II with its acceptance of the modern world and liberty of conscience. But in this modern world, conscience threatens to emancipate itself from the magisterium. His solution is to collapse the autonomy of conscience into the church's teaching authority. In so doing, he has reinvented the meaning of conscience.

Discussion Questions
PRIMACY OF CONSCIENCE

1. Has there ever been a time in your life when you, in a personal exercise of conscience, made a moral decision not in keeping with the teaching of the church? What process did you follow? Did you know the teaching of the church, or did you discover it only afterward? If you did know it, why did you decide to contravene it? Do you believe you did the right thing? Why or why not?

2. "Primacy of conscience" today, as reflected in the quotes from the *Catechism of the Catholic Church,* means that a person must seek to be informed about church teaching, open to it, and respectful of it. But

if, after careful reflection and prayer, a Catholic believes that he or she must decide differently, that person is bound to follow conscience even if it is contrary to church teaching. Did you know that this is current church teaching? Do you ever hear this preached? If so, how is it preached? If not, why do you think it is overlooked?

3. Teaching on conscience has at times stressed the role of the magisterium and at other times the dignity of the individual conscience. Which do you think needs to be emphasized in today's world?

4. Sheila Briggs notes that the ancient concept of conscience was that of "accuser." Later, it meant the exercise of reason and moral judgment. How do you think of the concept? Is it useful in both its meanings today?

5. Commentators on crime and public morality today often lament that people have lost a "sense of conscience." Religious educators talk about helping young people "form" good consciences. How would you help young people develop their consciences in today's milieu? How would you teach them about primacy of conscience?

Chapter 3

SCRIPTURAL
INTERPRETATION

For much of church history, Scripture was not directly accessible to the faithful, not only because of widespread illiteracy, but — especially after the Council of Trent — because church officials discouraged Scripture reading, fearing interpretations that might not accord with church doctrine. For centuries, they advocated an almost fundamentalist approach to the Bible, as exemplified in the Galileo Affair, when they insisted on a literal reading of Genesis (see chapter 15). But in 1943, with the publication of Pius XII's Divino Afflante Spiritu, the official approach shifted dramatically, as the church encouraged critical and historically informed methods of biblical scholarship.

Leo I, Letter 15 to Turribius, 447:

"And the apocryphal scriptures, which, under the names of Apostles, form a nursery-ground for many falsehoods, are not only to be proscribed, but also taken away altogether and burnt to ashes in the fire. For though there are certain things in them which seem to have a show of piety, yet they are never free from poison, and through the allurements of their stories they have the secret effect of first beguiling men with miraculous narratives, and then catching them in the noose of some error."

Context: The "Bible" was not always one defined volume, as we know it today. This letter exemplifies the long historical process of determining which books are "canonical" scripture and which are "apocryphal."

Gregory I, Letter to Leander, 594:

"At times we neglect to expound the obvious words of the narrative so as not to reach too late the obscure meanings. At times they cannot be understood literally because, when the obvious meaning is taken, they engender in the readers, not instruction but error.... In some instances, also, the words themselves militate against the possibility of their literal interpretation.... At times, however, he who fails to take the words of the story in a literal sense hides the light of truth that has been offered to him, and when he labors to find in them some other inner meaning, he loses what he could easily have arrived at on the surface."

Council of Toulouse, 1229:

"We prohibit also that the laity should be permitted to have the books of the Old or the New Testament; unless anyone from motives of devotion should wish to have the Psalter or the Breviary for divine offices or the hours of the blessed Virgin; but we most strictly forbid their having any translation of these books."

Context: "Translation" refers to vernacular languages, as opposed to Latin.

Clement V, Council of Vienne, 1311:

"Therefore, following the example of Him whose representative we are on earth, who wished that the Apostles, about to go forth to evangelize the world, should have a knowledge of every language, we earnestly desire that the church abound with Catholic men possessing a knowledge of the languages used by the infidels, who will be able to instruct them in Catholic doctrine and by holy baptism form them into a body of Christians. Therefore ... we ... direct that for the teaching of the languages learned below, schools be established ... decreeing that in each of these Catholic men possessing a sufficient knowledge of the Hebrew, Greek, Arabic, and Chaldaic languages be engaged."

Leo X, Fifth Lateran Council, *Supernae Majestatis Praesidio,* 1516:

"Nor shall [preachers] presume to announce or predict in their sermons any fixed time of future evils, the coming of Antichrist or the day of the last judgment.... Wherefore, no cleric, whether regular or secular, who engages in this work in the future is permitted in his sermons to foretell future events *ex litteris sacris* or to affirm that he has received his knowledge of them from the Holy Ghost or through divine revelation or to resort for proof of his statements to foolish divinations.... Let him preserve undivided the seamless garment of Christ, by abstaining from that scandalous practice of defaming the character of bishops, prelates, and other superiors before the people."

Council of Trent, 1546:

"No one relying on his own judgment shall, in matters of faith and morals pertaining to the edification of Christian doctrine, distorting the Holy Scriptures in accordance with his own conceptions, presume to interpret them contrary to that sense which holy mother church, to whom it belongs to judge of their true sense and interpretation, has held and holds, or even contrary to the unanimous teaching of the Fathers, even though such interpretations should never at any time be published."

Editors' Note: See Paul VI, 1971, for an updated version of this statement.

Clement XI, *Unigenitus,* 1713:

Clement XI condemned these statements of Pasquier Quesnel:

- "It is useful and necessary at all times, in all places, and for any kind of person, to study and to know the spirit, the piety, and the mysteries of Sacred Scripture."
- "The reading of Scripture is for all."
- "The sacred obscurity of the Word of God is no reason for the laity to dispense themselves from reading it."
- "The Lord's Day ought to be sanctified by Christians with reading of pious works and above all of the Holy Scriptures. It is harmful for a Christian to wish to withdraw from the reading."
- "It is an illusion to persuade oneself that knowledge of the mysteries of religion should not be communicated to women by the reading of Sacred Scriptures. Not from the simplicity of women, but from the proud knowledge of men has arisen the abuse of the Scriptures, and have heresies been born."
- "To snatch away from the hands of Christians the New Testament or to hold it closed against them by taking away from them the means of understanding it, is to close for them the mouth of Christ."

    Editors' Note: These statements were condemned by the pope.

Pius VII, Letter to the Archbishop of Mohileff, 1816:

"If the sacred books are permitted everywhere without discrimination in the vulgar tongue, more damage will arise from this than advantage.... Since in vernacular speech we notice very frequent interchanges, varieties and changes, surely by an unrestrained license of Biblical versions that changelessness which is proper to the divine testimony would be utterly destroyed, and faith itself would waver."

Pius IX, "Syllabus of Errors," 1864:

The "Syllabus of Errors" condemned the following propositions:

- "Divine revelation is imperfect and hence subject to continual and indefinite progress, which ought to correspond to the progress of human reason."
- "The prophecies and miracles set forth in the narration of the Sacred Scriptures are poetical fictions; the mysteries of the Christian faith are the outcomes of philosophical reflections; in the books of both Testaments mythical tales are contained; Jesus Christ Himself is a mythical fiction."

    Editors' Note: These propositions were condemned by the pope.

First Vatican Council, *Dei Filius,* 1870:

"In matters of faith and morals, affecting the building up of Christian doctrine, that is to be held as the true sense of Holy Scripture what Holy Mother the Church has held and holds, to whom it belongs to judge of the true sense and interpretation of Holy Scriptures. Therefore no one is allowed to interpret the same Sacred Scripture contrary to this sense, or contrary to the unanimous consent of the Fathers."

Leo XIII, *Providentissimus Deus,* 1893:

- "The sense of Holy Scripture can nowhere be found incorrupt outside the church and cannot be expected to be found in writers who, being without the true faith, only gnaw the bark of Sacred Scripture and never attain its pith."

- "It is absolutely wrong and forbidden, either to narrow inspiration to certain parts only of Holy Scripture, or to admit that the sacred writer has erred.... For all the books which the church receives as sacred and canonical are written wholly and entirely, with all their parts, at the dictation of the Holy Ghost; and so far is it from being possible that any error can coexist with inspiration, that inspiration not only is essentially incompatible with error, but excludes and rejects it as absolutely and necessarily as it is impossible that God himself, the supreme Truth, can utter that which is not true."

Leo XIII, *Vigilantiae,* Apostolic Letter on Institution of a Commission for Biblical Studies, 1902:

"Wherefore it has seemed good to Us to institute a council or, as it is termed, a Commission of men of learning whose duty shall be to effect that in every possible manner the divine text will find here and from every quarter the most thorough interpretation which is demanded by our times, and be shielded not only from every breath of error, but also from every temerarious opinion."

Congregation of the Inquisition, *Lamentabili,* 1907:

Lamentabili condemned these propositions:

- "The magisterium of the church cannot, even through dogmatic definitions, determine the genuine sense of the Sacred Scriptures."

- "Since in the deposit of faith only revealed truths are contained, under no respect does it appertain to the church to pass judgment concerning the assertions of human sciences."

- "Those who believe that God is really the authority of the Sacred Scriptures display excessive simplicity or ignorance."
  Editors' Note: The Holy Office condemned these ideas.

Pius X, *Praestantia Sacrae Scripturae*, 1907:

"Wherefore We find it necessary to declare and prescribe, as We do now declare and expressly prescribe, that all are bound in conscience to submit to the decisions of the Biblical Commission, which have been given in the past and which shall be given in the future, in the same way as to the Decrees which appertain to doctrine, issued by the Sacred Congregations and approved by the Sovereign Pontiff."

Pontifical Biblical Commission, *On the Historical Character of the First Three Chapters of Genesis*, 1909:

- "False exegesis — Whether the various exegetical systems, which have been elaborated and defended by the aid of a science falsely so-called, for the purpose of excluding the literal historical sense of the first three chapters of Genesis, are based upon solid argument.
  "Answer: In the negative."

But:

- "8. *Yom*. Whether the word *Yom* (day), which is used in the first chapter of Genesis to describe and distinguish the six days, may be taken either in its strict sense as the natural day, or in a less strict sense as signifying a certain space of time; and whether free discussion of this question is permitted to interpreters.
  "Answer: In the affirmative."
  Editors' Note: Modern biblical scholars no longer interpret Genesis in a literal way.

Code of Canon Law, 1917:

The 1917 Code of Canon Law "permitted Catholics to read non-Catholic editions of the Bible even without such approval as given to the Revised Standard Version, if the Catholics were in some way engaged in the study of Scripture and if the editions were complete and faithful and without notes that constituted an attack on Catholic dogma" (*New Jerome Bible Commentary*, p. 1111).

Benedict XV, *Spiritus Paraclitus*, 1920:

- "[Recent writers'] notion is that only what concerns religion is intended and taught by God in Scripture, and that all the rest ... God merely permits, and even leaves to the individual author's greater or less knowledge. Small wonder, then, that in their view a considerable number of things occur in the Bible touching physical science, history, and the like, which cannot be reconciled with modern progress in science!"
- "Some even maintain that these views do not conflict with what our predecessor laid down, since — so they claim — he said that the sacred

writers spoke in accordance with the external — and thus deceptive — appearance of things in nature. But the Pontiff's own words show that this is a rash and false deduction. For sound philosophy teaches that the senses can never be deceived as regards their own proper and immediate object. Therefore, from the merely external appearance of things...we can never conclude that there is any error in Sacred Scripture."

Editors' Note: See chapter 15, "Copernican Theory," and chapter 16, "Evolution."

Pius XII, *Divino Afflante Spiritu,* 1943:

- "Being thoroughly prepared by the knowledge of the ancient languages and by the aids afforded by the art of criticism, let the Catholic exegete undertake the task, of all those imposed upon him the greatest, that, namely, of discovering and expounding the genuine meaning of the Sacred Books."

- "Let the interpreter then, with all care and without neglecting any light derived from recent research, endeavor to determine the peculiar character and circumstances of the sacred writer, the age in which he lived, the sources written or oral to which he had recourse and the forms of expression he employed. Thus can he better understand who was the inspired author, and what he wishes to express by his writings."

- "In the immense matter contained in the Sacred Books — legislative, historical, sapiential, and prophetical — there are but a few texts whose sense has been defined by the authority of the church, nor are those more numerous about which the teaching of the Holy Fathers is unanimous. There remain therefore many things, and of the greatest importance, in the discussion and exposition of which the skill and genius of Catholic commentators may and ought to be freely exercised."

Pontifical Biblical Commission, 1943:

"Versions of Sacred Scripture translated into the vernacular either from the Vulgate or from the ancient texts may certainly be used and read by the faithful for their own private devotion, provided they have been edited with the permission of the competent ecclesiastical authority; moreover, if any version, after its text and notes have been seriously examined by men who excel in biblical and theological knowledge, is found more faithful or better expressed, bishops, either singly or jointly in provincial or plenary councils, may commend it to faithful entrusted to their special care, if they see fit."

Pontifical Biblical Commission, Letter to Cardinal Suhard, 1948:

"The question of the literary forms of the first eleven chapters of Genesis is far more obscure and complex. These literary forms correspond to none of our classical categories and cannot be judged in the light of Greco-Latin or modern literary styles. One can, therefore, neither deny nor affirm their historicity, taken as a whole, without unduly attributing to them the canons of a literary style within which it is impossible to classify them. If one agrees not to recognize in these chapters history in the classical and modern sense, one must, however, admit that the actual scientific data do not allow of giving all the problems they set a *positive* solution" [emphasis in original].

Editors' Note: This masterpiece of obfuscation was written in response to queries about the literal truth of the first chapters of Genesis. See Pontifical Biblical Commission, 1909, above.

Pius XII, *Humani Generis,* 1950:

- "Some go so far as to pervert the sense of the Vatican Council's definition that God is the author of Holy Scripture, and they put forward again the opinion, already often condemned, which asserts that immunity from error extends only to those parts of the Bible that treat of God or of moral and religious matters.... Further, according to their fictitious opinions, the literal sense of Holy Scripture and its explanation, carefully worked out under the church's vigilance by so many great exegetes, should yield now to a new exegesis, which they are pleased to call symbolic or spiritual."

- "In a particular way must be deplored a certain too free interpretation of the historical books of the Old Testament.... If ... the ancient sacred writers have taken anything from popular narrations (and this may be conceded), it must never be forgotten that they did so with the help of divine inspiration, through which they were rendered immune from any error in selecting and evaluating those documents. Therefore, whatever of the popular narrations have been inserted into the Sacred Scriptures must in no way be considered on a par with myths or other such things."

- "For the faithful cannot embrace that opinion which maintains ... that after Adam there existed on this earth true men who did not take their origin through natural generation from him as the first parent of parents. Now it is in no way apparent how such an opinion can be reconciled with that which the sources of revealed truth and the documents of the Teaching Authority of the church propose with regard to original sin, which proceeds from a sin actually committed by an individual Adam and which through generation is passed on to all and is in everyone as his own" (see chapter 16, "Evolution").

Second Vatican Council, *Dogmatic Constitution on Divine Revelation,* 1965:

- "Since everything asserted by the inspired authors or sacred writers must be held to be asserted by the Holy Spirit, it follows that the books of

Scripture must be acknowledged as teaching firmly, faithfully and without error that truth which God wanted put into the writings for the sake of our salvation."

- "But since Holy Scripture must be read and interpreted according to the same Spirit by whom it was written, no less serious attention must be given to the content and writing of the whole of Scripture, if the meaning of the sacred texts is to be correctly brought to light. The living tradition of the whole church must be taken in account along with the harmony which exists between elements of the faith. It is the task of exegetes to work according to these rules toward a better understanding and explanation of the meaning of Sacred Scripture, so that through preparatory study the judgment of the church may mature."

- "Easy access to Sacred Scripture should be provided for all the Christian faithful.... If, given the opportunity and the approval of church authorities, these translations [of the Bible] are produced in cooperation with the separated brethren as well, all Christians will be able to read them.... Editions of the Sacred Scriptures ... should be prepared also for the use of non-Christians and adapted to their situation. Both pastors of souls and Christians generally should see to the wise distribution of these in one way or another."

Paul VI, Apostolic Letter, 1971:

"Even though [scriptural] scholars must pursue their studies in accordance with recent scientific method, they know nevertheless that God has entrusted the Scriptures not to the private judgment of learned people, but to his church. The Scriptures, therefore, must always necessarily be interpreted according to the norms of Christian tradition and hermeneutics, under the guardianship and protection of the church's magisterium."

Context: This decree linked the Biblical Commission to the Congregation for the Doctrine of the Faith, whose prefect became the president of the Biblical Commission.

Pontifical Biblical Commission, "The Interpretation of the Bible in the Church," 1993:

- "In its attachment to the principle 'Scripture alone,' fundamentalism separates the interpretation of the Bible from the tradition which, guided by the Spirit, has authentically developed in union with Scripture in the heart of the community of faith.... The fundamentalist approach is dangerous, for it is attractive to people who look to the Bible for ready answers to the problems of life. It can deceive these people, offering them interpretations that are pious but illusory, instead of telling them that the Bible does not necessarily contain an immediate answer to each and

every problem. Without saying as much in so many words, fundamentalism actually invites people to a kind of intellectual suicide. It injects into
life a false certitude, for it unwittingly confuses the divine substance of
the biblical message with what are in fact its human limitations."

- "Exegesis is truly faithful to proper intention of biblical texts when it goes
not only to the heart of their formulation to find the reality of faith there
expressed but also seeks to link this reality to the experience of faith in
our present world."

- "In the last resort it is the magisterium which has the responsibility of
guaranteeing the authenticity of interpretation and, should the occasion arise, of pointing out instances where any particular interpretation
is incompatible with the authentic Gospel."

John Paul II, Message to Pontifical Academy of Sciences on Evolution, 1996:

"It is necessary to determine the proper sense of Scripture while avoiding
any unwarranted interpretations that make it say what it does not intend
to say. In order to delineate the field of their own study, the exegete and
the theologian must keep informed about the results achieved by the natural
sciences."

BIBLICAL REINTERPRETATION
Alice L. Laffey, SSD

Biblical interpretation is as old as the Bible itself. In the Old Testament,
the priestly authors of the books of Chronicles reinterpreted the books of
Kings for a later time. They idealized King David, omitting any reference to
his taking Bathsheba and orchestrating her husband Uriah's death (2 Sam.
11). Although Solomon built the temple, the chronicler credits David with
making all the preparations.

Similarly, books of the New Testament reinterpret passages from the
Old. Galatians 4:22–31 allegorically reinterprets Abraham's wives Hagar and
Sarah and their respective children. These women represent two covenants,
the Sinai covenant, which bears children for slavery (Hagar), and Christ's
covenant, which bears children of the promise (Sarah). When Matthew's
Gospel affirms that Jesus fulfills Hebrew prophecy, it is reinterpreting the
Old Testament. For example, it presents a genealogy that traces Jesus' ancestry back to Abraham (Matt. 1:1–17). It presents Mary as the young woman
whose son is named Emmanuel (cf. Isa. 7:14), and points out that Bethlehem

is the city from which Jesus, the ruler-shepherd, has come (cf. Mic. 5:2). It reinterprets the identity of the son called out of Egypt (Hos. 11:1), from the people of Israel to the person of Jesus, and it attributes the cause of Rachel's weeping (Jer. 31:15) at Judah's exile to the innocents' deaths at the hands of Herod. In other words, biblical (re)interpretation has always been an integral part of the Christian tradition.

The canon of books of Scripture developed over time. In the fourth century, St. Jerome did not consider the first extant books in Greek (such as Wisdom, Sirach, and Judith) to be on a par with the Hebrew Scriptures. Though he translated them for the Vulgate and considered them pious and recommended reading, they were not "canonical." In contrast, the church of Augustine's time (fifth century) did not distinguish between the Hebrew books, the Holy Scriptures of the Jews, and some of the Greek books. Eventually the larger canon, including 1–2 Maccabees, Tobit, Baruch, Judith, the Wisdom of Ben Sira (Sirach), and the Wisdom of Solomon, became normative. Leo I's 447 Letter to Turribius, condemning some apocryphal Scriptures, should be seen as part of a long historical process of determining the boundaries of canonical Scripture.

In the early centuries, the church interpreted Scripture literally, but it did not restrict itself to literal interpretation. Quite the contrary. A fuller sense of Scripture was encouraged. Gregory I's Letter to Leander (597) endorses both literal and symbolic interpretation, indicating that each can be useful for different members of the community. In his *Confessions* (12.18.27), Augustine reflects on the possibility of multiple interpretations of the Scriptures.

Symbolism, allegory, and typology were methods central to biblical interpretation.

Since many of the faithful were illiterate, they depended on the more educated clergy for the proclamation and interpretation of Scriptures. Interpretation took place not only through preaching and teaching but also through a variety of artistic and literary expressions. Canon 14 of the Council of Toulouse (1229) prohibited the laity from having access to translations of the Old or New Testaments, except the Psalms. Although the canon's historical context is unclear, a concern about the relatively uneducated making errors in handwritten copies may be the reason for the prohibition. At the Council of Vienne, only a century later, Clement V encouraged the evangelizing of the world by directing that Catholic men [sic] with sufficient knowledge of biblical languages be educated in the languages of the infidels, so that they might instruct them in Catholic doctrine and baptize them. Knowledge is a prerequisite for teaching.

At the Fifth Lateran Council (1516), Leo X affirmed that tradition is consistent with the church's Scriptures. Those who would preach should do so in a manner faithful to the Scriptures and consistent with the interpretations of the church's earliest theologians. The council wished to protect the Scriptures from false interpretation by condemning apocalyptic interpretations, which predicted future occurrences on the basis of specific biblical passages.

While assuming the literal meaning of biblical texts, the patristic and medieval church was open to multiple symbolic interpretations. Papal restriction on interpretation was limited and intended to ensure the competency of the interpreters.

Luther challenged "traditional" biblical interpretation, especially the existence of purgatory (see 2 Macc. 12:44–45) and the church's understanding of salvation through faith and good works (see Rom. 1–3). As a result, the Council of Trent declared that the magisterium, the official teaching authority of the church, was the "official interpreter" of Scripture. The church's focus shifted to protecting the Bible from erroneous interpretation. The consequence of Trent's emphasis was that the Bible was interpreted "seldom and by few." Clement XI's condemnations of personal biblical interpretation are expressions of the church's caution.

For almost four hundred years after the Council of Trent, Roman Catholic laity seldom read or interpreted the Sacred Scriptures. Even clergy were reluctant to use the Bible for preaching and teaching — lest they misinterpret. The Bible's use was limited to "proof-texting" by church authorities — that is, to quoting one or another verse from Scripture as a proof of the validity of one or another dogmatic or theological assertion.

Protestant churches, however, depended heavily on the Scriptures and encouraged personal interpretation. When Enlightenment philosophers challenged some of the Scriptures, such as miracles and prophecies, Protestant ministers set about developing "scientific" methods for studying the Scriptures. They assumed that the literal meaning of the biblical texts was significantly less important than what the original authors intended to say. Therefore they tried to develop ways of getting at who the original authors were, what their historical contexts were, and what their intentions were in producing the texts as we have them. These methods, consistent with the Enlightenment, depended on reason rather than faith.

Roman Catholic lay people were only minimally, if at all, knowledgeable about the gradual shift in biblical interpretation that was taking place among Protestants. As Catholic authorities became more aware of the Enlightenment's influence on biblical interpretation and the development of historical criticism among Protestants, they became increasingly skeptical and reacted negatively. Such attitudes continued through the First Vatican Council (1870), which reiterated Trent's assertion of the church's magisterium as the official interpreter of Scripture and which forbade any nontraditional interpretation. Both the nontraditional interpretation grounded in reason and the interpreter not grounded in faith were to be rejected.

Though Catholics seldom used the Bible for personal reading and prayer, they nevertheless continued to assert its importance and to assume that it was the word of God. It is not surprising, then, that church authorities viewed the proliferation of multiple translations negatively. Insofar as these were inaccurate, they could distort sacred meaning.

At the beginning of the twentieth century, Pope Leo XIII established the Pontifical Biblical Commission and the Pontifical Biblical Institute. Their purpose was to teach the Sacred Scriptures and guarantee that others who would teach them were competently prepared. Their objective was also to guard the traditional interpretations of Scripture against the onslaughts of "modernism." One such modern interpretation, fueled by Darwin's theory of evolution, challenged the literal meaning of Genesis 1–3.

Between 1909 and 1943, Roman Catholic Scripture scholars tried to accomplish the dual task of carrying forward traditional biblical interpretation and doing biblical scholarship in a post-Enlightenment historical context. Only with the publication in 1943 of Pius XII's *Divino Afflante Spiritu* were Catholic biblical scholars (exegetes) freed to use the tools of modern historical criticism and incorporate the results of recent Protestant biblical research into their work. The encyclical recognized that the church has determined the meaning of only a few scriptural passages in any doctrinal way, or even in any one way. Most passages are open to further study and interpretation. Only in 1943 were Catholics again allowed to read the Scriptures for "their own private devotion" with a less cautious attitude toward multiple translations and the possibility of erroneous interpretation.

After the Enlightenment, historical criticism, Darwin, and *Divino Afflante Spiritu*, Pius XII felt the need to reassert the sacred character of the Scriptures and church doctrine. This he did in the encyclical *Humani generis* (1950). He cautioned against failing to distinguish materials taken from popular narrations (ancient Sumerian and Babylonian creation and flood stories) and the inspired biblical versions of the narratives, and he warned against cavalierly imputing error to biblical materials. While acknowledging the discrepancy between the results of modern biblical scholarship regarding the creation and fall of human beings and the traditional doctrine of original sin, he asserted the legitimacy of the church's doctrine.

By 1965, the Second Vatican Council's *Decree on Sacred Revelation* had found a way to affirm what the Scriptures teach without error: "that truth which God wanted put into the writings for the sake of our salvation." The council not only encouraged the faithful to read Scripture, it even recommended Protestant translations.

Paul VI's Apostolic Letter and the Pontifical Biblical Commission's document, "The Interpretation of the Bible in the Church" (1993), both situate scientific biblical scholarship within a larger context. While affirming "the guardianship and protection of the church's magisterium," they reject fundamentalism and encourage exegetes and theologians to keep abreast of the "results achieved by the natural sciences." They recognize that "exegesis is truly faithful to the proper intention of the biblical texts when it goes to the heart of the texts to find the faith expressed there and also when it links that faith to the experience of faith in the present world."

This statement sets the stage for "postmodern" biblical interpretation. Practiced by Protestants and Catholics alike, its methods begin with the social location of the interpreter/interpreting community. If Catholic believers are making the interpretation, then revelation as defined by Vatican II (Scripture and tradition) may inform their interpretation. In an interesting *Commonweal* article, "So What's Catholic about It? The State of Catholic Biblical Scholarship" (January 16, 1998), Luke Timothy Johnson, OSB, suggests that modern biblical criticism be incorporated into the church's long tradition of biblical interpretation (as well as the church's contemporary "moment"). Struggling with some of the same intellectual concerns in *The Revelatory Text* (San Francisco: Harper, 1991), Sandra Schneiders argues for the privileged place of the believer/believing community in the art/act of interpretation.

Catholics educated between the Reformation and Vatican II were exposed to little biblical interpretation of any sort. Since Vatican II they have been exposed to considerably more biblical interpretation and modern methods of biblical study, especially historical criticism. But no matter what their age, Catholics reading this essay are still the products of the twentieth century. The church has a long and very rich history of biblical interpretation, one well worth studying. For most of that history, the popes fully supported biblical preaching and teaching. The shadow of the Reformation and Trent's response falls on only a few centuries during more than two thousand years. During that four-hundred-year period, papal pronouncements deprived Catholic believers of potentially life-giving interactions with the sources of their tradition. Let us rejoice that those days are gone; hopefully, they are gone forever.

Discussion Questions
SCRIPTURAL INTERPRETATION

1. What were you taught when you were young about the Bible? Were you encouraged to read the Bible? To interpret its meaning for your own life? To raise questions about the text? Or did you read it in the light of interpretations already done by someone else?

2. We live in a time when many fundamentalists publicly defend a literal reading of Scripture as the only proper "interpretation." Did you know that the Catholic Church does not agree with that? How do you react knowing that Catholicism today welcomes historical and textual criticism?

3. Scripture is a major source of revelation in Catholicism. How do you respond when you realize that it has been approached and interpreted in very different ways over the centuries?

4. Many popes maintained that scriptural interpretations had to be in line with church teaching. Some would reverse this, saying that church teaching must be compatible with the teaching of Scripture. What do you think about this paradox?

5. Biblical scholars interpret Scripture with an eye to its historical context, the literary genre of the books, the probable authorship of the text, the intention of the author and other factors. How does this affect scholarship? How does it affect prayer and reflection?

6. What has the Bible meant in your own spiritual development? What difference would it have made if you had not had access to it?

Chapter 4

RELIGIOUS FREEDOM

For centuries, the church taught that secular authorities were required to defend Catholicism as the established church and punish "heretics" accordingly. "Error had no rights," even in secular regimes. After World War II, pronouncements began to change. The major change occurred thanks largely to the U.S. experience of separation of church and state, and the work of John Courtney Murray, SJ, who defended separation of church and state. He was the major influence on the landmark Declaration on Religious Liberty of the Second Vatican Council, in which the church officially espoused religious liberty. Pope John Paul II has since decried the violence and intolerance that some earlier popes encouraged.

EARLY CHURCH

Augustine, Letter to the Tribune Boniface, 417:

"There is unjust persecution, which the impious commit against the church of Christ, and there is just persecution, which the churches of Christ commit against the impious.... The church persecutes out of love and the impious out of cruelty."

Theodosian Code, 438:

"There shall be no opportunity for any man to go out to the public and to argue about religion or to discuss it or to give any counsel. If any person hereafter, with flagrant and damnable audacity, should suppose that he may contravene any law of this kind or if he should dare to persist in his action of ruinous obstinacy, he shall be restrained with a due penalty and proper punishment.... All heresies are forbidden by both divine and imperial laws and shall forever cease."

Context: This Roman imperial law, promulgated when Christianity was the state religion, was the basis for later criminalization of heresy throughout Christendom (see Fourth Lateran Council, below).

MEDIEVAL CHURCH

Lucius III, *Ad Abolendam*, 1184:

Ad abolendam ordered bishops to "make inquisition" for heresy.
   Context: This marks the beginning of the Inquisition, which used the "secular arm" to punish heretics.

Innocent III, *Vergentis in Senium*, 1199:

"The goods of heretics are to be confiscated, and their children are to be subjected to perpetual deprivation for the sins of their parents."

Innocent III, *Cum ex Officii Nostri*, 1207:

"We decree as a perpetual law, that whatsoever heretic ... shall be found therein, shall immediately be taken and delivered to the secular court to be punished according to the law. All his goods also shall be sold. ... The house, however, in which a heretic has been received shall be altogether destroyed, nor shall anyone presume to rebuild it; but let that which was a den of iniquity become a receptacle of filth."

Fourth Lateran Council, 1215:

"We excommunicate and anathematize every heresy that raises itself against the holy, orthodox, and Catholic faith. ... Secular authorities, whatever office they hold, shall be admonished and induced and if necessary compelled by ecclesiastical censure, that as they wish to be esteemed and numbered among the faithful, so for the defense of the faith they ought publicly to take an oath that they will strive in good faith and to the best of their ability to exterminate in the territories subject to their jurisdiction all heretics pointed out by the church."

Gregory IX, *Excommunicamos*, 1231:

Excommunicamos specified punishment for unrepentant heretics: "*animadversio debita*," the debt of hatred (death penalty).

Innocent IV, *Ad Extirpanda*, 1252:

"The ... ruler ... is hereby ordered to force all captured heretics to confess and accuse their accomplices by torture which will not imperil life or injure limb, just as thieves and robbers are forced to accuse their accomplices, and to confess their crimes; for these heretics are true thieves, murderers of souls and robbers of the sacraments of God."
   Context: This bull authorized the state to torture accused heretics.

COUNTER-REFORMATION

Leo X, *Exsurge Domine*, 1520:

"The books of Martin Luther which contain these errors are to be examined and burned.... We give Martin sixty days in which to submit."

Context: If Luther had not had the protection and support of secular rulers, he probably would have been burned at the stake.

Leo X, Letter to Frederick the Wise, 1520:

"Beloved son, we rejoice that you have never shown any favor to that son of iniquity, Martin Luther.... We exhort you to induce him to return to sanity and receive our clemency. If he persists in his madness, take him captive."

MODERN ERA

Pius VI, *Quod Aliquantum*, 1791:

Quod aliquantum condemned "this absolute liberty which not only assures people of the right not to be disturbed about their religious opinions but also gives them this license to think, write, and even have printed with impunity all that the most unruly imagination can suggest about religion.... What could be more senseless than to establish among men equality and this unbridled freedom which seems to quench reason...?What is more contrary to the rights of the creator God who limited human freedom by prohibiting evil?"

Context: The French Revolution was at its height, and its anticlerical measures threatened the church.

Gregory XVI, *Mirari Vos*, 1832:

"The discipline sanctioned by the church must never be rejected or be branded as contrary to certain principles of natural law. It must never be called crippled, or imperfect or subject to civil authority.... This perverse opinion ['indifferentism'] is spread on all sides by the fraud of the wicked who claim that it is possible to obtain the eternal salvation of the soul by the profession of any kind of religion, as long as morality is maintained."

Editors' Note: For another view, see Vatican II in chapter 9, "Theological Dissent."

Pius IX, *Quanta Cura*, 1864:

Quanta cura condemned "that erroneous opinion which is especially injurious to the Catholic Church and the salvation of souls, called by our predecessor Gregory XVI insane raving, namely, that freedom of conscience and of worship is the proper right of each man, and that this should be proclaimed and asserted in every rightly constituted society."

Context: The famous "Syllabus of Errors" was appended to this encyclical.

Leo XIII, *Libertas Praestantissimum*, 1888:

"Since ... the profession of one religion is necessary in the State, that religion must be professed which alone is true. ... If unbridled license of speech and of writing be granted to all, nothing will remain sacred and inviolate. ... It is not of itself wrong to prefer a democratic form of government, if only the Catholic doctrine be maintained as to the origin and exercise of power. ... The church has always most faithfully fostered civil liberty."

Pius X, *Vehementer Nos*, 1906:

"That the state must be separated from the church is a thesis absolutely false, a most pernicious error, ... an obvious negation of the supernatural order."

Pius XI, *Mortalium Animos*, 1928:

"There are those who nurture the hope that it would be easy to lead people, despite their religious differences, to unite in the profession of certain doctrines accepted as a common basis of spiritual life. ... Such efforts have no right to the approval of Catholics, since they are based on this erroneous opinion that all religions are more or less good and laudable."

Pius XII, *Mystici Corporis*, 1946:

[Quoting canon law] "No one may be forced to accept the Catholic faith against his will. ... For faith, without which it is impossible to please God, must be an entirely free homage of the intellect and will. Hence, if it should happen that, contrary to the constant teaching of this Apostolic See, anyone should be brought against his will to embrace the Catholic faith, we cannot do otherwise, in the realization of our duty, than disavow such an action."

John XXIII, *Pacem in Terris*, 1963:

Everyone has the right "to worship God in accordance with the dictates of one's own conscience and to profess one's religion both in private and in public."

Second Vatican Council, *Declaration on Religious Liberty*, 1965:

- "This Vatican synod declares that the human person has the right to religious freedom."

- "To establish and strengthen peaceful relations and harmony in the human race, religious freedom must be given effective constitutional protection everywhere and people's supreme right and duty to be free to lead a religious life in society must be respected."

- "Although in the life of the people of God in its pilgrimage through the vicissitudes of human history there has at times appeared a form of behavior which was hardly in keeping with the spirit of the Gospel and was even opposed to it, it has always remained the teaching of the church that no one is to be coerced into believing."

Context: When the Vatican changes its position on an issue, it often claims that it has always proclaimed the new position. For contradictory statements, see Innocent III, Innocent IV, Paul IV, etc., in chapter 6, "The Jewish People."

PAPACY OF JOHN PAUL II

Vatican Secretariat of State, Letter to Cardinals, 1994:

"How can we keep silent about all the forms of violence that have been perpetrated in the name of faith? About the wars of religion, the inquisitorial tribunals, and other ways of violating the rights of the individual? It is significant that these coercive methods, which violate human rights, have subsequently been applied by the totalitarian ideals of the twentieth century.... The church too must make an independent review of the darker sides of its history."

John Paul II, *Tertio Millennio Adveniente*, 1994:

"Another painful chapter of history to which the sons and daughters of the church must return with a spirit of repentance is that of the acquiescence given, especially in certain centuries, to intolerance and even the use of violence in the service of truth."

SEPARATING CHURCH AND STATE
Charles E. Curran

It is almost inconceivable that less than thirty-five years ago, Catholic teaching did not accept religious liberty for citizens. Finally, at Vatican II in 1965, the Catholic Church accepted religious liberty as the right to immunity from external coercion that forces one to act against conscience or prevents one from acting in accord with conscience in religious matters.

The *Declaration on Religious Liberty* of Vatican II admits that divine revelation does not affirm this immunity in so many words, but Scripture has emphasized the dignity of the human person so that the teaching on religious liberty is rooted in revelation. Scripture insists that the human response to God should be free. God and Jesus have recognized the basic freedom of the person and call the person to respond freely to the truth and the spirit of the gospel. Jesus bore witness to the truth but refused to use force to impose it on those who spoke out against him. Taught by Jesus' word and example, the apostles followed the same path.

In the light of Vatican II's argument that religious liberty is rooted in the words and actions of Jesus, the historical evidence of texts supporting the use of force against heretics and denying religious freedom seems almost incredible. What happened? How can one explain the teachings and positions of the Catholic Church from the fourth century to the middle of the twentieth?

The statements in this chapter begin with the words of St. Augustine, who profoundly influenced subsequent church teaching. In the struggle with the Donatist heresy, Augustine moved from his earlier position — that the church should use only persuasion — to justifying the church's asking the state to use force and punish heretics and schismatics. Augustine argued from two New Testament passages. God used force to convert St. Paul; and, in the parable of the prepared banquet with no guests, the servants were sent out to compel people to come into the banquet (Luke 14:16–24). Augustine maintained that if the state can prevent people from killing themselves, it can prevent them from killing themselves spiritually. Behind this position lurks the temptation to use whatever means are necessary to achieve the end — especially if it is identified as God's will. Thus began the long history of the Catholic Church's using force and violence against heretics in the name of the gospel.

The statements from the medieval period show how total was the theory and practice of using force against heretics. But note that these texts are all limited to heretics and schismatics. Thomas Aquinas summarized the teaching and practice of the Middle Ages. Those who have never accepted the Catholic faith, such as non-Christian gentiles and Jews, should not be forced to believe, because to believe is an act of the free will. However, if these infidels impede or persecute the true Catholic faith, then the faithful can make war against them. The Spanish conquistadors' treatment of Native Americans shows how this teaching could be abused in practice. The church taught, however, that heretics and schismatics should be physically forced to fulfill what they had promised and to hold on to what they once had received. An important difference exists between those who once accepted the Catholic faith and those who never accepted it. How different from John Paul II, who today asks pardon for the past use of violence in the service of truth.

The statements from the modern period, before Vatican II, deal with religious liberty in the more restricted and precise sense described above. Citizens should not have religious liberty, they say. At best, religious liberty could be tolerated as the lesser of two evils, but it is always an evil and, if possible, should not exist.

What were the bases for this position? The first was the absolute value of spiritual truth (as identified with the Catholic Church), and the belief that "error has no rights." Just as you are not free to shout fire in a crowded theater, you are not free to engage publicly in a false religion. The second basis for the teaching concerns the role of the state or government. The state is paternalistic, authoritarian, and directly concerned with the moral and spiritual good of its members. Historically in the Western world, the union of church and state continued to exist well beyond the Reformation. Many thought that such religious unity was also necessary in order to achieve political and civic unity — a position still existing in many parts of the world.

A very significant historical factor also entered in. The Catholic Church in the eighteenth and nineteenth centuries strongly disagreed with the Enlightenment and liberalism, which emphasized individual rights and human freedom. The Catholic Church opposed the French Revolution's support of liberty, equality, and fraternity and backed the *ancien régime*. The nineteenth-century texts illustrate this strong Catholic opposition to freedom, equality, and individual rights in society.

The Catholic Church saw liberalism as its primary enemy. In the view of many Catholics in the nineteenth and early twentieth centuries, liberalism, with its emphasis on the individual, began with Martin Luther. Religious liberalism under Luther separated the Christian from the authority of the church. Philosophical liberalism made human reason supreme, especially in the ethical realm, and gave no role to God's law. Political liberalism in the form of democracy made majority vote the ultimate criterion of truth and once again gave no place to God's law. Catholic theologians also strongly opposed economic liberalism or capitalism, because it put no restraints on the individual's quest for profit and money at the expense of others.

As the twentieth century progressed, however, the enemy or — to use more restrained language — the dialogue partner changed. Totalitarianism of the right and, especially, of the left came to the fore. Slowly the Catholic Church began to support the freedom, dignity, and rights of the person by strongly opposing communism. In his encyclical *Rerum Novarum* (1891), Pope Leo XIII emphasized the rights of workers to earn a living wage and to organize. However, it was not until 1963 that Pope John XXIII, in *Pacem in Terris*, fully developed a papal approach to human rights. Likewise and for the same historical reason, the Catholic Church changed its attitude toward democracy and limited constitutional government. In 1944 Pope Pius XII maintained that a democratic form of government appears to many people as a demand imposed by reason itself. Government should not be authoritarian or paternalistic or directly involved in the spiritual realm, but must respect the freedom of the individual as far as possible and restrict it only insofar as necessary, as Vatican's II's *Declaration on Religious Liberty* later declared. Thus in the changing historical situation, the Catholic Church came to accept the fundamental rights and basic freedom of the person in civil life and to support limited constitutional government. In 1965 Vatican II could finally accept religious freedom.

The Catholic Church obviously learned much from the Enlightenment and liberalism, but Catholicism can never fully accept any individualistic approach. The human person is more than an isolated monad. Catholicism sees the person as a social being, related in special ways to many other people (family, neighborhood, community, nation, state, voluntary organizations) and in a general way to all other human beings. All humans are brothers and sisters because we are creatures of the same God, the mother and father of us all. There can be no doubt that papal teaching was quite late in systematically proclaiming a doctrine of human rights. But in 1962, Pope John XXIII, to his credit, insisted not only on political and civil rights such as freedom of religion, speech, and association, but also on social and economic rights such as the right to decent food, clothing, shelter, medical care, and necessary social services. These social and economic rights are grounded in the social aspects of the human person and were not emphasized by the Enlightenment or liberalism.

One final point. As noted in the statements, the pope has admitted past errors by the church. But it remains very difficult for the Catholic Church to admit explicitly that its papal teaching office, especially in the recent past, has made mistakes and has been in error. The *Declaration on Religious Liberty* and the history surrounding it illustrate well this unwillingness to admit error in papal teaching. The declaration nowhere acknowledges that past teaching up to Vatican II was wrong. It recognizes that "through the vicissitudes of human history there has at times appeared a form of behavior which was hardly in keeping with the spirit of the Gospel and was even opposed to it [although] it has always remained the teaching of the church that no one is to be coerced into believing" (n. 12). At best, this statement is disingenuous. Notice that it admits errors or problems with regard to forms of behavior but not with regard to official church teaching. However, there were official papal teachings accepting the use of torture and denying religious liberty. While church teaching did recognize that no one is to be coerced into believing, as the document states, the attitude toward heretics and schismatics was entirely different.

At the time of the Second Vatican Council, perhaps the most significant question involving religious liberty was not the substance of the issue itself but rather the question of change or development in church teaching. How could the church teach in the twentieth century what it denied in the nineteenth? Recall that the declaration itself admitted no error in past papal teaching. Many significant proponents of the newer teaching argued on the council floor that there was continuity between the teaching of the nineteenth-century popes and the new teaching. Changing historical circumstances explained the "development" in teaching. They did not want to admit that there had been discontinuity or that the earlier teaching had in any way been in error. I do not see how anyone today can deny some discontinuity, and therefore error, between the popes' teachings in the nineteenth century and the teaching of the Catholic Church today on religious liberty.

Discussion Questions
RELIGIOUS FREEDOM

1. If a secular state demands (or rewards) adherence to an official state religion like Catholicism (or Islam, Judaism, or another faith), what are the implications for the individual citizen of that state? What values are emphasized with such a policy? What values are considered unimportant?

2. Are there any tenets of Catholicism that are violated by *union* of church and state? If so, what are they?

3. John Courtney Murray, SJ, was the leading theological mind behind the church's change on issues of religious freedom. But before the Second Vatican Council officially adopted his thinking, church authorities censored him for his views. How do you respond to this fact? Does it affect how you think about the silencing of some theologians today? If so, how?

4. How would you describe the historical significance of this change in Vatican policy in today's world?

Chapter 5

ECUMENISM

Catholic policy on ecumenism has changed enormously in the last millennium. When Rome and Constantinople separated in 1054, rivalry between Eastern and Western Christians was so intense that Western zealots considered the Eastern churches mission territory. Mistrust of other Christians grew worse after the Reformation in the sixteenth century. Catholic officials identified Protestants and Anglicans as heretics, treated their liturgies as false worship, and suspected their ministers of bad faith.

Although Pope Leo XIII expressed concern about Christian unity, Rome's positions began to shift only under Pius XI and Pius XII. The major changes came with John XXIII, who assigned an ecumenical purpose to Vatican Council II, and with Paul VI, who "asked forgiveness" for the role of Catholics in the division of Christians and promulgated the council's Decree on Ecumenism. After the council, the church opened formal dialogues with Orthodox, Anglican, and Protestant churches. In his encyclical Ut unum sint, Pope John Paul II fully endorsed the ecumenical movement. But as yet the Vatican has taken no decisive steps to restore unity.

For another sampling of attitudes toward those judged to be "heretics" or otherwise outside the Catholic faith, see chapter 9, "Theological Dissent," chapter 4, "Religious Freedom," and chapter 6, "The Jewish People."

Leo IX, Bull of Excommunication of the Patriarch Michael Cerularius, 1054:

"By the authority of the Holy and Indivisible Trinity and of that of the Apostolic See ... by the authority of all the Orthodox Fathers of the seven ecumenical councils and of the whole Catholic Church, we [legates] subscribe the anathema pronounced by our Lord the most Holy Pope upon Michael [Cerularius] and his followers if they do not reform themselves ... and if they do not recant with all the heretics and with the devil and his angels, Amen, amen."

Context: This bull marked the beginning of the Great Eastern Schism, dividing the Latin and Eastern churches.

Boniface VIII, *Unam Sanctam,* 1302:

"We declare, affirm, and define as a truth necessary for salvation that every human being is subject to the Roman pontiff."

Council of Florence, Decree for the Jacobites, 1442:

"All who are outside the Catholic Church, not only pagans but also Jews, heretics, and schismatics, cannot partake of eternal life, but are doomed to the eternal fire of hell, if they do not enter the church before the end of their lives."

Pius IX, *Quanto Conficiamur*, 1863:

"It is necessary...to remember again and to condemn the very serious error into which some Catholics miserably fall, who think that men who live in error and are strangers to Catholic faith and unity can reach eternal life....Catholic dogma states that nobody outside of the Catholic Church can be saved."

Holy Office, *Ad Omnes Episcopos Angliae*, 1864:

"Of course, nothing is more important for a Catholic than that schisms and dissensions among Christians be radically abolished and that all Christians be united....But under no circumstances can it be tolerated that faithful Christians and ecclesiastics be under the leadership of heretics and, what is worse, that they should pray for Christian unity according to the intentions of the most depraved and contagious heresy."

Leo XIII, *Amantissimae Voluntatis*, 1895:

This apostolic letter, addressed "to the English who desire the kingship of Christ in the unity of faith," encouraged "a patient search for unity" and did not speak of submission but of "reconciliation and peace."

Leo XIII, *Provida Matris*, 1895:

Provida Matris "consecrated the nine days preceding Pentecost to prayer for Christian unity" (Tavard, 1960, p. 95).

Leo XIII, *Satis Cognitum*, 1896:

"Let all those...who detest the widespread irreligion of our times, and acknowledge and confess Jesus Christ to be the Son of God and the Savior of the human race, but who have wandered away from the Spouse, listen to Our voice. Let them not refuse to obey Our paternal charity....Let such as these take counsel with themselves, and realize that they can in no wise be counted among the children of God, unless they take Christ Jesus as their Brother, and at the same time the church as their mother."

Leo XIII, *Apostolicae Curae*, 1896:

"We pronounce and declare that ordinations carried out according to the Anglican rite have been and are absolutely null and utterly void."

Pius X, *Editae Saepe*, 1910:

"[During the Reformation] passions ran riot and knowledge of the truth was almost completely twisted and confused. A continual battle was being waged against errors. Human society, going from bad to worse, was rushing headlong into the abyss. Then those proud and rebellious men came on the scene who...were not concerned with correcting morals, but only with denying dogmas. Thus they increased the chaos. They dropped the reins of the law, and unbridled licentiousness ran wild. They despised the authoritative guidance of the church and pandered to the whims of the dissolute princes and people. They tried to destroy the church's doctrine, constitution, and discipline.... They called this rebellious riot and perversion of faith and morals a reformation, and themselves reformers. In reality they were corrupters."

Code of Canon Law, 1917:

"It is not licit for the faithful to assist in any way, that is, to take part, in the liturgies of non-Catholics."

Pius XI, *Discorsi agli Universitari*, 1927:

"For reunion it is above all necessary to know and to love one another. To know one another because if the work of reunion has failed so often, these failures have been due in large measure to the fact that neither side has known the other.... The errors and equivocations which exist and recur among our separated brethren against the Catholic Church seem simply incredible. But on the other hand, Catholics too have sometimes failed to have a proper appreciation of their responsibility; or, because of ignorance, they have lacked a fraternal spirit."

Pius XI, *Mortalium Animos*, 1928:

"Conventions, meetings, and addresses are frequently arranged...at which a large number of listeners are present, and at which all without distinction are invited to join in the discussion, both infidels of every kind, and Christians, even those who have unhappily fallen away from Christ or who with obstinacy and pertinacity deny His divine nature and mission. Certainly such attempts can nowise be approved by Catholics, founded as they are on that false opinion which considers all religions to be more or less good and praiseworthy.... The Apostolic See has never allowed Catholics to attend meetings of non-Catholics; the union of Christians can only go forward by encouraging the dissidents to return to the one true church."

Pius XI, *Caritate Christi*, 1932:

Caritate Christi called for "union of minds and forces of all who are proud of the Christian name...in order to ward off from mankind the great danger that threatens all alike."

Holy Office, *Cum Compertum*, 1948:

Cum compertum "reminded Catholics of canonical prohibitions against unauthorized participation in 'so-called "ecumenical" meetings' with non-Catholic Christians and in shared worship" (Minus, p. 166).

Holy Office, *Ecclesia Catholica*, 1950:

Ecclesia Catholica allowed Protestants and Catholics to say the "Our Father, Our Mother" together, but "non-Catholics may certainly be told that, should they return to the church, such good as the grace of God has already wrought in their souls will not be lost, but will be completed and brought to perfection. But they must not be given the impression that by their return they are contributing to the church something essential which formerly she lacked."

Pius XII, *Sempiternus Rex*, 1951:

"We foresee what a rich source of blessings for the common welfare of Christianity this return to the unity of the church would be."

Pius XII, Allocution of the Fifth National Convention of the Union of Italian Catholic Jurists, 1953:

"The affirmation: 'Religious and moral error must always be impeded when it is possible because toleration of them is in itself immoral,' is not valid absolutely and unconditionally. The duty of repressing moral and religious error cannot therefore be an ultimate norm of action. It must be subordinate to higher and more general norms, which in some circumstances permit, and even perhaps seem to indicate as the better policy, toleration of error in order to promote a greater good."

John XXIII, *Ad Petri Cathedram*, 1959:

"The outcome of the approaching Ecumenical Council will depend more on a crusade of fervent prayer than on human effort and diligent application. And so with loving heart We also invite to this crusade all who are not of this fold but reverence and worship God and strive in good faith to obey his commands."

Second Vatican Council, *Decree on Ecumenism*, 1964:

- "In humble prayer we beg pardon of God and of our separated sisters and brothers, just as we forgive those who trespass against us."

- "In certain circumstances, such as in prayer services 'for unity' and during ecumenical gatherings, it is allowable, indeed desirable, that Catholics should join in prayer with members of other Christian churches and communities.... Yet worship in common is not to be considered as a means to be used indiscriminately for the restoration of unity among Christians.... The concrete course to be adopted, when all the circumstances of time, place, and persons have been duly considered, is left to the prudent decision of the local episcopal authority, unless the bishops' conference according to its own statutes, or the holy See, has determined otherwise."

Second Vatican Council, *Dogmatic Constitution on the Church,* 1964:

- "All women and men are called to belong to the new people of God. This people, therefore, whilst remaining one and unique, is to be spread throughout the whole world and to all ages in order that the design of God's will may be fulfilled.... There are, legitimately in the ecclesial communion, particular churches which retain their own traditions, without prejudice to the Chair of Peter which presides over the entire assembly of charity while at the same time taking care that these differences do not diminish unity, but rather contribute to it."

- "Those who, through no fault of their own, do not know the Gospel of Christ or his church, but who nevertheless seek God with a sincere heart, and, moved by grace, try in their actions to do his will as they know it through the dictates of their conscience — these too may attain eternal salvation."

Paul VI, Address, 1970:

"You well know how Vatican Council II has awakened in the Catholic Church a new awareness of the links that already exist among the Christians who share the riches of Christ by faith and baptism."

Code of Canon Law, 1983:

"Whenever it is required by necessity or recommended by a true spiritual necessity and there is no danger of error or indifferentism, it is licit for the faithful who are in a material or moral impossibility of reaching a Catholic minister to receive the sacraments of penance, of the Eucharist, and of the unction of the sick from non-Catholic ministers in whose church these sacraments are valid."

John Paul II, *Ut Unum Sint,* 1995:

- "Dialogue has not only been undertaken; it *has become an outright necessity, one of the church's priorities*" [emphasis in original].

- "Legitimate diversity is in no way opposed to the church's unity, but rather enhances her splendor and contributes greatly to the fulfillment of her mission."

- "It is obvious that the lack of unity among Christians contradicts the truth which Christians have the mission to spread and, consequently, it gravely damages their witness."

John Paul II, Vespers Sermon, Church of St. Gregory of Rome, 1996:

"Thirty years ago the Catholic Church and the Anglican Communion, moved by the Holy Spirit, set out with determination along the path that would lead to the restoration of unity. It is a journey that is proving more difficult than was expected at its beginning. Sadly, we are faced with disagreements which have arisen since we entered into dialogue, including disagreement about conferring priestly ordination on women. This question puts into clear relief the need to reach an understanding of how the church authoritatively discerns the teaching and practice which constitute the apostolic faith entrusted to us."

John Paul II, *Tertio Millennio Adveniente,* 1996:

"The approaching end of the second millennium demands of everyone an examination of conscience and the promotion of fitting ecumenical initiatives so that we can celebrate the great jubilee, if not completely united, at least much closer to overcoming the divisions of the second millennium."

THE FLOWERING OF ECUMENISM
George H. Tavard

In earlier centuries, the church exhibited a basic hostility to heretics and schismatics. This was a side effect of the church's early struggle to protect the apostolic traditions, first from Gnostic distortions, and then from speculations about Christ and the Trinity that occasioned the great ecumenical councils. Later, a growing estrangement between Greek and Latin culture eventually brought about the schism of 1054 between Rome and Constantinople. Yet the popes never officially equated Byzantine Christians with heretics. It was Greek theologians who came to see the belief that "the Holy Spirit proceeds from the Creator and the Son" (the *Filioque*) as a heresy that Westerners introduced into their creed.

Throughout the Middle Ages, when Latin bishops and popes defended the church from pressure by emperors, kings, queens, and princes, they asserted a universal spiritual authority over all churches and secular realms and all individual believers. The Council of Florence's forceful language in a catechetical instruction endorsed what priests and faithful already believed about the supremacy of the pope's spiritual authority: "All who are outside the Catholic Church...cannot partake of eternal life." The standard medieval reaction to a number of lay movements that denied authority to the clergy ran along the same lines, and the axiom, "Outside the church, no salvation," was understood literally. So when the Albigensians denied basic Christian doctrines, they were massacred. Despite such conflict, close relations continued to exist between Catholics and Orthodox in many places, notably in the Lebanon.

As a coherent system of belief and life, centered on obedience to the bishop of Rome, Roman Catholicism came into being during the Counter-Reformation, in reaction to the Reformation of the sixteenth century and the parallel development of Anglican, Lutheran, Calvinist, and other churches, which are globally (though not always accurately) called Protestant. As diversity of churches and doctrines became a feature of European life, theology tended to define itself polemically, against others, even though some theologians and church leaders always felt deep concern about concord and unity among Christians. The fortress mentality of Roman Catholicism was strengthened by persecution of the church during the French Revolution and, in the nineteenth century, by the popes' ideological struggles with freemasons, socialists, and communists. The popes generally blamed the loss of the Papal States to the kingdom of Italy on the doctrines of the Reformation.

Leo XIII was the first pope to show any eagerness to promote both the unity of the Catholic Church and the reunion of all Christians. He recommended praying for unity in preparation for the feast of Pentecost. He formulated his hopes for reunion in the encyclical *Satis cognitum* (1896) and made tentative approaches toward Orthodox and Anglican Christians. According to his "unionist" theology, however, reunion of the churches could only come from their acknowledgment of the universal primacy of the Roman See. This precondition did not advance dialogue. Tragically, on the basis of an inconclusive historical and theological investigation by a special commission, Leo XIII also felt bound in 1896 to declare Anglican ordinations invalid. Although he expected that this decision would persuade large groups of Anglicans to make their submission to the Holy See, it became instead a lasting obstacle to reunion.

When the modern ecumenical movement was inaugurated in 1910, at a meeting of the International Missionary Council in Edinburgh, the Roman mind was not yet ready to be actively associated with it. Two organizations initiated there, "Life and Work" and "Faith and Order," vainly invited the Holy See to cooperate with them. In 1919, under Benedict XV, a Holy Office decree said all authorizations to take part in ecumenical meetings had to come from the Holy See.

Under Pius XI, however, Cardinal Désiré Mercier, archbishop of Malines (Belgium), sponsored the Malines Conversations (1921–26), in which several Catholic and Anglican theologians discussed some of the pending problems between their communions in an atmosphere of mutual respect and friendliness. Nonetheless, Pius XI did not authorize Catholic participation in the Lausanne meeting of Faith and Order in 1927. In the encyclical *Mortalium animos*, he accused its organizers of promoting a "pan-Protestantism" hostile to the true unity of the church. Some Catholics contributed unofficially to preparation of the Oxford meeting of Life and Work in 1937, and a few Catholics attended the Edinburgh meeting of Faith and Order that year in a strictly private capacity.

Pius XII began to break the ice in 1948, the year of the formation of the World Council of Churches (WCC) in Amsterdam, when a Holy Office decision gave bishops the responsibility of authorizing Catholics to attend ecumenical meetings in their diocese. Accordingly, in 1952 the vicar apostolic in Sweden sent official observers to the Faith and Order gathering of Lund. On the other hand, in 1954 Cardinal Samuel Stritch outlawed participation in the second meeting of the WCC in Evanston, Illinois.

A new phase in the Catholic Church's relations with other Christian churches began unexpectedly in 1960, when John XXIII created the Pontifical Secretariat for the Promotion of the Unity of Christians as one of the agencies to prepare Vatican Council II. In 1961 the Secretariat sent official observers to the WCC's third meeting, in New Delhi. At the Vatican Council the same secretariat hosted Orthodox and Protestant observers; it composed and presented the *Decree on Ecumenism*, the *Declaration on Religious Liberty*, and the *Declaration on the Relation of the Church to Non-Christian Religions*. It also provided half the members of the commission that wrote the *Dogmatic Constitution on Divine Revelation*. Pope Paul VI made the secretariat a permanent office in the Roman curia, and John Paul II eventually renamed it the Pontifical Council for the Promotion of the Unity of Christians.

Since Vatican II, Catholic participation in ecumenical activities has been taken for granted. Catholic observers attended the Montreal meeting of Faith and Order (1963), and they have been present at all later meetings of the WCC, as well as the Lambeth Conference of Anglican Bishops and the Anglican Consultative Council. In addition, the Catholic Church has taken the initiative in holding bilateral theological dialogues with all major Christian churches, both at the international level and in a number of countries. Catholic theologians are now active in the Faith and Order Commission, they work closely with the International Missionary Council, and they are involved in ecumenical translations of the Bible. A joint working group

brings together representatives of the WCC and the Council for the Unity
of Christians on a regular basis.

Some of the bilateral dialogues have issued valuable statements — notably,
in the United States, *Justification by Faith,* issued by Lutherans and Catholics
in Dialogue in 1983. Internationally, they produced the final report of the
First Commission of ARCIC (Anglican-Roman Catholic International Conversations) in 1981. Unfortunately, the Congregation for the Doctrine of the
Faith's critique of it illustrated the Roman curia's continuing inability to read
ecumenical documents in the spirit in which they have been composed.

At the end of Vatican II, the Secretariat for Christian Unity published the
Directory for Ecumenism (1967 and 1970), for the guidance of bishops, priests,
and people in their ecumenical activities. This was replaced in 1993 by a
new directory. It is now common for each Catholic diocese to have an active ecumenical commission to promote contacts with other Christians, and
seminaries and faculties of theology are expected to offer courses on the history and theology of the ecumenical movement. Parishes are encouraged to
take part in ecumenical programs of social action, Bible studies, and theological conversations with ministers and laity of the other churches in their
neighborhood.

Regardless of recurring problems — not surprising given the long history
of estrangement between the churches — since Vatican II the Holy See has
promoted a progressive opening of Catholic hearts and minds to the requirements of Jesus' prayer for the unity of his disciples (John 17:21). It has also
fostered greater awareness of the Catholic Church's partial responsibility for
the separations of the past and realization that prolonged Christian disunity
sends the wrong message to the world. Such a development can only be
the work of the Holy Spirit, as all the popes since Pius XII have acknowledged. In numerous addresses and in the encyclical *Ut unum sint* (1995),
John Paul II has shown that he fully shares the commitment to Christian
unity of John XXIII and Paul VI (and presumably John Paul I, who hosted
ecumenical dialogues when he was patriarch of Venice). John Paul II has expressed the hope that the year 2000 will mark a point of no return in the
process of reconciliation between the Catholic and Orthodox churches.

The passage from polemic to friendship among divided Christians has the
marks of a true conversion. The reasons for the change in the twentieth
century need to be examined in relation to theories of doctrinal development
that are not yet fully elaborated.

Pius XII once remarked that *Catholicism* should not be confused with
Catholicity. He was referring to the medieval idea of "two swords, spiritual
and temporal," a notion related to an aspect of Catholicism that was not part
of the church's essential Catholicity. In other words, a deep logic of Catholicity breaks through the superficial aspects of Catholicism once these are no
longer nurtured by the conditions of society. This change has now happened

to the militancy of the Counter-Reformation, which became dysfunctional when the world began to search for unity beyond national rivalries and conflicting philosophies of life. The church and the churches are being guided by the Spirit toward new forms of communion. This movement is far from over.

At this time, however, new difficulties seem to loom on the horizon in regard to the reconciliation of Christians. Despite the consensus reached in some of the major dialogues, especially with Anglicans and Lutherans, regarding problems that prompted the separations of the past, the authorities of the churches hesitate to take concrete steps toward organic unity. The slow pace of visible results threatens to lead priests and people to give up hope in the reunion of Christians. Another peril is that the church could bow to the urging of some of its members to define new dogmas. All proclamations that a given doctrine is necessary to salvation necessarily throw a new and serious obstacle in the way of Christian unity. Finally, recent changes in the theology of the church's mission, a new appreciation of spiritual dimensions outside Christianity, and new dialogues of Asian and African Catholics with the faithful of other religions, should not be allowed to erode the sense of urgency inherent in ecumenical dialogues among the Christian churches. These dialogues constitute the Christian response to Christ's prayer that his disciples may be one.

Discussion Questions
ECUMENISM

1. What has been your personal experience of people in other Christian denominations?

    • Have you worshiped with them?

    • Have you worked with them on social issues?

    • Have you engaged them in dialogue about theological issues, ethics, or worship?

    • If so, how did you find these experiences?

2. What factors in the contemporary world seem to be leading the Roman curia in the direction of advocating Christian unity?

3. As you view the churches and the world, what are the major obstacles to Christian unity?

4. Do you believe that Christian unity is an imperative of our time? If so, why? If not, why not?

5. The curia has said that unity is possible only when other Christians recognize the primacy of Rome and the pope. Is this a helpful approach? Why or why not?

6. Envision for a moment a world in which Christendom is unified. What does it look like? What is the essence of that "unity"? How is that "unity" structured? Do non-Christians have anything to fear from Christian unity?

Chapter 6

THE JEWISH PEOPLE

Catholic Church pronouncements provided a theological underpinning for anti-Semitism for centuries. Although the history is mixed, with a few popes upholding Jewish rights, official pronouncements are replete with requirements that Jews dress differently and references to Jewish guilt for the death of Christ. In the twentieth century, many have criticized Pope Pius XII for not using the power of the church to condemn the Holocaust. With Pope John XXIII and the Second Vatican Council, however, the church condemned anti-Semitism as a sin. Pope John Paul II has been especially strong in reaching out to the Jewish community to establish better relations.

SCRIPTURE

Genesis 25:23:

"[Rebekah] went to consult God, who answered her:

'Two nations are in your womb,
    two peoples are quarreling while still within you;
But one shall surpass the other,
    And the older shall serve the younger.'"

Context: This passage is quoted in Romans 9:12. Church officials used both passages to justify God's preference for Christians (Jacob) over Jews (Esau).

Galatians 4:21–25:

"I ask you, you who strive to be subject to the Law — do you understand what the Law asks of you? For Scripture says that Abraham had two children — one by Hagar, who was a slave, and the other by Sarah, who was freeborn. The child of the slave had been begotten in the course of nature, but the child of the free woman was the fruit of the promise. All this is clearly an allegory: the two women stand for the two Covenants. One is from Mt. Sinai, and she gave birth to children in slavery: this is Hagar. Hagar represents Mt. Sinai in Arabia — which corresponds to the present Jerusalem, which is in slavery like Hagar's children."

1 Corinthians 5:6–8, 10:16–21:

"This boasting of yours is an ugly thing. Don't you know that a little yeast has its effect all through the dough? Get rid of the old yeast to make for yourselves fresh dough, unleavened bread, as it were; Christ our Passover has been sacrificed. So let us celebrate the feast — not with the old yeast, the yeast of corruption and wickedness, but with the unleavened bread of sincerity and truth.

"The cup of blessing which we bless — is it not a sharing in the blood of Christ? The bread we break — is it not a sharing in the body of Christ? Because the loaf of bread is one, we who are many are one body, for we all partake of the one loaf. Or look at the people of Israel: those who eat the sacrifices are in communion with the altar. Now I don't mean to imply that a sacrifice offered to an idol is anything, or that the idol itself is anything; it's just that pagans make sacrifices to demons, not to God, and I do not want you to be in communion with demons. You cannot drink the cup of our Savior and the cup of demons too; you cannot partake of our Savior's table and the table of demons."

Editors' Note: See the accompanying essay for the way church leaders interpreted this passage.

CHURCH FATHERS

Origen, c. 230:

"And therefore the blood of Jesus falls not only on the Jews of that time, but on all generations of Jews up to the end of the world."

John Chrysostom, c. 400:

"The synagogue is a bordello, . . . a hiding place for unclean beasts."

Augustine, c. 425:

"The Jews are dispersed throughout all nations, as witnesses to their iniquity and of our truth."

MIDDLE AGES

Gregory I, c. 600:

"Just as license must not be granted to the Jews to presume to do in their synagogues more than the law permits them, so they should not suffer curtailment in that which has been conceded to them."

Calixtus II, *Constitutio pro Judeis,* 1120 or 1123:

Constitutio pro Judeis condemned forced baptisms, assaults on Jews and their property, and desecration of synagogues and cemeteries; it upheld rights and practices.

Context: This decree, based on a lost pronouncement by Nicholas II (1061), was reissued by Innocent III, Honorius II, Innocent IV, Alexander IV, Urban IV, Gregory X, Nicholas III, Martin IV, Honorius IV, Nicholas IV, Urban V, Martin V, and Eugenius IV. Gregory IX incorporated it into his Decretals, one of the bases of canon law, in 1234.

Council of Auvergne, in Gratian, *Decretum,* c. 1140:

"If anyone joins himself to the Jewish wickedness in conjugal partnership, or if any Christian woman mixes in carnal union with a Jew, or any Jewish woman with a Christian, let whoever is known to have committed such wickedness forthwith be separated from Christian company and fellowship and from the communion of the church."

Innocent III, *Licet Perfidia Judeorum,* 1199:

"Although the Jewish perfidy is in every way worthy of condemnation, nevertheless, because through them truth of our own Faith is proved, they are not to be severely oppressed by the faithful.... Thou shalt not destroy the Jews completely, so that the Christians should never by any chance be able to forget Thy Law."

Innocent III, Letter to Archbishop of Arles, 1201:

[Even if torture or intimidation is used, the convert] "does receive the impress of Christianity and may be forced to observe the Christian Faith as one who expressed a conditional willingness though, absolutely speaking, he was unwilling.... [Once] the grace of Baptism had been received and they had been anointed with the sacred oil, and had participated in the body of the Lord, they might properly be forced to hold to the faith which they had accepted perforce, lest the name of the Lord be blasphemed, and lest they hold in contempt and consider vile the faith they had joined."

Innocent III, Letter to Archbishop of Sens and Bishop of Paris, 1205:

"Christian piety receives [into its midst] the Jews who, by their own guilt, are consigned to perpetual servitude."

Innocent III, Letter to the Count of Nevers, 1208:

"Thus the Jews, against whom the blood of Jesus Christ calls out — although they ought not to be killed, lest the Christian people forget the Divine Law — yet as wanderers ought they to remain upon the earth, until their countenance be filled with shame and they seek the name of Jesus Christ, the Lord. That is why blasphemers of the Christian name ought not to be aided by Christian princes to oppress the servants of the Lord, but ought rather be forced into the servitude of which they made themselves deserving when they raised sacrilegious hands against Him who had come to confer true liberty upon them, thus calling down His Word upon themselves and upon their children."

Council of Arles, 1234:

"We decree that male Jews from the age of thirteen and up, when outside their homes, except when on a journey, must wear upon the outer garment, upon the breast, a round badge of three or four fingers in width. Jewish women from the age of twelve and up shall wear veils when outside their homes. If the Jews shall, under any pretext, act contrary, they shall be denied intercourse with the Christians."

Editors' Note: In the twentieth century, the Nazis forced Jews and other persecuted minorities to wear badges, such as the Star of David or the pink triangle.

Gregory IX, 1239:

"If what is said about the Jews ... is true, no punishment would be sufficiently great or sufficiently worthy of their crime."

Gregory IX, Letter to the Bishop of Paris, 1239:

"We, through Apostolic letters, order Your Discretion to have the Jews who live in the Kingdoms of France, England, Aragon, Navarre, Castile, Leon, and Portugal, forced by the secular arm to give up their books. Those books, in which you will find errors of this sort, you shall cause to be burned at the stake. By Apostolic Power, and through use of ecclesiastical censures, you will silence all opponents."

Innocent IV, *Lachrymabilem Iudaeorum*, 1247:

"While solemnizing the Passover ... they are falsely accused ... that they share the heart of a murdered child."

Context: Accusations in the eleventh and twelfth centuries that Jews killed Christians and used their blood to make Passover matzohs or in circumcision rituals led to pogroms (systematic armed attacks on Jewish communities) and expulsions of Jews from several countries.

Alexander IV, Letter to Duke of Burgundy, 1257:

"You must cause those books which are popularly called Talmud, in which are contained errors against the Catholic faith and horrible and intolerable blasphemies against our Lord Jesus Christ and the Holy Virgin Mary, His mother, to be surrendered by all the Jews in the aforesaid land."

Clement IV, *Turbato Corde,* 1267:

- "A number of bad Christians have abandoned the true Christian faith and wickedly transferred themselves to the rites of the Jews.... We order your organization [Inquisition], within the territories entrusted to you by the Apostolic See for searching out heretics, to make diligent and thorough inquiry into the above."
- "Against Christians whom you find guilty of the above you shall proceed as against heretics. Upon Jews...you shall impose fitting punishment. By means of appropriate ecclesiastical censure you shall silence all who oppose you. If necessary, you may call on the secular arm."

Nicholas III, *Vineam Soreth,* 1278:

Vineam Soreth enjoined Franciscans and Dominicans to "summon [the Jews] to sermons where they live, in large and small groups, repeatedly, as many times as you may think beneficial. Inform them of evangelical doctrines with salutary warnings and discreet reasonings."

Context: This decree led to book burnings, synagogue invasions, and mob attacks. It was discontinued in 1846 by decree of Gregory XVI.

Clement VI, 1348:

"Let no Christian compel Jews to come to baptism by violence, these same unwilling or refusing.... For he, indeed, who is known to come to Christian baptism, not spontaneously but unwillingly, is not considered to possess authentic Christian faith. Too, let no Christian have the presumption to wound or to kill those same Jewish persons, nor to take their money from them, apart from the lawful sentence of the lord of the region, or city, or countryside which they inhabit."

Council of Basel, *Decree on Jews and Converts,* 1434:

"[Jews] are to be forced under threat of heavy penalties to take on a form of dress by which they can be clearly distinguished from Christians. Moreover, in order to avoid excessive social intercourse, they must be made to dwell separate from Christians in their cities and towns, in places as far distant from the churches as possible. Nor may they on Sundays and other solemn feast days open their shops or work in public."

Innocent VIII, 1489:

Innocent VIII absolved the magistrates of Siena who had taken in and employed several Jewish lenders and pawnbrokers, doing so for "the good of the city's poor" (Lapide, p. 56).

Context: This action was characteristic of Renaissance popes dealing with lending money at interest in Italy. It was a pragmatic solution sanctioned even by canon lawyers (see chapter 18, "Usury").

Paul IV, *Cum Nimis Absurdum*, 1555:

- "Since it is absurd and improper that Jews — whose own guilt has consigned them to perpetual servitude — under the pretext that Christian piety receives them and tolerates their presence, should be ingrates to Christians, so that they attempt to exchange the servitude they owe to Christians for domination over them."

- "It has lately come to our notice that these Jews, in our dear City and in some other cities, lands, and places of the Holy Roman Church, have erupted into insolence: they presume not only to dwell side by side with Christians and near the churches, with no distinct habit to separate them, but even to erect homes in the more noble sections and streets of the cities, lands, and places where they dwell, and to buy and possess fixed property, where they dwell, and to have nurses, housemaids, and other hired Christian servants and to perpetrate many other things in ignominy and contempt of the Christian name.... We sanction ... that all Jews should live solely in one and the same location [in what would come to be called ghettoes]."

Benedict XIV, A *Quo Primum*, 1751:

[To Polish bishops] "Neither your property nor your privileges are [to be] hired to Jews; furthermore you do no business with them and you neither lend them money nor borrow from them."

Context: He cites statements by Nicholas IV, Paul IV, Pius V, Gregory VIII, and Clement VIII, forbidding Christians from living in the same cities with Jews.

Pius IX, Letter to Edgardo Mortara, 1867:

"You are very dear to me, my little son, for I acquired you for Jesus Christ at a high price. So it is. I paid dearly for your ransom. Your case set off a worldwide storm against me and the Apostolic See. Governments and peoples, the rulers of the world as well as the journalists — who are the truly powerful people of our times — declared war on me. Monarchs themselves entered the battle against me, and with their ambassadors they flooded me with diplomatic notes, and all this because of you.... People lamented the harm done to your parents because you were regenerated by the grace of holy baptism and brought up according to God's wishes. And in the meantime no one showed any concern for me, father of all the faithful."

Context: Edgardo Mortara was forcibly taken from his Jewish parents at age six, in 1858, on the order of the Inquisitor of Bologna, to be raised as a Christian because he allegedly had been secretly baptized as an infant by a servant. He was taken to Rome, where Pius IX oversaw his education. He later became a priest and died at age eighty-eight, in Belgium, one month before the Nazis invaded in 1940.

Holy Office, Decree Suppressing Opus Sacerdotale Amici Israel, 1928:

- "The Catholic Church, in fact, has always been accustomed to pray for the Jewish people, which was the depository of divine promises up until Jesus Christ, in spite of the continual blindness of this people, and indeed precisely because of this blindness. With what charity the Apostolic See has protected this people against unjust persecutions!"

- "Because it disapproves of all hatreds and animosities among peoples, it condemns in the highest decree hatred against the people formerly chosen by God, the hatred that is commonly designated today under the name of 'anti-Semitism.'"

Pius XI, Address to Pilgrims, 1938:

"No, it is not possible for Christians to take part in anti-Semitism. We recognize that anyone has the right to defend himself, to take steps to protect himself against anything that threatens his legitimate interests. But anti-Semitism is inadmissible. We are spiritually Semites."

Context: This extempore declaration had "no official character" and was not published in L'Osservatore Romano.

[About] Paul VI, [as Msgr. Montini,] 1945:

"In a long conversation with Msgr. Montini...in October 1945 in Rome, during which I pleaded with him to help us obtain the return of Jewish children who had been saved by Catholics or Catholic institutions, I was shocked when the Catholic prelate contested the accuracy of my statement that at least 1.5 million Jewish children had perished in the Holocaust. It took more than half an hour to explain and justify my statement and for him to accept it....It seems to me fair to say that high Vatican diplomacy never really understood the extent of the tragedy that had befallen the Jewish people" (Gerhart Riegner, "A Warning to the World: The Efforts of World Jewish Congress to Mobilize Christian Churches against the Final Solution," 1983).

Prayer for the Conversion of the Jews, Withdrawn after 1959:

"Almighty and eternal God, who drivest not away from Thy mercy even the faithless Jews [*Judaicam perfidiam*], hear our prayers, which we offer for the blindness of that people...that...they may be delivered from their darkness."

Editors' Note: This prayer used to be part of the Good Friday liturgy. John XXIII ordered the phrase "perfidious Jews" removed in 1959. The entire prayer was eliminated after Vatican II.

John XXIII, Meeting with United Jewish Appeal Leaders, 1960:

"I am Joseph, your brother."

[John XXIII, Prayer, n.d.: "The mark of Cain is stamped upon our foreheads. Across the centuries, our brother Abel has lain in blood which we drew, and shed tears we caused by forgetting Thy love. Forgive us, Lord, for the curse we falsely attributed to their name as Jews. Forgive us for crucifying Thee a second time in their flesh. For we knew not what we did."]

Editors' Note: This prayer is probably a hoax, perpetrated after John's death, during Vatican II.

Second Vatican Council, *Declaration on the Relation of the Church to Non-Christian Religions,* 1965:

- "Even though the Jewish authorities and those who followed their lead pressed for the death of Christ ... neither all Jews indiscriminately at that time, nor Jews today, can be charged with the crimes committed during his passion. It is true that the church is the new people of God, yet the Jews should not be spoken of as rejected or accursed as if this followed from Holy Scripture."

- "Indeed, the church reproves every form of persecution against whomsoever it may be directed. Remembering, then, its common heritage with the Jews and moved not by any political consideration, but solely by the religious motivation of Christian charity, it deplores all hatreds, persecutions, displays of anti-Semitism leveled at any time or from any source against the Jews."

John Paul II, Address in the Synagogue of Rome, 1986:

"Speaking through me, the church deplores, in the words of *Nostra aetate,* the hatreds, the persecutions, and all the manifestations of anti-Semitism directed against the Jews at any time by whomever."

John Paul II, 1990:

"For Christians the heavy burden of guilt for the murder of the Jewish people must be an enduring call to repentance; thereby we can overcome every form of anti-Semitism and establish a new relationship with our kindred nation of the Old Covenant."

John Paul II, 1994:

"In the face of the perils which threaten the sons and daughters of this generation, Christians and Jews together have a great deal to offer to a world struggling to distinguish good from evil."

John Paul II, Remarks on the Fiftieth Anniversary of the Liberation of Auschwitz, 1995:

"God does not want us to be weeping tomorrow over other Auschwitzes of our own day. Let us pray and work so that this does not happen.... Never again anti-Semitism! Never again the arrogance of nationalism! Never again genocide!"

Commission for Religious Relations with the Jews, "We Remember: A Reflection on the Shoah," 1998:

- "The history of relations between Jews and Christians is a tormented one.... In effect, the balance of these relations over two thousand years has been quite negative."

- "During and after the war, Jewish communities and Jewish leaders expressed their thanks for all that had been done for them, including what Pope Pius XII did personally or through his representatives to save hundreds of thousands of Jewish lives. Many Catholic bishops, priests, religious, and laity have been honored for this reason by the State of Israel."

- "Nevertheless ... alongside such courageous men and women, the spiritual resistance and concrete action of other Christians was not that which might have been expected from Christ's followers.... For Christians, this heavy burden of conscience of their brothers and sisters during the Second World War must be a call to penitence. We deeply regret the errors and failures of those sons and daughters of the church."

ST. PAUL'S CONUNDRUM
Kenneth Stow

In recent years Pope John Paul II has confronted the Catholic Church's relationship to the Jews with almost unprecedented determination. This may reflect his moral sense of the evils of anti-Semitism and his response to the actions — or inaction — of Pius XII during the Shoah [Holocaust]. The impact of the Shoah itself is profound, as both non-Jews and Jews come to grips with the Jewish people's near-total destruction, which changed the social and cultural map of Europe, as well as the map of Jewish life.

But is the pope's new determination truly revolutionary? Has he finally rejected problematic ancient beliefs or merely created a new attitude out of old cloth? The answer is yes and no.

The first important, and ambivalent, statements about Jews came from Pope Gregory the Great, following St. Paul, who said in the Epistle to the Romans that the Jews were both "friends because of their ancestors" and "enemies of the Gospel." Following the laws of the late Christian-Roman Empire, Gregory stipulated that Jews had rights as well as limitations. Pope Alexander II repeated Gregory's ideas in 1063, by saying that Jews were unique among those who were not enemies. They should be allowed to live safely in Christendom, since "they were always prepared to serve" (to accept church rule).

Alexander's pronouncement evolved in two directions. First, in the twelfth century, the *Constitutio pro iudaeis* restated Gregory's notion that the Jews were to be both protected and limited. Then in 1205, Pope Innocent III, who reissued the *Constitutio,* said that Jews were consigned to "perpetual servitude."

This is a most misunderstood term. It has nothing to do with slavery, as the canon lawyers of the Middle Ages pointed out. However, it *did* mean the Jews were to accept a large number of disabilities, especially regulations constraining social interaction with Christians. For instance, during Holy Week, Jews were to remain indoors. Jews and Christians were not to dine together. Christians were not to live in Jews' homes as their servants, and sexual mingling of any sort was strictly forbidden. The reason for these specific prohibitions was to prevent the Christian body — the body of the individual Christian as well as that of the church — from being "sullied." This concept comes from St. Paul, this time in Galatians (4:21–25) and 1 Corinthians (5:6–13, 10:16–21).

In these epistles, Paul worried about Christians' compromising their faith, through circumcision, for instance. Paul also warned against idolatrous sacrifice, which he compared to Jewish sacrifice in the ancient Jerusalem Temple, in contrast to the Christian celebration of the Eucharist. Paul spoke, too, against sharing the "cup of demons" and uniting sexually with the unsaved. His intention may have been metaphorical and allegoric — he implicated Jews only indirectly — but later commentators took him literally. Hence dining with Jews and uniting sexually were anathema, for they compromised — indeed "polluted" — the Christian's faith. One way of preventing such "evils" was to enact laws prohibiting them. Most of these prohibitions were already in place by 1012, in the so-called *Decretum,* a collection of laws composed by Bishop Burchard of Worms. The Fourth Lateran Council of 1215 decreed the infamous Jewish badge (a type of special clothing). The badge (strips of cloth or a circle) was originally intended to prevent sexual contact. However, this special clothing and the badge quickly assumed pejorative overtones.

The particulars of papal policy fall between avoiding impurity and insults to the faith and protecting Jewish rights. Thus, in the thirteenth century, Innocent IV, following Gregory IX, ordered confiscation and examination of the Talmud (the prime body of Jewish legal discussion), to judge whether its contents were blasphemous and whether they contradicted the Law of Moses (the Torah). The church willingly tolerated the Torah, which it saw as a precursor of Christian truth.

Yet Innocent IV also warned that Jewish books should not be confiscated or destroyed to the extent that the Jews could no longer practice Judaism. This decision did not please the Talmud's opponents. The Talmud already had been burned at Paris in about 1240, with royal encouragement. In 1257, Alexander IV ordered a new confiscation of the Talmud. But Jewish books were not really attacked again until about 1415 in Spain and 1553 in the Papal States of Italy.

This "balance" or "restraint" — in medieval terms, one should stress; in contemporary terms it is all intolerable — appeared again on the subject of preaching. Franciscan and Dominican preachers wanted the right to preach to Jews and even force them to hear sermons. But Pope Nicholas III said only that if Jews failed to come, he was to be informed, so he could think of a solution. This policy shows that popes hesitated to violate longstanding traditions that conceded to the Jews the right to observe their religion unhindered.

The popes would not compromise in matters related to baptism, however. Technically, forced baptism was illegal. But when could one say force had been applied? Innocent III clarified this by distinguishing "conditional" from "absolute" force. The former, effectively, was anything short of the latter. Even a person who accepted baptism to save his or her life was considered legally baptized. People who reneged on baptism, as well as willing converts, were the subject of Clement IV's 1267 letter, *Turbato corde,* which instructed the papal inquisition to try "apostates," as well as any Jews who may have been "fautors" (promoters) of heresy.

On the other hand, the popes were consistent in discrediting charges that Jews murdered Christian children to use their blood in matzohs or circumcision rituals. Innocent IV's letter of 1247 denied that Jews ate these children's hearts. This defense is all the more interesting, because popes did believe that Jews might kill Christian children deliberately. Innocent III said so.

Boniface VIII, among others, believed that Jews were capable of desecrating the consecrated eucharistic host. It is no exculpation, but we must evaluate this accusation in the context of a world where the Eucharist was a starkly present and binding symbol, the fundamental expression of the Christian faith.

After the Protestant Reformation, the church's drive to reform itself led the papacy to make its first-ever attempt at a mass conversion of Jews in 1555. Paul IV ordered the Jews of Rome to enter a ghetto (the term comes from the site in Venice where the first ghetto was established in 1516). He was convinced that social isolation under a regimen of strictly applied canon law would ensure conversion. He was wrong. The forced sermons that Gregory XIII ordered in 1584 were equally ineffective in achieving conversions. No more than ten Jews a year, on average, converted at Rome during the entire ghetto period, which lasted until 1870. (Many were not Romans by origin.) Moreover, the zeal for mass conversion flagged quickly, and most popes were content just to leave the ghetto in place.

Under the challenge of the eighteenth-century Enlightenment, which the church intuited to be opposed to religion, and especially to the Catholic Church, the popes applied greater pressure. Benedict XIV, in particular, sought to enforce ghetto regulations rigidly. In addition, his letter to Polish bishops in 1751 reveals his fear of Jewish power over Christians, aligning him with those guarding against the subjection and alleged "contamination" of the individual Christian. The pope may have been most exercised by the fact that the Christians he accused of lending Jews money were bishops of the Polish church. The Jews then lent the money anew, making both themselves and the bishops recipients of interest. (All interest is called usury in the papal texts, not only the exorbitant rates that constitute illegal usury today.) Some earlier commentators had also been much concerned about the activities of clerical lenders, called, unflatteringly "our Jews." But it is important to note that Pope Benedict was reversing the normal papal policy, which found a pragmatic way to allow Jewish lending: it was always forbidden, but no punishments were meted out.

The threat that the Jews of Poland may have symbolized for Benedict XIV became clearer in the nineteenth century, during the long reign of Pius IX. This was the period of emancipation, when Jews throughout western and central Europe were being freed of limitations and enfranchised as full citizens. Yet Pius IX rigidly kept the Jews in the ghetto of Rome.

To protect his prerogatives vis-à-vis Jews, Pius IX was adamant in the famous case of Edgardo Mortara, willing even to lose the support of the French troops who protected the Papal States against incipient Italian nationalism. The French government opposed the keeping of Edgardo Mortara, a little boy who had allegedly been baptized as an infant by his nurse in Bologna, part of the Papal States. When he was six, church officials forcibly took him from his parents and whisked him off to a convent in Rome. Pius IX refused to return him. The French government withdrew its troops from Rome as a result, and Pius IX could not hold the Papal States. He obviously subscribed to the words of Benedict XIV, who, in 1751, lauded a sixteenth-century conciliar decision that "prohibited the principle of freedom of conscience."

Loss of power, or imminent loss of power, moved Pius IX to take extreme positions in the Mortara case. In the thirteenth century — as canon lawyers sharply reminded Pius IX — Pope Clement IV had ordered that a child baptized under similar conditions be returned to its parents until, at age seven, it could decide its faith for itself. This decision may have been somewhat casuistic, but it took into account parental feelings of loss, the very feelings Pius IX

reserved to himself as "father of all the faithful." Another factor in the Mortara case was the pope's sense of being under siege, since Italian nationalist
forces were threatening his control of the Papal States at the time.

In this rigid resistance to modernity and change, we may find the origins of the church's unfortunate positions during the fascist period in Spain,
Italy, and, most of all, Nazi Germany. As many critics have pointed out,
Pius XII took no clear position on the fate of the Jews under the Nazis. He
remained notoriously silent. Others, like Paul VI, seem to have failed to grasp
the dimensions of the Shoah's horror. After the war, the claim was made —
still repeated by Pius XII's defenders — that his was the only way to save
the Jews who could be saved and that the church would have suffered ir-
reparable damage otherwise. However much one rationalizes it historically,
this argument still begs the moral and theological question: When is one required to sacrifice — as no small number of Catholic clergy did during those
dark times?

In recognition of this failure, the present-day church has rejected anti-
Semitism. This change began with the Second Vatican Council's *Nostra
Aetate* on Judaism. But in the footnotes, which refer again and again to Paul's
Epistle to the Romans, one can see that the traditional theology of the True
Israel (Christianity) as opposed to the Carnal Israel (the rejected Jews) has
not been abandoned.

Likewise, no matter what John Paul II — clearly a true enemy of anti-
Semitism — intended, I cannot fail to recall the biblical verse this pope
alluded to in his famous visit to the Roman synagogue. You are our "elder
brothers," the pope said, but the entire verse states that "the elder shall
serve the younger." This verse was often used during the long centuries of
anti-Jewish polemic.

Nostra Aetate was written more than thirty years ago, and the fateful visit
to the synagogue happened well over a decade ago. Today few if any in the
church would rest at these points, not even John Paul II himself. Surely nobody would subscribe any longer to Benedict XIV's words decrying freedom
of conscience. More representative is the statement of Jesuit Father Drew
Christiansen in testimony (September 1997) before a committee of the U.S.
House of Representatives: "In Catholic teaching, religious liberty is universal
and indivisible."

Does this teaching extend to the idea that all religious teachings are
equally valid? One commentator tried to put words implying as much into
the mouth of Pope John XXIII. The imputed statement said: "We realize that
the mark of Cain stands upon our foreheads" — reversing what St. Augustine
said when he placed the brand of Cain on the foreheads of the Jews. Had
John XXIII really made this statement, no Catholic thenceforth could call
"the other" an enemy of the faith. Unfortunately, this imputed statement is
a fiction.

After 1959 an infamous prayer for the conversion of the Jews was removed from the Catholic Good Friday liturgy. Did this really herald a new era? To condemn anti-Semitism, not to offend Jews publicly, is one thing; to change theological fundamentals radically is another, and that is what a full reversal of the traditional view of Jews would demand.

The Vatican's "We Remember: A Reflection on the Shoah," of March 1998, left all the important questions unanswered. It did not consider whether the church as an institution played a negative role in the Shoah. It failed utterly to grasp the link between traditional Christian views of Judaism and the racial anti-Judaism of the Nazis, which included the ancient notion that a Jewish presence might be "polluting." Given the general optimism preceding its publication, "We Remember" was a disappointment.

Ten years ago, as the Vatican began work on this "apology," Cardinal Ratzinger, president of the Congregation for the Doctrine of the Faith, said in an interview with the Italian Catholic journal *Il Sabato*, "The pope has offered respect, but also a theology: Christ is the fulfillment of Abraham." This is exactly what St. Paul argued in Romans. It is this conundrum that Catholics must resolve in order truly to modify past attitudes toward Jews.

Discussion Questions
THE JEWISH PEOPLE

1. What has been your experience with Jewish people?

   • Have you ever participated in services at a synagogue?

   • Have you ever worked with Jewish people on issues of justice and peace?

   • Have you ever discussed Scripture, theology, or moral teachings with Jewish friends or acquaintances?

   • If so, how did you find your experience? Did you find that you shared common ideals and values? If so, what?

2. When you read the history of official pronouncements laced with anti-Semitism, how do you respond? Why do you think that Catholic leaders fostered this type of thinking for so many centuries?

3. What have been the long-term implications of Christian anti-Semitism? Did the church advance or hinder its primary religious objectives because of it?

4. Imagine that you were pope during World War II. You knew that the Shoah (Holocaust) was taking place, and that the Nazis were sending millions of Jews to gas chambers. At the same time, you were worried about the church in Nazi Germany and Fascist Italy, and what

might happen if you spoke out publicly against this slaughter. What would you do? What do you believe Pius XII should have done in this circumstance?

5. In his essay, Kenneth Stow argues that a fundamental theological change is necessary to rid the church completely of anti-Semitism. Do you agree? Why or why not? If you agree, what kind of change is necessary?

Chapter 7

SLAVERY

From the beginning until the nineteenth century, church pronouncements often justified the practice of slavery. As late as 1866, the Holy Office said, "Slavery itself... is not at all contrary to the natural and divine law." But when Leo XIII condemned slavery in 1890, he ignored the long church justification, claiming that the church had worked strenuously for centuries to abolish slavery. Both Rerum Novarum (1891) and the Second Vatican Council (1965) unequivocally condemned slavery.

EARLY CHURCH

Council of Gangra, c. 340:

"If anyone, on the pretext of religion, teaches another man's slave to despise his master, and to withdraw from his service, and not to serve his master with good will and all respect, let him be anathema" (see *Decretum*, below).

Context: This was a reaction to Manichean incitement of slaves to emancipate themselves. It was incorporated into canon law and cited for the next fourteen hundred years.

Gregory I, Deed of Manumission, 595:

"It is most fitting that by a grant of manumission, masters should restore those whom nature had set free into the world, but who had been condemned to the yoke of slavery by the *jus gentium*, to the freedom in which they were born."

Gregory I, *Pastoral Rule*, c. 600:

"Slaves should be told... not [to] despise their masters and recognize that they are only slaves."

Gregory I, *Expositio in Librum B. Job*, c. 600:

"All men are equal by nature but... a hidden dispensation of providence has arranged a hierarchy of merit and rulership, in that the differences between classes of men have arisen as a result of sin and are ordained by divine justice."

Ninth Council of Toledo, 655:

Children of clerics were to be enslaved.

Context: This was an early attempt to enforce clerical celibacy. It was later incorporated into canon law.

MEDIEVAL CHURCH

Urban II, Council of Melfi, 1089:

"We remove from every sacred order those who from the subdiaconate wish to have leisure for wives, and we decree that they be without office and benefice of the church. But if, warned by the bishop, they fail to correct themselves, we give permission to rulers that they subject their women to servitude."

Context: This was part of the effort to enforce mandatory clerical celibacy. It was incorporated into canon law.

Decretum, 1140:

"If anyone, on the pretext of religion, teaches another man's slave to despise his master, and to withdraw from his service and not to service his master with goodwill and all respect, let him be anathema."

Alexander III, 1174:

"Everyone has the same God in heaven who created all men to be equal and not slaves by nature."

Context: This was an appeal to a Moorish king to release Christian prisoners of war.

Third and Fourth Lateran Councils, Alexander III and Innocent III, twelfth and thirteenth centuries:

The Lateran Councils permitted enslavement of Christians who helped Saracens during the Crusades.

Nicholas V, *Dum Diversas,* 1452/54:

"We grant to you [Kings of Spain and Portugal] by these present documents, with our Apostolic Authority, full and free permission to invade, search out, capture, and subjugate the Saracens and pagans and any other unbelievers and enemies of Christ wherever they may be, as well as their kingdoms, duchies, counties, principalities, and other property...and to reduce their persons into perpetual slavery."

Context: Pope Calixtus III confirmed this decree in 1456. Sixtus IV renewed it in 1481. Alexander VI extended it from Africa to America in 1493, and Leo X renewed it in 1514.

Pius II, Letter to a Bishop, 1462:

Pius II condemned "wicked Christians who were taking the recently baptized adult converts away into slavery."

COUNTER-REFORMATION

Paul III, *Sublimis Deus*, 1537:

Although Indians were non-Christians, they had not been deprived of their freedom or of ownership of possessions; they should not be reduced to slavery.

Context: This decree was not considered to contradict earlier papal pronouncements because it did not apply to hostile non-Christians enslaved in just wars.

Paul III, *Motu Proprio*, 1548:

"Each and every person of either sex, whether Roman or non-Roman, whether secular or clerical...may freely and lawfully buy and sell publicly any slaves whatsoever of either sex...and publicly hold them as slaves and make use of their work, and compel them to do the work assigned to them....Slaves who flee to the Capitol and appeal for their liberty shall in no wise be freed from the bondage of their servitude, but...shall be returned in slavery to their owners and if it seems proper...punished as runaways."

Context: Slaves in Rome were seeking sanctuary on church property.

Pius V, *Motu Proprio*, 1566:

Pius V restored local officials' right to emancipate slaves who sought sanctuary in the Capitol.

Gregory XIV, *Cum Sicuti*, 1591:

Cum sicuti decreed the emancipation of all indigenous slaves in the Philippines, a Spanish possession.

Urban VIII, *Commissum Nobis*, 1639:

Commissum Nobis forbade enslavement and trade in Indians in Paraguay, Brazil, and the Rio de la Plata region.

Urban VIII, 1629, Innocent X, 1645, Alexander VII, 1661:

All of these popes were personally involved in buying Muslim galley slaves.

Holy Office, 1686:

The Holy Office decreed that Africans enslaved in unjust wars should be freed.

Context: When the church learned how the cruelty of Portuguese and Spanish conquerors alienated Indians from Christianity, it tried to back away from Nicholas V's blanket authorization of 1452/54 (see above).

MODERN ERA

Benedict XIV, *Immensa Pastorum*, 1741:

Immensa pastorum condemned the unjust enslavement of non-Christian and Christian Indians.

Sacred Congregation of the Index, eighteenth and nineteenth centuries:

Numerous antislavery tracts were placed on the *Index of Forbidden Books.*

Gregory XVI, *In Supremo Apostolatus*, 1839:

"[We] do ... admonish and adjure in the Lord all believers in Christ, of whatsoever condition, that no one hereafter may dare unjustly to molest Indians, Negroes, or other men of this sort; or to spoil them of their goods; or to reduce them to slavery; or to extend help or favor to others who perpetrate such things against them; or to exercise that inhuman trade by which Negroes, as if they were not men, but were animals, howsoever reduced into slavery, are, without any distinction, contrary to the laws of justice and humanity, bought and sold, and doomed sometimes to the most severe and exhausting labors."

Context: The British Parliament outlawed slavery and slave trade in all dominions in 1838. Gregory did not condemn "just" enslavement or slave trade; nor did he excommunicate slave traders. Bishops in the U.S. South decided his prohibition did not apply to U.S. slavery.

Holy Office, 1866:

"Slavery itself ... is not at all contrary to the natural and divine law. ... For the sort of ownership which a slave owner has over a slave is understood as nothing other than the perpetual right of disposing of the work of a slave for one's own benefit — services which it is right for one human being to provide for another. ... The purchaser should carefully examine whether the slave who is put up for sale has been justly or unjustly deprived of his liberty, and that the vendor should do nothing which might endanger the life, virtue, or Catholic faith of the slave."

Context: The U.S. Emancipation Proclamation was issued in 1863, the U.S. Civil War ended in 1865, and the thirteenth amendment to the U.S. Constitution, adopted at that time, abolished slavery. "Rome had never unequivocally condemned slavery, mostly out of fear of offending Spanish and Portuguese royalty. Gregory XVI finally condemned the slave trade in 1839, but not slavery itself. If pressed, the Vatican fell back on the medieval argument that, while slavery was an evil, it was not an unmitigated evil, for it allowed slaves to be Christianized. Although the Vatican was officially neutral during the Civil War, Pius IX made no secret of his sympathies for the Confederacy. However deplorable its social system, the South at least was not infected with the virus of liberalism" (Morris, p. 78).

Pius IX, 1873:

"...attached an indulgence to a prayer for the 'wretched Ethiopians in Central Africa that Almighty God may at length remove the curse of Cham [Ham] from their hearts'" (Maxwell, p. 20).

Context: In Genesis 9:22–27, Noah cursed his son Ham for seeing his nakedness and declared Ham would be his brothers' slave. Theologians later used this passage to justify the enslavement of Africans.

Leo XIII, Letter to the Brazilian Bishops, 1888, Letter to All Bishops, 1890, and *Catholicae Ecclesiae*, 1890:

"From the beginning, almost nothing was more venerated in the Catholic Church... than the fact that she looked to see a slavery eased and abolished which was oppressing so many people.... She... stood forth as a strenuous defender of liberty.... Indeed the more slavery flourished from time to time, the more zealously she strove [to liberate slaves].... Many of our predecessors, including St. Gregory the Great, Hadrian I, Alexander III, Innocent III, Gregory IX, Pius VII, and Gregory XVI, made every effort to ensure that the institution of slavery should be abolished where it existed and that its roots should not revive where it had been destroyed."

Context: Brazil was the last country in the Western Hemisphere to abolish slavery, in May 1888. Maxwell (1975) comments, "With the greatest respect to Pope Leo XIII, [his statement] is historically inaccurate." Popes had condemned only "unjust" slavery (of captives taken in unjust wars), not all slavery.

Leo XIII, *Rerum Novarum*, 1891:

"The active force inherent in the person cannot be the property of anyone other than the person who exerts it, and it was given to him in the first place by nature for his own benefit."

Code of Canon Law, 1917:

"A lay person who has been legitimately declared guilty of the crime of...
selling a human being into slavery or for any other evil purpose...shall auto-
matically be deprived of the right to legal ecclesiastical actions and of every
position which he may have in the church....If a cleric has committed [the
above crime]...he shall be punished by the ecclesiastical court...even with
disposition, if the circumstances demand it."

Second Vatican Council, *Pastoral Constitution on the Church in the Modern World*, 1965:

"Whatever violates the integrity of the human person, such as mutilation,
torture inflicted on body or mind, attempts to coerce the will itself, whatever insults human dignity, such as subhuman living conditions, arbitrary
imprisonment, deportation, slavery, prostitution, and selling of women and
children...all these things and others like them are infamous....Human
institutions...should be bulwarks against any kind of political or social
slavery and guardians of basic rights under any kind of government."

*Context: "It should be noticed how very slender and scarce is the Catholic
antislavery documentation since 1888 as compared with the very large volume
of Catholic proslavery documentation right up to the time of the Second Vatican
Council" (Maxwell, p. 125). John Paul II quoted this passage in* Veritatis splendor
(1993).

REFLECTIONS ON SLAVERY
Diana Hayes

Human slavery has existed as long as human beings have struggled for power
and authority over one another. Historically the most usual forms of slavery resulted from wars, in which the defeated population became part of the
spoils for the victors, or from poverty or indebtedness that forced the poor to
sell themselves or their offspring. Although this state was seen as lasting the
lifetime of the enslaved person, a slave had many ways to obtain his or her
freedom, through marriage to a free person, as a result of exemplary work,
through self-purchase, among others. More important, these forms of slavery
did not carry with them, for the most part, the stigma of dehumanization or
racial inferiority (as racial categories had not yet been invented). Once having obtained their freedom, former slaves were usually at liberty to live their
lives as they chose in the same society in which they had been enslaved.

The most significant shift in the institution of slavery occurred with the
opening of the Americas to European colonization. It brought with it a

stigma that has lasted to this day, especially for people of African descent. As Fr. Cyprian Davis noted,

> Slavery was very much an accepted institution in the world of the six-teenth and seventeenth centuries. It was accepted as an institution by the church leaders of the time, despite the efforts of popes to regu-late trafficking in slaves and of Catholic theologians to determine the legitimate basis for the enslavement of certain peoples. (Davis, 1990, p. 20)

The Roman Catholic Church's history with regard to the institution of slavery in the New World is, clearly, not an unblemished one. Although, as the records show, efforts were made at various times to control slavery and its harshest impact upon the enslaved, "as is often the case, however, there was often a vast discrepancy between the theory and the practice. The fact that one individual had ownership of the person and the labor of another provided the framework for inevitable acts of oppression and brutality" (Davis, 1990, p. 20). Just like today, the Catholic faithful and the hierarchy interpreted not only Scripture and tradition but papal and curial statements to fit their own situations and understandings.

It is often asserted that slavery in Catholic nations was more benign, since the enslaved were recognized as persons because of their baptism, with rights and privileges in accordance with their human dignity. The fact remains that they had little or no control over their lives and those of their husbands, wives, or children.

For centuries, the church saw slavery as a feature of the natural law: some people were meant to be slaves, while others were meant to be their mas-ters. Theologians believed that Sacred Scripture, especially the writings of St. Paul, and tradition in a seemingly unbroken line from the early church fa-thers through the popes and councils supported slavery. This "unbroken" line did have breaks in it, when the Vatican exposed and condemned the sinful nature of slavery and of those who profited from the trade in human lives. But this perspective was rarely acknowledged until recent times, when we see a dramatic shift from the affirmation to the condemnation of slavery.

As the statements cited in this book show, from its very beginning, the church not only acknowledged but actively supported the "natural order" of slavery. As Pope Gregory I (c. 600) noted: "A hidden dispensation of provi-dence has arranged a hierarchy of merit and rulership, in that the difference between classes of men has arisen as a result of sin and is ordered by divine justice." The enslaved were slaves because of their own faults and failures, and the church did not see its role or responsibility to change this state of affairs.

Thus, when the Americas were first opened to exploration and colo-nization, it was assumed that the people found in those lands, so radically different from the claimants, were fit only to serve rather than be served or accepted as equals. Once again, slavery's defenders used Sacred Scripture to support the enslavement of the native peoples of both the Americas and Africa. They interpreted the curse of Ham and his son Canaan and the curse of Cain as especially significant prophecies of both the existence of people of color and the divine mandate for their capture and enslavement. Thus, slavery became an accepted part of the church's expansion in Africa and the Americas, as a result, it was believed, of God's providence. Less importance was given to the explorers' and colonizers' desire to exploit the riches of these lands, which required a massive application of cheap and abundant labor.

The spread of the faith was also a critical factor in this new understanding of slavery, transforming it into a huge global market that traded in human lives. The church itself used enslavement to punish those who questioned or contradicted church teachings. Proponents saw slavery as an instrument of God's salvific plan for a great harvest of souls, because it brought pagan Africans and indigenous people in contact with the teachings of Christ. The doctrine of just war was a further justification. Theologians upheld enslavement of those defeated in a just war, and condemned enslavement of those captured in an unjust war.

In his first sermon, Jesus proclaimed the realization of Isaiah's prophecy that one would come who would proclaim "good news to the poor . . . release to the captives [and that] the oppressed [would] go free" (Luke 4:18). It is ironic indeed that a church founded on such principles would become the legitimizer of a form of slavery that dehumanized native and African peoples and established a mindset that differentiated people on the basis of race. This consciousness fostered the rise of racism, an ideology that haunts humanity, especially in the United States, to the present day, both in and outside the church, as the U.S. bishops acknowledged in their 1974 pastoral letter on racism, *Brothers and Sisters to Us*.

As Maxwell notes, Leo XIII's assertion that the church always opposed slavery is sadly inaccurate. Before the end of the slave trade in the nineteenth century, with few exceptions, the Roman Catholic Church did support and maintain with all its power, secular and spiritual, the enslavement not only of non-Catholics but of its own Catholic faithful. Although England and the United States abolished the slave trade in 1807 and 1808, slavery itself did not end in the U.S. until 1865, and the Catholic nations of Spain and Portugal continued engaging in the illegal slave trade. The denial of slaves' human dignity and baptism in Christ, which affirmed that dignity, meant that until this century, the church denied people of color, male and female, rights granted to all other faithful in the church, including access to parochial schools, the religious life, and the priesthood.

The impact has been global, but it is in the United States that we can see some of the most harmful effects. Fr. Cyprian Davis carefully sets out the extreme bias that many U.S. bishops in the nineteenth and early twentieth centuries showed toward people of African descent. This bias clearly affected their interpretation of mandates issued by Rome calling for the elimination of the slave trade and slavery itself, as well as an intensive evangelization effort among the newly freed slaves. In the South and throughout the United States, overt resistance to more recent church teachings opposing slavery and racism culminated in segregation, discrimination, and second-class citizenship for Black Catholics. This resistance was so widespread that discrimination is still being dismantled today, with great difficulty.

We must admit, however, that today the church is trying to erase the failures of the past. It is critical that these failures be acknowledged as the sins they were and continue to be (see the 1989 report, *The Church and Racism*, by the Pontifical Commission on Peace and Justice). Despite claims to the contrary, the church was instrumental in the spread of a new and vastly more horrific form of slavery to the New World and in the establishment of a racial caste system that haunts us to this day.

The interpretation of Scripture and tradition by which the church supported such acts was a product of the times and the conditions of society during those times. Nonetheless, this interpretation was immoral then and still is today. Since all of humanity, in its great diversity, was created in the image and likeness of God, there can be no rationale for slavery. To differentiate among human beings based on the color of their skin or any other factor is a sin against God and must be condemned. "Whatever violates the integrity of the human person, . . . whatever insults human dignity, . . . all these things and others like them are infamous" (*Pastoral Constitution on the Church in the Modern World*).

Evidence of conversion in the hearts and minds of the leaders of our church, albeit late, is welcome. For slavery has not ended. It exists in Africa on both the west coast, where children are kidnapped, and the east coast, where Christians are enslaved by non-Christians. We continue to reap the horrors of what was sown so many years ago. When people are brutalized and dehumanized, whether by their own or others, in the name of God, there can be no peace. Their souls cry out to heaven and we ignore them at our peril.

Thus the church's complicity in the enslavement of countless millions cannot be ignored. Nor can we rewrite history to place the church in a better light. Instead, our knowledge serves to help us recognize the humanity of those in the church who falter and stumble as the rest of us do. Recounting this history enables Catholics throughout the world to realize that what once may have seemed acceptable was not and never can be.

The church's understanding of itself and its role has changed continually throughout its history and continues to change today. Further change is still necessary and will occur, because no human institution, even one graced by the Holy Spirit, can remain static. The church is both the unchanging body of Christ and the fallible creation of fallible human beings. As such, we continue to seek perfection while recognizing that only God is perfect. We strive for perfection and approach it most closely when we acknowledge the sins of the past, learn from them, and strive to do better.

Discussion Questions
SLAVERY

1. Why do you think that the official church was so slow in condemning slavery?

2. Imagine that you are a Catholic in the nineteenth century at the height of the antislavery movement in the U.S. You want to speak out about your church's tolerance of this wretched institution.

   • Is this situation similar to situations faced by Catholics today? If so, how?

   • What arguments do you think that defenders of the official position might have used if you had spoken out?

   • Do you think that the church's position affected the debate about slavery? If so, how?

   • What risks are involved in speaking out in matters such as this?

   • Would the risks have been worth it in the nineteenth century where slavery was concerned?

   • Are the risks worth it today?

3. Why do you think that Leo XIII, when he finally condemned slavery, did not acknowledge the church's full historical record on this issue? Should he have apologized for the church's historical tolerance of slavery? Should the current pope apologize?

Chapter 8

DEMOCRACY IN THE CHURCH

The political structures of the church and definitions of how church authority should operate have changed significantly through the centuries. The egalitarian ideals of Scripture and the early centuries eroded gradually as a monarchical system became established. Medieval and modern debates over the selection of bishops, papal centralization, the role of church councils, infallibility, and collegiality reflect an ongoing struggle over differing models of church governance.

SCRIPTURE

Luke 22:25–27:

"But Jesus said to them, 'Earthly rulers domineer over their people.... This must not happen with you. Let the greatest among you be like the youngest. Let the leader among you become the follower. For who is the greater? The one who reclines at a meal, or the one who serves it? Isn't it the one reclining at table? Yet here I am among you as the one who serves you.'"

John 15:15:

"I no longer speak of you as subordinates, because a subordinate doesn't know a superior's business. Instead I call you friends, because I have made known to you everything I have learned from Abba God."

Matthew 23:8–10:

"But as for you, avoid the title 'Rabbi.' For you have only one Teacher, and you are all sisters and brothers. And don't call anyone on earth your 'Mother' or 'Father.' You have only one Parent — our loving God in heaven. Avoid being called leaders. You have only one leader — the Messiah."

1 Corinthians 12:13:

"It was by one Spirit that all of us, whether we are Jews or Greeks, slaves or citizens, were baptized into one body. All of us have been given to drink of the one Spirit. And that Body is not one part; it is many."

Galatians 2:11:

"When Peter came to Antioch, however, I opposed him to his face, since he was manifestly in the wrong."

Context: Paul, as the Apostle to the Gentiles, was concerned that some church leaders were demanding that new Christians follow Jewish customs and laws. Read Galatians 2:1–21 for Paul's account of the First Council of Jerusalem.

EARLY CHURCH

Celestine I, c. 425:

"No bishop should be installed against the will of the people."

Leo I, Letter 10, No. 6, c. 450:

"The consent of the clergy, the testimony of those held in honor, the approval of the orders and the laity should be required. He who is to govern all should be chosen by all."

Council of Toledo, 633:

"He whom the clergy and people of his own city have not elected, and whom neither the authority of the metropolitan nor the consent of the provincial bishops has chosen — he shall not be a bishop."

MEDIEVAL AND EARLY RENAISSANCE CHURCH

Leo IX, Synod of Rheims, 1049:

Bishops are to be elected by clergy and people.

Nicholas II, Election Decree, 1059:

"Concerning the election of a Supreme Pontiff: That, on the death of a bishop of this universal Roman church, the cardinal bishops, having first very thoroughly discussed the matter together, shall then summon the cardinal clerks to them, and then the rest of the clergy and people shall in the same way come to consent to the new election.

" ... The churchmen shall take the lead in electing the pope and the others shall merely follow.... Since the Apostolic See is set among all the other churches in the world and so cannot have a metropolitan over it, the cardinal bishops undoubtedly perform the office of a metropolitan, that is, they promote the chosen bishop to the summit, the apostolic throne."

Context: This decree changed the method of electing the pope to give preeminence to the cardinals, who were bishops in the diocese of Rome.

Gregory VII, *Dictatus Papae*, 1074:

"(2) Only the Roman pontiff is rightly called universal. (3) He alone can depose or absolve bishops. (9) The pope is the only man to whom all princes bend the knee. (12) He is allowed to depose emperors. (16) No general synod (council) can be convened without a [papal] order. (18) His sentence cannot be repealed by anyone and he alone can repeal all other sentences. (19) He must not be judged by anyone. (22) The Roman church has never erred; and according to the testimony of Scripture it never will err."

Context: Gregory VII was one of the papal "centralizers" of church history.

Second Lateran Council, 1139:

"We forbid under anathema the canons of the episcopal see to exclude religious men from the election following on the death of the bishop.... Because if an election is held with these religious persons excluded, where this is done without their knowledge and consent, it is null and void."

Boniface VIII, *Unam Sanctam*, 1302:

"It is altogether necessary to salvation for every human creature to be subject to the Roman pontiff."

Clement VI, *Acta Clementis*, c. 1350:

The pope has the same earthly power as Christ.

Council of Constance, *Frequens*, 1417:

"By a perpetual edict, we establish, enact, decree, and ordain that henceforth general councils shall be held ... from ten years to ten years for ever."

Context: To end proliferation of popes and antipopes, as occurred at the time of the Avignon popes, this council established the supremacy of councils over popes with this decree and the following one. These statements are products of the conciliar movement of the age.

Council of Constance, *Sacrosancta*, 1417:

"This holy synod ... ordains, defines, enacts, decrees, and declares ... that ... it holds power directly from Christ; and that everyone of whatever state of dignity he be, even papal, is obliged to obey it in those things which belong to the faith ... and to the general reform of the said church of God in head and in members."

Context: Sacrosancta came up again during the First Vatican Council, when papal infallibility was debated (see below).

Pius II, *Execrabilis*, 1460:

"Some imbued with a spirit of rebellion ... suppose that they can appeal from the pope, vicar of Jesus Christ ... to a future council.... We condemn appeals of this kind, reject them as erroneous and abominable, and declare them to be of no effect."

Editors' Note: See chapter 1, "Infallibility."

MODERN ERA

First Vatican Council, *Pastor Aeternus,* 1870:

"We teach and define... that the Roman Pontiff, when he speaks *ex cathedra,* that is, when in the exercise of his office as pastor and teacher of all Christians, he defines, by virtue of his supreme apostolic authority, a doctrine of faith or morals to be held by the whole church — is, by reason of the divine assistance promised to him in blessed Peter, possessed of that infallibility with which the Divine Redeemer wished his church to be endowed in defining doctrines of faith and morals; and consequently that such definitions of the Roman Pontiff are irreformable of their own nature, and not by reason of the church's consent."

Context: This is the first dogmatic declaration of the pope's infallibility. The council declared that the pope has "full and supreme jurisdiction of the church in those matters which concern discipline and direction of the church dispersed throughout the world" and based this claim on earlier popes and councils. But the Council of Constance (see above) had said that popes were subject to councils.

Pius X, *Vehementer Nos,* 1906:

"This church is in essence an unequal society, that is to say, a society comprising two categories of persons, the shepherd and the flock.... These categories are so distinct that the right and authority necessary for promoting and guiding all the members toward the goal of society reside only in the pastoral body; as to the multitude, its sole duty is that of allowing itself to be led and of following its pastors as a docile flock."

Pius XI, *Quadragesimo Anno,* 1931:

[Definition of subsidiarity] "That which individual men and women can accomplish by their own initiative and their own industry cannot be taken away from them and assigned to the community; in the same way, that which minor or lesser communities can do should not be assigned to a greater or higher community. To do so is a grave injury and disturbance of the social order, for social activity by its nature should supply help to the members of the social body, never destroy or absorb them." Subsidiarity is "a fundamental principle of social philosophy, fixed and unchangeable."

Context: This was one of the great "social encyclicals." Its definition of subsidiarity was meant to apply to secular states, but calling it a "fundamental principle" of social philosophy suggests it should also apply to the church.

Pius XII, *Humani Generis*, 1950:

"If the Supreme pontiffs in their official documents purposely pass judgment on a matter debated until then, it is obvious to all that the matter, according to the mind and will of the same pontiffs, cannot be considered any longer a question open for discussion among theologians."

Second Vatican Council, *Dogmatic Constitution on the Church*, 1964:

- The church is the "People of God" (title, Chapter II).

- There is "a true equality with regard to the dignity and to the activity common to all the faithful for the building up of the body of Christ."

  Editors' Note: See the difference between this and the statement as it appears in the Code of Canon Law, below.

- [Collegiality espoused] "Just as, by God's will, St. Peter and the other apostles constituted one apostolic college, so in a similar way the Roman Pontiff as the successor of Peter and the bishops as the successors of the apostles are joined together. The collegial nature and meaning of the episcopal order found expression in the very ancient practice by which bishops...were lined with one another and with the bishop of Rome...also, in the conciliar assemblies which made common judgments about more profound matters in decisions reflecting the views of many. The ecumenical councils held through the centuries clearly attest to this collegial aspect."

  Context: The Second Vatican Council (1962–65) was a progressive, reforming council, promoting wide participation in church life by all sectors.

Paul VI, *Ecclesiam Suam*, 1964:

"The church is not a democratic association established by human will."

Synod of Bishops, *Justice in the World*, 1967:

"While the church is bound to give witness to justice, it recognizes that everyone who ventures to speak to people about justice must first be just in their eyes. Hence we must undertake an examination of the modes of acting and of the possessions and lifestyle found within the church herself."

John Paul II (as Karol Wojtyla), *The Acting Person*, 1969:

"Conformity means death for any community. A loyal opposition is a necessity in any community."

  Context: As Karol Wojtyla, John Paul II was confronting the communist regime in Poland, where he eventually aided in the rise of Solidarity, an opposition movement. See his contradictory statement in Veritatis splendor, *below.*

Code of Canon Law, 1983:

- "The Supreme Pontiff freely appoints bishops or confirms those who have been legitimately elected. . . . Whenever a diocesan bishop or a coadjutor bishop is to be named, . . . it is the responsibility of the pontifical delegate to seek out individually the suggestions of the metropolitan and the suffragans of the province . . . and of the president of the conference of bishops and to communicate them to the Apostolic See together with his own preference. . . . And if he judges it expedient, he shall also obtain, individually and in secret, the opinion of other members of the secular and religious clergy as well as of the laity who are outstanding for their wisdom."

- "In virtue of their rebirth in Christ, there exists among all the faithful a true equality in regard to dignity and activity whereby all cooperate in the building up of the Body of Christ in accord with each one's own condition and function."

John Paul II, *Veritatis Splendor,* 1993:

"*Dissent,* in the form of carefully orchestrated protests and polemics carried on in the media, *is opposed to ecclesial communion and to a correct understanding of the hierarchical constitution of the People of God*" [emphasis in original].

Context: Pope John Paul II stands in the tradition of the "centralizing" popes, demanding obedience to papal authority and seeking to silence dissent.

THE CHURCH ISN'T A DEMOCRACY, BUT SHOULDN'T IT BE?

Rosemary R. Ruether

Whenever groups of Catholics assert rights of popular decision-making in the church, some bishop typically intones, "The church is not a democracy." This is a relatively accurate statement about the Roman Catholic Church today. But the assumption that it is either a comprehensive historical statement or a biblically and theologically normative statement needs to be challenged. One should reply, "Yes, the church isn't democratic, but shouldn't it be?"

Those who seek to cut off this question assume that the Roman Catholic Church has always possessed a centralized, monarchical form of government, and that this form of government was given to it by Jesus Christ. It is therefore divinely mandated and unchangeable. Both of these assumptions are incorrect. Democratic elements have always existed in the church. More important, democratic polity better expresses the theological meaning of church as redemptive society than monarchical hierarchy does.

The New Testament shows no evidence of monarchical hierarchy as practiced in the early church or as intended by Christ. Rather it witnesses to the opposite vision: the church as a discipleship of equals. The church was ordered primarily on the local level. Local congregations chose their own leaders through a combination of elections and discernment of gifts. There was no hierarchical structure above the local level. Relations between churches were based on a sense of spiritual communion between them and connections established by itinerant apostles.

In the second century, the church moved toward a patriarchal ordering of local congregations; then, in the next three centuries, to an increasing approximation of the hierarchical system of the Roman imperial bureaucracy. The papacy shaped its own bureaucracy to imitate the Roman emperor's rule over the empire. But this structure was never accepted by the Eastern Church, which continued to see the pope as bishop of Rome with collegial authority over Western churches, but not ruling over the church as a whole.

Moreover, local control on the metropolitan and provincial levels remained the norm into the late Middle Ages, with election of bishops by the local clergy, popular acclamation by the laity, and validation by regional assemblies of bishops. The election of the pope by the College of Cardinals descends from this practice, since the college originally was not a worldwide body but the clergy of the local churches of the diocese of Rome.

The late Middle Ages and the Reformation era saw the rise of conciliarism, with its concerted effort to renew a democratic form of church government based on a European-wide church parliament, with the papacy reformed as a constitutional monarchy elected by, and responsible to, this church parliament. But the papacy resisted all such efforts. It reasserted its claims to autocratic power without accountability to others, harking back to imperial Rome and foreshadowing the absolute monarchies of the early modern era.

In practice, however, the papacy of this period was weak and depended on playing powerful Catholic monarchs, such as the French, Spanish, and Austrians, against one another. The national episcopacies and Catholic princes largely controlled clerical appointments.

It was only when the democratic revolutions of the nineteenth century dismantled Catholic monarchies and separated church from state that the papacy could emerge from the tutelage of these princes. The papacy responded to these democratic revolutions by declaring its unchangeable hostility to them, proclaiming itself to be infallible apart from church councils. It thus tried to wipe out the remnants of the conciliar tradition that had sought to democratize the church itself.

The Second Vatican Council partially returned to a conciliar concept of the church as a vehicle of reform. Its definition of the church as "people of God" marked a decisive shift from the concept of church as "perfect society," identified only with the hierarchy as a "corporation." "People of God" means starting with the whole *laos* as the basic meaning of church, placing leaders within, not above, the community. Vatican II also promoted the principle of collegial subsidiarity, which reversed the hierarchical ordering of church government. Priest and people in parishes, bishop and clergy in dioceses, bishops and the bishop of Rome, all meet as equals to make decisions, with a preference for the local and regional levels in most cases.

But the Roman curia had no intention of implementing such reform. As soon as the council fathers returned home, the Vatican reasserted the top-down system of government. With the advent of John Paul II, the center has made a continual effort to repress local and national church government in favor of global papal monarchy, with every bishop and church institution directly responsible to Rome. There has been an effort to extend papal infallibility by putting all decisions of the pope, even in matters of policy, beyond question.

Implications of Recent Trends

Catholics today should recognize that this effort to reify papal monarchy as an unchangeable divine order is a form of idolatry of the church institution. It bears evil fruits in untruth, abusive relationships, corruption, and lovelessness. We must see that the papal system itself is the product of a long process of historical changes that emerged from the suppression of earlier democratic forms of church government and developed through continual suppression of new efforts at democratic reform that have arisen in the church from the fifteenth to the twentieth centuries.

Once we recognize that all forms of church government are relative and historical, we can then turn to the normative question. What form of church government is best? What form of church government would most authentically manifest the nature of the church as redemptive community? Surely the essential characteristics of redemptive community are those that foster just, loving, and truthful relations between people based on mutual respect. A church whose system of power fosters the opposite of these traits falls below, rather than rises above, the "world" to which it seeks to speak a saving word.

Democratic church reform is more than an adaptation to passing forms of government of the modern world. This is so not only because democratic patterns are early and continual in church history, but also because the drive for democracy itself represents a moral quest for political forms that better express and guarantee just and good government in the interest of all the people. Thus democratic reform is a search for redemptive society. Democratic participatory forms of government better express respect for all persons and guard against abuse of power than hierarchies and monarchies that treat the "governed" as dependents without rights.

Of course, not every form of government today that claims the name "democratic," including that of the United States, is in fact just and respectful of all persons equally. Much of what is called democracy by Americans, both at home and internationally, is simply a way of covering up political, cultural, and economic oligarchies with a facade of electoral politics. This generates increasingly unjust societies, split between wealthy, powerful elites, and a vast underclass of poor and powerless people. We need to rethink how to organize genuine participatory democracies in our political communities.

But this failure of much of what is called democracy does not excuse similarly abusive power relations in the church. It simply means that both in society and the church we need to reexamine what sort of organizing relations between people best assure justice and curb abuse of power.

What does redemption mean on the level of social relations? What kind of social ordering best approximates, even if always imperfectly, redemptive relationality? How can the very process of continual repentance and renewal, as the essential way of keeping the Spirit alive in our midst, be built into our understanding of political order in church and society? These are the questions to be probed as Catholics shake off the papal claim of sacral hierarchy and examine the meaning of redemption, not simply as theological theory and personal spirituality, but also as reform of structures.

Discussion Questions
DEMOCRACY IN THE CHURCH

1. What is your experience of authority in the Roman Catholic Church? At the parish or diocesan level? At the level of the universal church? Has this been a positive or negative experience for you? Why?

2. How would you describe the political structure of the church today? Does it reflect the ideals of the gospel as you understand them?

3. What difference does it make to you to know that authority structures and policies have varied widely during church history?

4. How has reading these quotations and Rosemary Ruether's commentary altered, if at all, your understanding of the church?

5. Rosemary Ruether raises pivotal issues in her commentary. How would you answer the following questions?

   • What form of church government would most authentically manifest the nature of the church as a redemptive community?

- How can the process of continual repentance and renewal be built into the political order of the church?

6. If someone today confronted you with the statement, "The church is not a democracy," how would you respond?

7. If you were to dream about new, democratic political structures for the Roman Catholic Church, what would they look like?

Chapter 9

THEOLOGICAL DISSENT

Many pronouncements from popes and councils have outlawed dissent and punished dissenters. The "Holy Inquisition" used the secular state to imprison, torture, or even execute those suspected of unorthodox teaching. In modern times, the church has used ecclesiastical penalties such as the condemnation of books, silencing, and excommunication. With the Second Vatican Council and Pope Paul VI's address to the International Theological Commission in 1969, the official approach to theological research changed significantly, as the church recognized theologians' right to free inquiry. Under the administration of Pope John Paul II, however, the Vatican has resurrected older policies of condemnation and silencing.

EARLY CHURCH

Augustine, Letter to the Tribune Boniface, 417:

"There is unjust persecution, which the impious do to the church of Christ; and there is just persecution, which the church of Christ does to the impious. ... The church persecutes out of love, and the impious out of cruelty."

Theodosian Code, 438:

"There shall be no opportunity for any man to go out to the public and to argue about religion or to discuss it or to give any counsel. If any person hereafter, with flagrant and damnable audacity, should suppose that he may contravene any law of this kind or if he should dare to persist in his action of ruinous obstinacy, he shall be restrained with a due penalty and proper punishment. ... All heresies are forbidden by both divine and imperial laws and shall forever cease."

Context: This Roman imperial law, promulgated when Christianity was the state religion, was the basis for later criminalization of heresy throughout Christendom (see Fourth Lateran Council, below).

MEDIEVAL CHURCH

Decretum, c. 1140:

"The first See cannot be judged by anyone except when he is convicted of deviation from the faith."

Context: At least four popes were accused of heresy: Honorius, Marcellinus, Vigilius, and John XXII.

Third Lateran Council, 1179:

"Heretics and all who defend and receive them are excommunicated. If they die in their sin, they shall be denied Christian burial and are not to be prayed for."

Lucius III, Ad Abolendam, 1184:

Ad abolendam ordered bishops to "make inquisition" for heresy.

Innocent III, Cum ex Officii Nostri, 1207:

"In order altogether to remove from the patrimony of St. Peter the defilement of heretics, we decree as a perpetual law, that whatsoever heretic ... shall be found therein shall immediately be taken and delivered to the secular court to be punished according to the law. All his goods also shall be sold. ... The house, however, in which a heretic has been received shall be altogether destroyed, nor shall anyone presume to rebuild it; but let that which was a den of iniquity become a receptacle of filth."

Fourth Lateran Council, 1215:

"We excommunicate and anathematize every heresy that raises itself against the holy, orthodox, and Catholic faith."

Gregory IX, Excommunicamos, 1231:

Excommunicamos specified punishment for unrepentant heretics: "*animadversio debita,*" the debt of hatred (death penalty).

Innocent IV, Ad Extirpanda, 1252:

"The ... ruler ... is hereby ordered to force all captured heretics to confess and accuse their accomplices by torture which will not imperil life or injure limb, just as thieves and robbers are forced to accuse their accomplices, and to confess their crimes; for these heretics are true thieves, murderers of souls and robbers of the sacraments of God."

Context: This bull authorized torture of accused heretics. Amended versions by Alexander IV (1260) and Urban IV (1262) "allowed the inquisitors themselves to be present at the torturing, to direct it, and to have confessions made during it taken down by their notaries" (Guirard, p. 86).

Alexander IV, Bull of 1256:

"Bishop Alexander, the servant of the servants of God, fondly sends greetings and apostolic blessings to the fraternal sons of the Order of Preachers, who are inquisitors of the terrible depraved heresy [Catharism] in Tholosa and in all the lands of that noble man, the Count of Poitou. So that you may proceed more freely in carrying out the business of faith, we grant that, by the present authority, if out of human weakness, in some cases you incur a sentence of excommunication and irregularity, or you remember that you may have incurred such, and because of the exercise of the office that you bear you are not able to go to your superiors, we grant that you can absolve yourselves according to the form of the church and dispense by your own authority, in the same manner as was granted by the apostolic see to your superiors."

Context: Here the pope authorized inquisitors to absolve each other for crimes committed during interrogations. The historian Henry Charles Lea maintained, "It was this bull which enabled inquisitors to administer torture."

John XXII, 1317:

John XXII required a bishop's agreement before torture could begin.

John XXII, Bull of 1319:

The Bull of 1319 absolved an inquisitor whose torture by fire led to an accused heretic's death.

John XXII, *Cum inter Nonnullos*, 1323:

"Since it happens among learned men that doubt is raised as to whether the persistent assertion that our Redeemer and Lord Jesus Christ and his apostles did not possess any goods or other property, either privately or in common, should be designated heretical... we, desiring to put an end to this controversy, ... declare by this everlasting edict that a persistent assertion of this kind shall henceforth be designated as erroneous and heretical, since it expressly contradicts Holy Scripture, which expressly states in some places that [Christ and the apostles] did possess some things."

Context: Four Franciscans who insisted that Christ and the apostles were poor and owned nothing were burned as heretics by the Inquisition. John XXII was later condemned as a heretic at the University of Paris for his unorthodox positions on other issues, and he recanted on his deathbed.

COUNTER-REFORMATION

Leo X, Fifth Lateran Council, *Supernae Majestatis Praesidio*, 1516:

"Nor shall [preachers] presume to announce or predict in their sermons any fixed time of future evils, the coming of Antichrist or the day of the last judgment.... Wherefore, no cleric, whether regular or secular, who engages in this work in the future is permitted in his sermons to foretell future events *ex litteris sacris* or to affirm that he has received his knowledge of them from the Holy Ghost or through divine revelations or to resort for proof of his statements to foolish divinations.... Let him preserve undivided the seamless garment of Christ by abstaining from that scandalous practice of defaming the character of bishops, prelates, and other superiors before the people."

Leo X, *Exsurge Domine*, 1520:

"The books of Martin Luther which contain these errors are to be examined and burned.... We give Martin sixty days in which to submit."

Leo X, Letter to Frederick the Wise, 1520:

"Beloved son, we rejoice that you have never shown any favor to that son of iniquity, Martin Luther.... We exhort you to induce him to return to sanity and receive our clemency. If he persists in his madness, take him captive."

Council of Trent, 1563:

"And if anyone should read or possess books by heretics or writings by any author condemned and prohibited by reason of heresy or suspicion of false teaching, he incurs immediately the sentence of excommunication."

MODERN ERA

Pius VI, *Quod Aliquantum*, 1791:

Quod aliquantum condemned "this absolute liberty which not only assures people of the right not to be disturbed about their religious opinions but also gives them this license to think, write, and even have printed with impunity all that the most unruly imagination can suggest about religion.... What could be more senseless than to establish among men equality and this un-bridled freedom which seems to quench reason...? What is more contrary to the rights of the creator God who limited human freedom by prohibiting evil?"

   Context: The French Revolution was at its height, and its anticlerical measures threatened the church.

Gregory XVI, *Mirari Vos*, 1832:

"The discipline sanctioned by the church must never be rejected or be branded as contrary to certain principles of natural law. It must never be called crippled, or imperfect or subject to civil authority.... This perverse opinion ['indifferentism'] is spread on all sides by the fraud of the wicked who claim that it is possible to obtain the eternal salvation of the soul by the profession of any kind of religion, as long as morality is maintained."

Pius IX, *Quanta Cura*, 1864:

- "Our Predecessors have, with Apostolic fortitude, constantly resisted the nefarious enterprises of wicked men, who, like raging waves of the sea foaming out their own confusion, and promising liberty whereas they are the slaves of corruption, have striven by their deceptive opinions and most pernicious writings to raze the foundations of the Catholic religion and of civil society, to remove from among men all virtue and justice, to deprave persons, and especially inexperienced youth, to lead it into the snares of error, and at length to tear it from the bosom of the Catholic Church."

- *Quanta cura* condemned "that erroneous opinion which is especially injurious to the Catholic Church and the salvation of souls, called by our predecessor Gregory XVI insane raving, namely, that freedom of conscience and of worship is the proper right of each man, and that this should be proclaimed and asserted in every rightly constituted society."

   Context: The famous "Syllabus of Errors" was appended to this encyclical.

First Vatican Council, *Dei Filius*, 1870:

"If anyone says that it is possible that the dogmas propounded by the church can, as a result of the progress of science, be given a meaning different from that which the church has understood and continues to understand, let him be anathema."

Leo XIII, *Instructio SCNNEE*, 1902:

"It is impossible to approve in Catholic publications of a style inspired by unsound novelty which seems to deride the piety of the faithful and dwells on the introduction of a new order of Christian life, on new directions of the church, on new aspirations of the modern soul, on a new vocation of the clergy, on a new Christian civilization" (quoted by Pius X in *Pascendi* [1907]; see below).

Pius X, *Pascendi Dominici Gregis*, 1907:

"Their system [modernism] means the destruction not of the Catholic religion alone but of all religion.... Anybody who in any way is found to be imbued with Modernism is to be excluded without compunction from these offices [directors and professors in seminaries and Catholic universities], and those who occupy them are to be withdrawn.... We bid you do everything in your power to drive out of your dioceses, even by solemn interdict, any pernicious books that may be in circulation there.... In the future bishops shall not permit congresses of priests except on very rare occasions." Councils of Vigilance were to be established, to meet secretly and "watch most carefully for every trace and sign of Modernism both in publications and in teaching."

Context: Modernism was a late nineteenth-century attempt by Catholic intellectuals to reconcile the Catholic faith with contemporary culture. The Vatican defined it as a heresy in the early twentieth century.

Pius XI, 1923:

"In those matters in which there is a division among the best authors in Catholic schools, no one is to be forbidden to follow that opinion which seems to him [or her] to be nearer the truth."

Pius XI, *Mortalium Animos*, 1928:

"There are those who nurture the hope that it would be easy to lead people, despite their religious differences, to unite in the profession of certain doctrines accepted as a common basis of spiritual life.... Such efforts have no right to the approval of Catholics, since they are based on this erroneous opinion that all religions are more or less good and laudable.... The Apostolic See has never allowed Catholics to attend meetings of non-Catholics; the union of Christians can only go forward by encouraging the dissidents to return to the one true church."

Pius XII, *Mystici Corporis*, 1946:

[Quoting canon law] "No one may be forced to accept the Catholic faith against his will.... For faith, without which it is impossible to pleasure God, must be an entirely free homage of the intellect and will. Hence, if it should happen that, contrary to the constant teaching of this Apostolic See, anyone should be brought against his will to embrace the Catholic faith, we cannot do otherwise, in the realization of our duty, than disavow such an action."

John XXIII, *Pacem in Terris*, 1963:

"Also among humanity's rights is that of being able to worship God in accordance with the right dictates of one's own conscience and to profess one's religion both in private and in public."

Second Vatican Council, *Dogmatic Constitution on the Church,* 1964:

"To the extent of their knowledge, competence, or authority the laity are entitled, and indeed sometimes duty-bound, to express their opinion on matters which concern the good of the church."

Second Vatican Council, *Declaration on the Relation of the Church to Non-Christian Religions,* 1965:

"People look to their different religions for an answer to the unsolved riddles of human existence.... The Catholic Church rejects nothing of what is true and holy in these religions."

Second Vatican Council, *Declaration on Religious Liberty,* 1965:

- "This Vatican synod declares that the human person has the right to religious freedom."

- "The individual must not be forced to act against conscience nor be prevented from acting according to conscience, especially in religious matters."

- "Although in the life of the people of God in its pilgrimage through the vicissitudes of human history there has at times appeared a form of behavior which was hardly in keeping with the spirit of the Gospel and was even opposed to it, it has always remained the teaching of the church that no one is to be coerced into believing."

  Editors' Note: When the Vatican reverses its position on an issue, it often claims that it has always proclaimed the new position. For contradictory statements, see Innocent III, Innocent IV, Paul IV, etc., in chapter 8, "The Jewish People."

Second Vatican Council, *Pastoral Constitution on the Church in the Modern World,* 1965:

"With the help of the Holy Spirit, it is the task of the entire People of God, especially pastors and theologians, to hear, distinguish, and interpret the many voices of our age, and to judge them in the light of the divine Word. In this way, revealed truth can always be more deeply penetrated, better understood, and set forth to greater advantage."

Paul VI, Address to the International Theological Commission, 1969:

"We wish to assure you by our words that we want to recognize completely the laws and exigencies that are proper to your studies, that is, to respect that freedom of expression which belongs to theological science and that ability to do the research required for the progress of this science.... In this respect we want to remove from your spirits any fear that the service requested of you ought so to limit and restrict the broad range of your studies as to impede legitimate investigation or suitable formulations of doctrine."

PAPACY OF JOHN PAUL II

Congregation for the Doctrine of the Faith, *Professio Fidei*, 1989:

"Moreover, with a religious *obsequium* of will and intellect I adhere to the teachings which either the Roman Pontiff or the College of Bishops enunciate when they exercise the authentic magisterium even if they intend to proclaim them with a nondefinitive act."

Context: The Vatican required this profession of faith and loyalty oath of seminary presidents, theology professors, rectors, and pastors. Hundreds of U.S., Canadian, and British theologians protested.

Congregation for the Doctrine of the Faith, "Instruction on the Ecclesial Vocation of the Theologian," 1990:

- Mission of the magisterium: "to affirm and define the character of the Covenant"; to "protect God's people from the danger of deviation and confusion"; to guarantee them "the objective possibility of professing the authentic faith free from error."

- "The freedom of the act of faith cannot justify a right to dissent."

John Paul II, *Tertio Millennio Adveniente*, 1994:

"Another painful chapter of history to which the sons and daughters of the church must return with a spirit of repentance is that of the acquiescence given, especially in certain centuries, to intolerance and even the use of violence in the service of truth."

Congregation for the Doctrine of the Faith, Notification to Tissa Balasuriya, OMI, 1997:

"The author arrives at the foundation of principles and theological explanations which contain a series of grave errors and which, to different degrees, are distortions of the truths of dogma and are, therefore, incompatible with the faith.... In publishing this notification, the congregation is obliged also to declare that Fr. Balasuriya has deviated from the integrity of the truth of the Catholic faith and, therefore, cannot be considered a Catholic theologian; moreover, he has incurred excommunication *latae sententiae*."

Context: Fr. Balasuriya, a seventy-two-year-old priest from Sri Lanka, published a book supporting unorthodox positions including the ordination of women. He was excommunicated without a hearing, which led to worldwide protests by theologians and others. The excommunication decree was lifted in January 1998.

FROM HERESY TO DISSENT
Richard A. McCormick, SJ

Consider the following two statements:

> In order altogether to remove from the patrimony of St. Peter the defilement of heretics, we decree as a perpetual law, that whatsoever heretic . . . shall be found therein shall immediately be taken and delivered to the secular court to be punished according to the law. All his goods shall be sold. . . . The house, however, in which a heretic has been received shall be altogether destroyed, nor should anyone presume to rebuild it. (Innocent III, *Cum ex officii nostri*, 1207)

> The church has always opposed these errors. Frequently she has condemned them with the greatest severity. Nowadays, however, the Spouse of Christ prefers to make use of the medicine of mercy rather than that of severity. She considers that she meets the needs of the present day by demonstrating the validity of her teaching rather than by condemnations. (John XXIII, opening speech at Vatican II, 1961)

These remarkably different texts, separated by 756 years, reveal the diverging attitudes popes have taken toward theological dissent over the centuries. Most topics in this book have undergone more or less gradual changes. Positions formerly regarded as correct are now seen as gravely inadequate (on usury and religious freedom, for example). This is not quite the developmental path we see where theological dissent is concerned. Church attitudes toward dissent have ebbed and flowed, according to sociological variables that constitute the context in which the People of God lives its pilgrim life.

But first a word about the term "theological dissent." As I treat it here, it refers to modification of, or disagreement with, authoritative, but not infallible, teachings. Growth in understanding of defined teaching and departure from earlier, less profound understandings may occur. But since day-to-day authoritative church teaching is not infallible, I shall limit my consideration to dissent from noninfallible teaching.

Calling dissent "theological" seems to imply that only professional theologians deal with it. Vatican II, however, encouraged the faithful to become conversant with the sacred sciences, and the term has come to include others besides professional theologians. In this sense, "theological" means "in theological matters."

What then are the variables that determine how the church views and treats dissent? I shall mention five:

1. *Self-definition of the church.* This has varied enormously over the centuries. Early in church history, when Christianity became the state religion,

authorities were much more likely to proceed triumphantly and punitively against dissenters. In the sixteenth century the church adopted a fortress mentality against reformers. This mentality endured and generated the one-sided juridical model of church that prevailed for four hundred years, until the time of Vatican II (1962–65). During those four centuries the church described itself in ways that closely resembled civil society. The pyramid was the dominant model. In this structure, truth and authority descended from the summit down.

Vatican II provided a new self-definition of the church as the People of God, a *communio*. In this concentric, rather than pyramidal, model, the People of God are the repository of Christian revelation and wisdom. As Cardinal Leo Suenens pointed out,

> The church, seen from the starting point of baptism rather than that of the hierarchy, thus appeared from the first as a sacramental and mystical reality first and foremost, rather than — which it also is — a juridical society. It rested on its base, the people of God, rather than on its summit, the hierarchy. The pyramid of the old manuals was reversed.

Obviously such a model suggests, among other things, the need for broad communication if the church is to gather, formulate, and reflect wisdom to the world. Such dialogical communication is inseparable from dissent.

2. *Educational status of the clergy and laity.* For centuries the clergy were the best-educated people in the world. Many cultural factors — among them the broad, nonspecialized character of education — explained this phenomenon. This meant that the clergy assumed responsibilities they would not bear in a later era, and they showed a concomitant intolerance of dissent.

In our times, educational specialization and the widespread availability of higher education mean that the clergy is no longer the best-educated group in the church. Many lay people have special expertise, are capable of relating this expertise to doctrinal issues, and can often express themselves articulately in religious and theological matters. Vatican II explicitly recognized this competence when it stated:

> Lay people should also know that it is generally the function of their well-formed Christian conscience to see that the divine law is inscribed in the life of the earthly city.... Let the lay people not imagine that their pastors are always such experts that to every problem which arises, however complicated, they can readily give a concrete solution, or even that such is their mission. Rather, enlightened by Christian wisdom and giving close attention to the teaching authority of the church, let lay people take on their own distinctive role. (*Pastoral Constitution on the Church in the Modern World*, 43)

With their level of education today, lay people are not likely to turn to their pastors with every new and complicated problem and acquiesce humbly and passively to their decisions.

3. *Status of relations between ecclesial groups.* After the Reformation, many in the church took an apologetic or defensive attitude. Catholic attitudes were simply unecumenical. Viewing other ecclesial groups as in some sense "the adversary," we would not turn to those groups for Christian or theological enlightenment. They were not regarded as reliable sources of religious knowledge. They embodied and defined dissent.

Now we live in an ecumenical age. The church shows new willingness to seek answers from, and association with, non-Catholic ecclesial groups. As Vatican II noted, "In fidelity to conscience, Christians are joined with others in the search for truth and for the genuine solution to the numerous problems which arise in the life of individuals and from social relationships" (*Pastoral Constitution on the Church in the Modern World*, 16). Those who used to be considered adversaries and dissenters are now potential sources of wisdom in elaborating Christian life. This stance requires the church to view dissent itself differently.

4. *The manner of the exercise of authority in the church.* In the past several centuries, authority in the church was highly centralized, both at the Roman and the diocesan level. Popes consulted with few theologians in drafting their statements. What little consultation occurred was often the product of a single theological emphasis. Furthermore, in the decades after Vatican I defined papal infallibility, theologians were overawed by the documents of the ordinary, noninfallible magisterium. They tended to be exegetical in their approach to these teachings, and it was almost unthinkable (and certainly very risky) to question the formulation of such documents.

With its teaching on the nature of the church and the collegiality of bishops, Vatican II began a process of decentralization of authority in the church. The postconciliar church lives in a secular world whose institutions are increasingly sensitive to the values of participatory democracy. It is easy to agree with the French bishops, who declared in 1969, "We have reached a point of no return. From now on the exercise of authority demands dialogue and a certain measure of responsibility for everyone. The authority needed for the life of any society can only be strengthened as a result." Sadly, the Holy See seems to have forgotten this in our time.

5. *The situation of church-state relations.* When Christianity is the state religion, dissent is much less likely to exist or be tolerated. Officialdom tends to view it as a threat to the state itself. Given that state of affairs, many fear that the secular arm will prosecute and persecute dissent, or at least powerfully support the church's doing so. Pluralism of thought is not one of the identifying characteristics of the religious state. This was as true of European states at the time of the Inquisition as it is in present-day Iran.

Interestingly, a similar state of affairs exists when a state is officially atheistic. Anyone out of step with official atheism is marginalized and put on the defensive. That is one reason why Karol Wojtyla, later Pope John Paul II, wrote in *The Acting Person:* "The structure of a human community is correct only if it admits not just the presence of a justified opposition, but also that effectiveness of opposition which is required by the common good and the right of participation" (pp. 286–87).

Theologians have pointed out that this applies also to the church. Referring to *The Acting Person,* Ronald Modras asserts that "loyal opposition can serve the well-being of a church as well as of a state" (*Commonweal* 106 [1979]: 493–95).

Developments like these reveal the meaning of theological dissent at any point in time. Instead of interpreting dissent as ecclesial disloyalty or doctrinal corruption, theologians and others should weigh underlying factors such as the ones listed above. By doing so, they will nearly always arrive at a different and healthier analysis of dissent's significance and validity.

Discussion Questions
THEOLOGICAL DISSENT

1. What were you taught in the course of your religious education about dissent in the church? Has your view changed at any time in your life? Why or why not?

2. How have you responded when you heard in the news that a theologian (or anyone) has lost a position, been silenced, or been excommunicated because of dissent?

3. Should the church permit public theological dissent? Are there any limits? If so, what are they?

4. What benefits does the church receive if it permits dissent? What are the negative consequences of dissent?

5. Richard McCormick discusses the factors that have influenced official attitudes toward dissent in the history of the church. How would you describe the official attitude toward dissent in the church today? Which factors (those McCormick lists, or others) seem most important in shaping the current climate?

Chapter 10

WOMEN IN THE CHURCH

In biblical times, women served as deaconesses, and recent research suggests that they often performed priestly functions as the leaders of "house churches" in the early centuries.

By the fourth century, however, official church pronouncements condemned women as unclean because of the menstrual cycle and childbirth and kept them out of all sacramental and decision-making functions in the church. In 1977, the Declaration on the Admission of Women to the Ministerial Priesthood said that women could not be priests because they do not "image" Christ. Official church pronouncements since then have tried to proclaim this opinion infallible.

Attitudes toward women have been very slow to change, but negative rhetoric about women has alternated with theoretical declarations in favor of gender equality and Vatican II's condemnation of "all discrimination . . . based on sex . . . as contrary to God's intent." Many observers read these contradictions as an official tradition struggling with itself, and perhaps on the brink of major change.

SCRIPTURE

Galatians 3:28:

"In Christ there is no Jew or Greek, slave or citizen, male or female. All are one in Christ Jesus."

1 Corinthians 11:5, 10:

"Any woman who prays or prophesies with her head uncovered brings shame upon her head. . . . A woman ought to have a sign of submission on her head."

1 Corinthians 14:34–35:

"According to the rule observed in all the assemblies of believers, women should keep silent in such gatherings. They may not speak. . . . If they want to learn anything, they should ask their husbands at home."

Ephesians 5:22:

"Wives should be submissive to their husbands."

Editors' Note: The translations above are from the New American Bible. The Inclusive New Testament, by Priests for Equality, translates the last three passages this way: 1 Corinthians 11:5, 10: "If a woman prays or prophesies with her head uncovered, it's a sign of disrespect for her 'head.'... Women are to have an outward sign of prophetic authority — the covering of their 'head.'" 1 Corinthians 14:34– 35: "As in all the churches of the holy ones, only one spouse has permission to speak. The other is to remain silent.... If the silent one has questions to ask, ask them at home." Ephesians 5:22: "Those of you who are in committed relationships should yield to one another as if to Christ."

Romans 16:1–7:

"I commend to you our sister Phoebe, a deacon of the church at Cenchrea. Welcome her, in the name of Our God, in a way worthy of the holy ones, and help her with her needs. She has looked after a great many people, including me.

"Give my greetings to Prisca and Aquila; they were my co-workers in the service of Christ Jesus.

"My greetings to Mary, who has worked hard for you, and to Andronicus and Junia, my kin and fellow prisoners; they are outstanding apostles."

CHURCH FATHERS

Tertullian, c. 200:

- "One hopes that the mad insolence of women, who have dared to wish to teach, will not go so far as to claim the right to baptize as well."
- "*You* are the devil's gateway; *you* are the unsealer of that (forbidden) tree; *you* are the first deserter of the divine law; *you* are she who persuaded him whom the devil was not valiant enough to attack. *You* destroyed so easily God's image, man. On account of *your* desert — that is, death — even the Son of God had to die."

Cyril of Jerusalem, c. 350:

"The virgins should silently read the Psalms.... They should speak only with their lips so that nothing can be heard.... Women should do just this. When they pray they are to move their lips, but their voices should not be heard."

Ambrose, c. 380:

"Let the woman cover her head, so as to secure her modesty even in public."

John Chrysostom, c. 400:

Women were "to be veiled not only at the time of prayer, but continuously."

EARLY CHURCH

Didascalia Apostolorum, third century:

"Thou hast need of the ministry of a deaconess for many things.... Let a woman be devoted to the ministry of women and a male deacon to the ministry of men."

Context: This document ("The Teaching of the Apostles") is one of the precursors of canon law.

Constitutiones Apostolicae, fourth century:

- "Now as to women's baptizing, we let you know that there is no small peril to those who undertake it. Therefore we do not advise you to do it; for it is dangerous, or rather wicked and impious" (see Urban II, below).

- "The deaconess cannot impart a blessing, nor does she carry out any of the functions which the priest or the deacons exercise; she is only a doorkeeper and helps the priests in administering baptism, simply for the sake of decency."

- Women could take communion only while wearing a veil.

- "We do not permit women to exercise the office of teaching in the church; rather they are simply to pray and listen to the teachers. For our teacher and lord Jesus himself sent only the Twelve to us, to teach the people and the gentiles. But he never sent women, although there was no lack of them.... If it had been seemly for women, he would have called them himself."

  Context: This document ("Apostolic Constitutions") is one of the precursors of canon law.

Synod of Laodicea, fourth century:

"Women are not allowed to approach the altar."

Gelasius, Letter to the Bishops of Lucania, 494:

"Nevertheless we have heard to our annoyance that divine affairs have come to such a low state that women are encouraged to officiate at the sacred altars, and to take part in all matters imputed to the offices of the male sex, to which they do not belong."

Gregory I, Letter to the English Bishop Augustine, Tenth Answer, c. 600:

- "When a woman has given birth...she should abstain [from entering a church] for thirty-three days if she had a boy, sixty-six if she had a girl."

- "During the time she is menstruating she should not be hurried to enter a church."

- "A woman should not be forced to receive the sacrament of holy communion [during her menstrual period]."

- "As for the man who sleeps with his wife, he should not enter a church without washing."

- "Because even licit union with his wife cannot be done without fleshly desire, he must abstain from entering the sacred place, since this desire cannot exist completely without sin."

Synod of Paris, 829:

"In some provinces it happens that women press around the altar, touch the holy vessels, hand the clerics the priestly vestments, indeed even dispense the body and blood of the Lord to the people. This is shameful and must not take place. . . . No doubt such customs have arisen because of the carelessness and negligence of the bishops."

MEDIEVAL CHURCH

Urban II, *Epistola 271*, c. 1090:

"If it is to be baptized, if the moment requires, a woman will baptize a child in the name of the Trinity."

Decretum, c. 1140:

"The image of God is in man in such a way that there is only one lord, the origin of all others, having the power of God as God's vicar, for everything is in God's image; and thus woman is not made in God's image."

Hadrian IV, c. 1155:

"We forbid that in the said monastery [Herford] any bishop outside the Roman pontiff exercise jurisdiction, and indeed in the sense that he never — unless he will be so invited by the abbess — may presume to celebrate solemn Mass there."

Innocent III, *On the Misery of the Human Condition*, 1195:

"According to the Mosaic law, a woman during her menstrual period is considered unclean. . . . Because of this uncleanness it is further commanded that a woman keep away from the entrance to the temple for forty days if she bear a male child but for eighty days if she bear a female."

Context: This book was a medieval bestseller and is thought to have influenced Geoffrey Chaucer in writing The Canterbury Tales. *It was typically medieval in its deep pessimism, condemnation of anything new, and horror of sexuality.*

Gregory IX, *Decretals*, c. 1230:

"Our daughter beloved in the Lord, and Abbess of Bubrigen, has set forth the following in a petition sent to us: Sometimes when she suspends her canonesses and the clerics who are subject to her jurisdiction, because of disobedience and other lapses, from their office and benefice, they do not observe a suspension of this sort because they are strongly convinced that she cannot excommunicate, hence, their excesses remain uncorrected. So that the said canonesses and clerics show obedience and respect to the above named abbess and obey her good admonitions, we consign therefore to your [the abbot's] discrimination to what extent you — according to previous admonition — wish to inflict on them ecclesiastical censure under exclusion of appeal."

Context: Within their abbeys, abbesses had the same authority as bishops.

Boniface VIII, *Periculoso*, 1298:

"We command by this present constitution, whose validity is eternal and can never be questioned, that all nuns, collectively and individually, present and to come, of whatsoever order of religion, in whatever part of the world they may be, shall henceforth remain in their monasteries in perpetual enclosure."

Editors' Note: Both the Council of Trent, in the sixteenth century, and the First Vatican Council, in the nineteenth century, reaffirmed this pronouncement.

Paul III, Letter on Herford Abbey, 1549:

"The abbess's right as proper judge to pronounce due penalties remains undisputed."

MODERN ERA

Pius X, *Motu Proprio de Musica Sacra*, 1903:

"Women, therefore, being incapable of such an office, cannot be admitted to the choir. If high voices, such as treble and alto, are wanted, these parts must be sung by boys, according to the ancient custom of the church."

Code of Canon Law, 1917:

"A female person may not minister. An exception is allowed only if no male person can be had and there is good reason. But female persons may in no case come up to the altar, and may only give responses from afar."

Pius XII, *Musicae Sacrae*, 1955:

"It is allowed that 'a group of men and women or girls, located in a place outside the sanctuary set apart for the exclusive use of this group, can sing the

liturgical texts at Solemn Mass, as long as the men are completely separated
from the women and girls, and everything unbecoming is avoided.'"

Context: He was quoting from Decrees of the Sacred Congregation of Rites.

John XXIII, *Pacem in Terris,* 1963:

"Human beings have the right to set up a family, with equal rights and duties
for men and women, and also the right to follow a vocation to the priesthood
or the religious life."

Paul VI, *E Motivo,* 1964:

"We have given orders that some devout ladies are to attend as auditors
several of the ... ceremonies and several of the general congregations of the
coming third session of the second Vatican Council.... Women will thus
know just how much honor the church pays to them in the dignity of their
being and of their mission on the human and the Christian levels."

*Context: The pope permitted women only to observe, not to participate, in
Vatican II.*

Second Vatican Council, *Pastoral Constitution on the Church in the Modern World,* 1965:

"Any type of social or cultural discrimination in basic personal rights on the
grounds of sex, race, color, social conditions, language, or religion, must be
curbed and eradicated as incompatible with God's design."

Paul VI, *Ministeria Quaedam,* 1972:

"Mother Church earnestly desires that all the faithful should be led to that
full consciousness and active participation in liturgical celebrations which is
demanded by the very nature of the liturgy. Such participation by the Christian people as 'a chosen race, a royal priesthood, a holy nation, a purchased
people' (1 Peter 2:9) is their right and duty by reason of their baptism. In
the restoration and promotion of the sacred liturgy, this full and active participation by all the people is the aim to be considered before all else.... In
accordance with the venerable tradition of the church, installation in the
ministries of lector and acolyte is reserved to men."

Paul VI, *Soyez les Bienvenues,* 1975:

"We defined the task of the Study Commission on Women in Society and the
Church. The task was concerned with documentation and with reflection
on the ways of promoting the dignity and responsibility of women.... The
fulfillment of the task of promotion must be gradual and none of the stages
in the process may be bypassed. Prudent discernment is called for, for the
question with which you deal requires tact. Nothing is gained by talking of
the equalization of rights, for the problem goes far deeper."

Commentary on Paul VI, *Declaration on the Question of the Admission of Women to the Ministerial Priesthood*, 1976:

"It is precisely because the priest is a sign of Christ the savior that he must be a man and not a woman.... [Quoting Aquinas] 'The priest enacts the image of Christ, in whose person and by whose power he pronounces the words of consecration.' Only a man can take the part of Christ, be a sign of his presence, in a word 'represent' him (that is, be an effective sign of his presence) in the essential acts of the covenant."

Congregation for Sacraments and Divine Worship, 1980:

"Women are not...permitted to act as altar servers" (approved by John Paul II, April 17, 1980).

Editors' Note: In 1994 this congregation changed its mind and left to individual bishops the decision as to whether females could be altar servers.

John Paul II, *Mulieris Dignitatem*, 1988:

"Virginity and motherhood [are the] two particular dimensions of the fulfillment of the female personality."

John Paul II, 1994:

"Women have been misunderstood in their dignity, misrepresented in their prerogatives, marginalized and even reduced to slavery."

John Paul II, *Ordinatio Sacerdotalis*, 1994:

"I declare that the church has no authority whatsoever to confer priestly ordination on women and that this judgment is to be definitively held by all the faithful."

John Paul II, *Christi Fidelis Laici* (quoting 1987 Synod on the Laity), 1995:

"Without discrimination women should be participants in the life of the church and also in consultation and the process of coming to decisions."

Congregation for the Doctrine of the Faith, Reply to the *Dubium* [Doubt], 1995:

"*Dubium:* Whether the teaching that the church has no authority whatsoever to confer priestly ordination on women, which is presented in the Apostolic Letter *Ordinatio Sacerdotalis* to be held definitively, is to be understood as belonging to the deposit of the faith.

"*Responsum:* In the affirmative.

"This teaching requires definitive assent, since, founded on the written Word of God, and from the beginning constantly preserved and applied in the Tradition of the church, it has been set forth infallibly by the ordinary and universal magisterium (cf. Second Vatican Council, *Dogmatic Constitution on the Church, Lumen Gentium* 23, 2). Thus, in the present circumstances, the Roman Pontiff, exercising his proper office of confirming the brethren (cf. Luke 22:32), has handed on this same teaching by a formal declaration, explicitly stating what is to be held always, everywhere, and by all, as belonging to the deposit of the faith."

GENDER EQUALITY: THEORY AND PRACTICE

Maureen Fiedler, SL

When I was ten years old, I saw a woman with a scarf on her head and a lighted candle in her hand, kneeling at Mary's altar in our parish church. "Why is she doing that?" I asked. My mother explained, "She just had a baby, and this is her 'churching' ceremony. It's a form of purification." "Purification from what?" I wondered.

Years later, as a young nun in Titusville, Pennsylvania, I can remember scratching my (veiled) head when the mistress of novices explained that the sister who gave the prayer responses to the priest at Mass could not kneel near the altar. She had to remain at a distance because church law forbade women to approach the altar during Mass. This made no sense either.

Years later, I connected the dots. "Churching" and keeping one's distance from the altar were remnants of a powerful patriarchal tradition in a church that regards men as the norm for human beings and treats women as unclean, inferior, and sources of temptation and sin. This tradition is very much alive in the church today, although some of its expressions, like "churching," praying at a distance, and the required wearing of veils, have been abandoned.

But it is not the only Catholic tradition about women, even in the realm of official teaching. The patriarchal tradition has been in constant struggle with the egalitarian tradition of the gospel for much of the past two millennia.

The Basic Struggle

In the early Christian writings attributed to Paul, contradictory statements reflect the struggle of these traditions. The Letter to the Galatians, for example, espouses an egalitarian view: "In Christ, there is no Jew or Greek, slave or free, male or female. All are one in Christ Jesus" (Gal. 3:28). The Epistle to the Romans acknowledges that women, including Phoebe, a deacon, are the co-workers of male apostles (Rom. 16:1–6). But the First Epistle to the Corinthians and the Letter to the Ephesians reflect the norms of the dominant culture, telling women to be silent in the assembly (1 Cor. 14:34–35), assigning them an inferior role in marriage (Eph. 5:22–24), and requiring them to cover their heads at worship as a "sign of submission" (1 Cor. 11:5–10).

The struggle depicted in the Pauline letters was writ large in the first centuries of the Christian community. On one hand, Jesus in the gospel represented the egalitarian ideal by emphasizing love and ministerial service rather than law and tradition. Jesus spoke with women in public despite strong taboos to the contrary (John 4:4–42). He ignored the ancient "blood taboo" and cured a woman who had been bleeding for eighteen years, although this made him unclean under Jewish law (Luke 8:43–48). He told parables that encouraged women to demand their rights from the unjust (Luke 18:1–8). He welcomed women and men equally to ministry, even calling Mary Magdalen to be the first to preach the Resurrection to the disciples (John 20:17–18). Since he never ordained anyone — male or female — to a "ministerial priesthood" as we understand it today, his counter-cultural attitude toward gender roles suggests that he intended women to minister in the community as the equals of men.

But the Greco-Roman world surrounding the early Christian communities operated as a patriarchal order. It treated women as inferiors who existed largely to please men, procreate the species, and keep house. Women were "naturally" destined for the private sphere and excluded from public functions or leadership roles. A philosophical dualism prevailed in which men represented the intellect, the soul, and things spiritual. Women were associated with the senses, the body, and things carnal. Their bodies and sexual functions defined their roles: they were either mothers, virgins, or whores. This thinking provided a strong rationale for power relationships that defined men as superior to women.

Comfortable in such patriarchal roles, many men in the church adopted this philosophical approach to gender, wedded it to theology, and relegated women to severely restricted roles in the Christian church. Christian communities that did practice gender equality were in a tenuous, counter-cultural position. The patriarchal norms of the larger culture eroded and eventually submerged the Christian egalitarian practice of the first centuries. But this process took a long time.

Women in the First Centuries

Although today's opponents of women's ordination maintain that patriarchy has always prevailed in the "unbroken tradition" of the all-male priesthood, recent scholarship shows that the egalitarian tradition in ministry lived on in many Christian communities for centuries. In her monumental work *In Memory of Her*, Elisabeth Schüssler Fiorenza describes how the early Christian community tried to live out the ideal of a "discipleship of equals."[1] Women led eucharistic worship in house churches, preached the gospel, went on missionary journeys, and filled leadership functions in early Christian communities.

Iconographic evidence in the catacombs suggests that women celebrated the Eucharist and possibly even served as bishops. The Catacomb of St. Priscilla in Rome has a third-century fresco with figures that are almost certainly women celebrating the Eucharist. The Chapel of St. Zenonia in the Roman Basilica of St. Prassede has a beautiful mosaic of four women, one of whom is named "Episcopa Theodora," *Bishop* Theodora.

In *When Women Were Priests*, Karen Torjesen explains that women filled priestly roles when the Roman authorities persecuted the church and Christians celebrated the Eucharist mostly in private homes.[2] After the Edict of Milan (313 C.E.), Christianity became the state religion of the Roman Empire and religious rituals moved to public places. Male church leaders began to assert the patriarchal values that reserved public roles in religious ritual and leadership for men alone.

Yet research by Dr. Georgio Otronto shows that the egalitarian tradition withstood this onslaught for centuries.[3] Women filled priestly roles as late as the fifth and sixth centuries in southern Italy and along the Dalmatian coast (present-day Croatia). In his letter to the bishops of Lucania in 494, Pope Gelasius I complained that bishops were ordaining and appointing women to fill *actual* priestly roles in their communities.

During these early centuries, a chorus of church fathers preached patriarchy. They told women to veil themselves in public, to be "seen and not heard" when reading the Psalms (Cyril of Jerusalem), and to refrain from teaching and baptizing (Tertullian).

Some wanted to restrict the ministry of women to women, to prevent deaconesses from imparting blessings, and to allow women to fill only the most minor roles. Others wanted women to stay away from the altar altogether. (Shades of that convent in Titusville!)

The writings of the church fathers and other early documents reveal the underlying rationale for restricting women's religious roles. Tertullian's famous charge, "You are the devil's gateway," essentially blamed Eve, and all women as her descendants, for original sin, the destruction of "man," and the death of Jesus. As temptresses of men, women were ultimately held responsible for the sins of men. Other influential thinkers such as Ambrose, Augustine, and later Thomas Aquinas, reinforced these negative and restrictive views of women.

---

1. Elisabeth Schüssler Fiorenza, *In Memory of Her* (New York: Crossroad, 1984).

2. Karen Jo Torjesen, *When Women Were Priests* (San Francisco: HarperSanFrancisco, 1993).

3. For the translation of Otronto's work, see Mary Ann Rossi, "Priesthood, Precedent, and Prejudice," *Journal of Feminist Studies in Religion* (May 1991): 73–94.

Gregory I seized on the ancient blood taboo, inherited from Judaism, which treated women as fundamentally unclean because of menstruation and childbirth. Gregory I and Innocent III even said that bearing a female child made the mother unclean for a *longer* time than bearing a male child! Of course unclean women could not touch sacred vessels, distribute communion, or approach the altar (Synod of Paris, 829).

This dominant patriarchal view denigrated women's body, sexuality, intellect, and spirituality.

The Middle Ages

Despite this powerful patriarchal tradition, remnants of egalitarianism remained alive during the Middle Ages among abbesses. They exercised the "power of jurisdiction," usually ascribed to bishops. They could not celebrate the Eucharist or administer the sacraments, but they appointed priests to nearby churches, granted and removed priestly faculties, and suspended those who were disobedient. As late as the nineteenth century, women exercised such power in European religious communities.

But abbesses were an exception, and a limited one at that, since much of an abbess's jurisdictional power was over other women, not men. Patriarchy remained dominant. Women's chastity took on far greater importance than men's chastity, and the church emphasized practices to "protect" it, such as veiling, cloistering of nuns, and preaching the importance of women's domestic role. Women who obeyed such rules implicitly recognized the superior status of the men who imposed these regulations.

The Modern Era

In the nineteenth and twentieth centuries, change in official teaching or practice regarding women has been glacial. But powerful forces are pushing the church to revisit the egalitarian model. These include the ordination of women in all mainstream Protestant denominations, the rise of a vocal women's movement in the Catholic Church, and the rich scholarship of feminist theological and biblical studies. They have forced even patriarchal churchmen to admit today what they would *never* have admitted only half a century ago: that women are — in *theory* at least — the equals of men in the eyes of God.

The Second Vatican Council said, "Every type ... of discrimination ... based on sex, race, color, social conditions, language, or religion ... is to be overcome and eradicated as contrary to God's intent."[4] This strong and unqualified statement preceded the example of a woman having the right to choose her state in life.

---

4. Second Vatican Council, *Pastoral Constitution on the Church in the Modern World*, 29.

The church has made serious attempts to overcome racism and anti-Semitism, but the same is not true with sexism. Instead, the official church has been struggling to "define" what the council meant. It has wrestled not only with the actual roles that women may fill, but with the theological and philosophical underpinnings of its historic discrimination against women. This struggle is evident in papal encyclicals, Vatican documents, and bishops' pastoral letters, where most recent statements about gender equality have been *qualified* — they speak of "appropriate" or "suitable" equality. But however much some prelates might wish that Vatican II had qualified its declaration against all forms of discrimination, it did not.

The church's official teaching and practice on women are clearly in flux. The Vatican does not want to oppose "equality," but it has not applied the teaching on nondiscrimination to ecclesial roles of any significance. Moreover, Vatican officials still repeat the central message of the Vatican's *Declaration on the Question of the Admission of Women to the Ministerial Priesthood*, that women cannot "image Jesus" in the priesthood. They seem blithely unaware that this assertion is discriminatory and contrary to the teaching of the *Pastoral Constitution on the Church in the Modern World*. They ignore the theological community that has, by and large, dismissed this contention as specious and unfounded. They ignore the tradition that has always affirmed that women are made in the image of God and that Christ is the paradigmatic *imago Dei*, thus making it logical that women can represent Christ as *imago Dei*. And they confuse many Catholics for whom "imaging Jesus" means living a virtuous life, not having the physical characteristics of a male.

In spite of this, some pastoral practices have begun to change, inch by inch. Catholic women today are rarely, if ever, "churched." Women serve close to the altar as lectors and touch the host as ministers of the Eucharist. In most dioceses, females are altar servers, a function related to the minor order of the priesthood known as the "acolyte." Women serve on parish councils and in diocesan offices. A few are chancellors. Hundreds serve as pastoral administrators, essentially acting as pastors in all functions except administration of the sacraments.

But these changes do not yet touch the central questions: priesthood and the nexus of decision-making power in the institution. Women still may receive only six of the seven sacraments solely because of their gender. Only the ordained — that is, males — are permitted to exercise real decision-making authority, or "jurisdiction." The Vatican's continued refusal to break that link between ordination and jurisdiction, or even discuss the ordination of women to the diaconate or the ministerial priesthood, shows that the patriarchal tradition still dominates the thinking of the hierarchy.

But the rapidly changing roles of women in today's world, the strength of feminist voices in the church, and increasing pastoral needs in the face of a chronic, worldwide shortage of male celibate clergy are clear "signs of the times" that beckon the church to change. They increase pressure on the Vatican daily. Cardinal Ratzinger's attempt in 1995 to declare infallible the Vatican's insistence on the all-male priesthood may signal a "last-ditch" attempt to bolster the patriarchal tradition. Meanwhile, calls for change become more compelling and egalitarian ideals more attractive to the People of God worldwide.

Feminist theological analyses are not easily answered. They point out that an all-male priesthood is out of synchrony with the gospel, discriminatory and therefore sinful, injurious to the faith of believers, and scandalous to many inside and outside the church.

Perhaps most devastating of all, feminists point out fundamental contradictions in current church teaching and practice. If, as Vatican II declared, women are indeed the equals of men and if all sex-based discrimination is contrary to God's intent, then why does the church refuse to admit women to the ministerial priesthood? Why are they not equals in decision-making?

Now the Vatican is quite capable of advocating one thing (equality) and practicing another (exclusion) — as is also the case with religious liberty, which it espouses for secular states but does not practice internally. But when compelling historical events finally *do* force change, I predict that Vatican II's seemingly small alteration in teaching, that women are the theoretical equals of men, will provide the rationale for the decision to ordain women. The first line of the triumphant press release will probably read, "As we have always maintained throughout the ages..."

Discussion Questions
WOMEN IN THE CHURCH

1. What is your experience of the ministries of women in the Catholic Church today? How have you experienced the work of women who are priests, ministers, or rabbis in other denominations? How did you find these ministries? Is being a woman a hindrance or a help to ministry?

2. When you read that women filled priestly roles in the early church, how do you respond? Does this have any relevance today?

3. When you read some of the quotations from the church fathers and other officials that express negative views of women or seek to restrict their roles, how do you respond? What stance toward women do you believe is closest to the behavior of Jesus in the gospel?

4. The Vatican has said that women cannot "image Jesus" in the priesthood and that Jesus never authorized it. In 1995, Cardinal Joseph Ratzinger tried to claim that the Vatican insistence on an all-male priesthood is infallible. How do you respond? How does this hierar-

chical position affect your attitude toward church? Toward your faith? How does it fit your understanding of the gospel?

5. Imagine a Catholic parish in the twenty-first century with a woman serving as priest and pastor. How would that be different from a parish today? Would the fact that the priest is a woman change the ministry? Would it change your attitude toward the priest? Would you like to participate in such a parish? Why or why not?

Chapter 11

MARRIED CLERGY

Church policy on clerical celibacy has reversed itself in the past thousand years. Roman Catholic clergy were permitted to marry during the first eleven centuries of Christianity. However, the passage of church lands from father to son (and thus out of the hands of the institutional church), a negative view of sex and women, and the rise of the celibate ideal in monastic orders led to the official proclamation of clerical celibacy. Enforcement took centuries. In the last decades of the twentieth century, the church is showing signs of being ready to revert to its earlier tradition.

SCRIPTURE

Matthew 8:14:

"Entering Peter's house, Jesus found Peter's mother-in-law in bed with a fever. Jesus touched her hand and the fever left."

1 Corinthians 9:5:

"Don't we have a right to have Christian spouses with us on our travels — as do all the other apostles, and Jesus' own family members, and Cephas?"

1 Timothy 3:

"Bishops must be irreproachable, married only once, even-tempered, self-controlled, modest, and hospitable.... They must be good managers of their own households, keeping their children under control without sacrificing their dignity. For if bishops don't know how to manage their own households, how can they take care of the church of God? ... In the same way, deacons must be dignified and straightforward.

"... Their spouses, similarly, should be serious, mature, temperate, and entirely trustworthy. Deacons must have been married only once and must be good managers of their children and their households."

Titus 1:6:

"Presbyters must be irreproachable, married only once, and the parents of children who are believers and are known not to be wild and insubordinate."

Editors' Note: Presbyters were those who filled priestly roles.

EARLY CHURCH

Council of Elvira, 306:

"Bishops, presbyters, and deacons and all other clerics having a position in the ministry are ordered to abstain completely from their wives and not to have children."

Council of Gangra, 345:

"If anyone shall maintain, concerning a married presbyter, that [it] is not lawful to partake of the oblation when he offers it, let him be anathema."

Leo I, *Epistles*, 440–61:

"Therefore, so that a spiritual bond may grow from the physical marriage, [deacons] may not send their spouses away and must live as though they had none, whereby the love of the married couple remains intact and the conjugal acts cease."

Hilarius, Letter to the Bishop of Tarragona, 465:

"Especial care must be taken — as already prescribed in previous decrees — that no one who has married a wife who was not a virgin aspires to higher ordinations. Those too must be debarred who have contracted a second marriage, contrary to the apostolic directives."

Gregory I, Letter to Augustine, Bishop of England, c. 600:

"If... there are any clerics not in sacred orders who cannot contain themselves, they ought to take themselves wives."

Council in Trullo II, 692:

- "He who has been joined in two marriages after his baptism, or has had a concubine, cannot be bishop, or presbyter, or deacon, or at all on the sacerdotal list; in like manner... he who has taken a widow, or a divorced person, or a harlot, or a servant, or an actress, cannot be bishop, or presbyter, or deacon, or at all on the sacerdotal list."

- "We, preserving the ancient rule and apostolic perfection and order, will that the lawful marriages of men who are in holy orders be from this time forward firm, by no means dissolving their union with their wives nor depriving them of their mutual intercourse at a convenient time. Wherefore, if anyone shall have been found worthy to be ordained sub-deacon, or deacon, or presbyter, he is by no means to be prohibited from admittance to such a rank, even if he shall live with a lawful wife. Nor shall it be demanded of him at the time of his ordination that he promise to abstain from lawful intercourse with his wife.... But we know, as they who assembled at Carthage (with a care for the honest life of the clergy) said, that subdeacons, who handle the Holy Mysteries, and deacons and presbyters should abstain from their consorts according to their own course [of ministration].... For it is meet that they who assist at the divine altar should be absolutely continent when they are handling holy things."

- "Since it is declared in the apostolic canons that of those who are advanced to the clergy unmarried, only lectors and cantors are able to marry; we also, maintaining this, determine that henceforth it is in nowise lawful for any subdeacon, deacon, or presbyter after his ordination to contract matrimony, but if he shall have dared to do so, let him be deposed. And if any of these who enter the clergy wishes to be joined to a wife in lawful marriage before he is ordained subdeacon, deacon, or presbyter, let it be done."

   Context: The canons of this Eastern church council were accepted by Pope Hadrian I (772–95.) The later split between Eastern and Western churches was partly caused by the Western insistence on clerical celibacy.

MEDIEVAL CHURCH

Council of Pavia, eleventh century:

"Se non caste, tamen caute" (If you can't leave your wife, be discreet).

Gregory VII, Letter to Otto of Constance, c. 1079:

"Those who are guilty of the crime of fornication are forbidden to celebrate Mass or to serve the altar if they are in minor orders. We prescribe, moreover, that if they persist in despising our laws, which are, in fact, the laws of the Holy Fathers, the people shall no longer be served by them. For if they will not correct their lives out of love for God and the dignity of their office, they must be brought to their senses by the world's contempt and the reproach of their people."

Urban II, 1089:

"We remove from every sacred order those who from the subdiaconate wish to have leisure for wives, and we decree that they be without office and benefice of the church. But if, warned by the bishop, they fail to correct themselves, we give permission to rulers that they subject their women to servitude."

   Context: This was part of efforts to enforce mandatory clerical celibacy. It was incorporated into canon law, along with an order by Benedict VIII (1012–24) to enslave clerics' children.

Innocent II, Synod of Clermont, 1130:

"Since priests are supposed to be God's temples, vessels of the Lord and sanctuaries of the Holy Spirit...it offends their dignity to lie in the conjugal bed and live in impurity" (see Pius XI, below).

Second Lateran Council, 1139:

"We also decree that those in the orders of subdeacon and above who have taken wives or concubines are to be deprived of their position and ecclesiastical benefice. For since they ought to be in fact and in name temples of God, vessels of the Lord and sanctuaries of the Holy Spirit, it is unbecoming that they give themselves up to marriage and impurity."

Context: Councils had to declare the institution of clerical celibacy and the outlawing of clerical marriage several times before bishops would enforce it.

Council of Trent, 1563:

"If anyone says that clerics with higher orders can enter into a valid marriage, let him be anathema." And "If anyone says that the married state excels the state of virginity or celibacy, and that it is better and happier to be united in matrimony than to remain in virginity or celibacy, let him be anathema."

MODERN ERA

Pius XI, *Ad Catholici Sacerdotii*, 1935:

"Since 'God is a spirit,' it is only fitting that he who dedicates and concentrates himself to God's service should in some way 'divest himself of his body.'"

Paul VI, *Sacerdotalis Caelibatus*, 1967:

Vatican II "foresaw the possibility of conferring the holy diaconate on men of mature age who are already married.... All this, however, does not signify a relaxation of the existing law, and must not be interpreted as a prelude to its abolition."

Paul VI, *Abbiamo Bisogno*, 1970:

Celibacy "can neither be abandoned nor discussed."

John Paul II, 1990:

John Paul II approved ordination of two married Brazilian men "as long as they gave up sexual intercourse." The Vatican issued a statement listing conditions for "a dispensation from the impediment of the marriage bond in view of ordination to the priesthood":

"1. total separation from the wife in the matter of cohabitation;
"2. acceptance of celibacy;
"3. written consent of the wife and children (if any)."

John Paul II, 1993:

"Jesus did not promulgate a law, but proposed celibacy as an ideal."

PRACTICE OF THE CHURCH IN EARLIER AGES

Pope Sixtus I (c. 116–25) was the son of a priest.

Pope Damasus I (366–84) was the son of a priest.

Pope St. Anastasius I (395–401) was the father of Pope St. Innocent I (401–17).

Pope Boniface I (418–22) was the son of a priest.

Pope Sixtus III (432–40) was the son of a priest.

Pope Felix III (483–92) was the son of a priest and a widower with two children when elected. One of his descendants was Pope Gregory I.

Pope Hormisdas (504–23) was the father of Pope Silverius (532–35).

Pope Agapitus I (535–36) was the son of a priest.

Pope Adeodatus I (615–18) was the son of a subdeacon.

Pope Theodore I (642–49) was the son of a bishop.

Pope Marinus (832–84) was the son of a priest.

Pope Boniface VI (896) was the son of a bishop.

Pope John XI (931–35) was the illegitimate son of Pope Sergius III (904–11).

Pope John XV (985–86) was the son of a priest.

NONCELIBATE POPES:

Adrian II (867–72, last married pope), Benedict V (964), Sergius III (904–11), John X (914–28), John XII (955–63), Benedict VII (974–83), Benedict IX (1032–44; 1045; 1047–48), Clement V (1305–14), Clement VI (1342–52), Sixtus IV (1471–84), Pius II (1458–64), Innocent VIII (1484–92), Alexander VI (1492–1503), Julius II (1503–13), Paul III (1534–49), Julius III (1550–55), Gregory XIII (1572–85), Gregory XV (1621–23), Urban VIII (1623–44), Innocent X (1644–55), Alexander VII (1655–67), among others.

THE MARRIED PRIESTHOOD, ON THE RECORD

Anthony T. Padovano

The biblical teaching is clear: Jesus did not link celibacy with ministry. The New Testament church accepted married ministers. There is no ambiguity here. The Letters to Timothy and Titus present family life as crucial for pastoral care. Jesus did not see celibacy as a preferred choice for ministry. He chose married apostles. They remained married, as St. Paul tells us in his first letter to the Corinthians, and took their wives with them on missionary journeys. Indeed, Paul tells us that Jesus gave no rule on celibacy or marriage to the disciples but left this to their choice. Jesus never refers to his own celibacy and does not make it normative for full and faithful following of him.

Furthermore, there is no clear evidence that Jesus was celibate. Assuming, however, that he was, he grew up in a tradition that saw marriage as a right and a value for all. He endorsed marriage and never challenged or denigrated the marital status of the Jewish patriarchs, prophets, and kings.

The New Testament presents a profound incarnational approach to ministry, in which marriage and family life, children and sexuality are celebrated. Ephesians teaches that the love of husband and wife symbolizes the love of Christ for the church.

The biblical teaching and apostolic practice are so clear that there have been married priests for two thousand years in all the Eastern churches, Catholic and Orthodox, and in the Latin church until the twelfth century. The twentieth century has seen a return to the linkage between ordained ministry and marriage. Vatican II began the change by declaring that marriage was neither a lesser sacrament than orders nor a lesser charism than celibacy. It taught that there is no essential relationship between priesthood and celibacy. It went further and recommended the ordination of married men as deacons.

Six years after the close of Vatican II, Paul VI expressed a willingness to ordain married men as priests in mission countries. In the 1980s John Paul II extended married priesthood to converts from Episcopal and Protestant churches and to lifelong Catholics who kept their marriages but renounced sexual expression after ordination. In 1997 the Vatican decision to allow deacons to remarry after ordination in certain circumstances reversed a centuries-old prohibition.

National hierarchies (Brazil, Canada, Sri Lanka) have asked for ordination of married men, as have many cardinals and bishops and a vast number of Catholics in several countries. Cardinal Basil Hume of Westminster, England, led the bishops of England and Wales in requesting the pope to offer amnesty to priests who married after ordination, were willing to continue ministry, and were judged adequate to the task.

The teaching has changed, dramatically, irreversibly, quietly, incrementally. In 1960 the Catholic world would never have believed that the following forty years would see married Catholic priests and their families (converts from the Anglican or the Lutheran Church) serving Western-rite Catholic churches, a married diaconate, and many cardinals and bishops calling for the end of mandatory celibacy. In 1993, even the pope admitted that there was no scriptural mandate for priestly celibacy.

It is clear from the historical record that a married priesthood is not a reform but a restoration and, indeed, a restoration to biblical teaching and apostolic practice. If the record is so clear, however, why did the Vatican impose mandatory celibacy, and why does the pope continue to insist on it?

It is commonplace to observe that the antisexual biases of Greco-Roman culture influenced the gentile Christian community. These biases are rooted in the idea that an intellectual, emotionally controlled, unearthly spirituality is superior to the incarnational, affective, and concrete spirituality of the gospel. In the second century, Origen, one of the greatest Christian thinkers of all time, castrated himself to please Christ. A few centuries later, the great Augustine, writing of Christian wives, cried out: "How sordid, filthy, and horrible a woman's embrace!" There is a direct line from Origen and Augustine to the mandatory celibacy of the twelfth century, but it does not pass through the gospel.

As the official church denigrated sexuality and women, its teaching became increasingly artificial and convoluted. Jerome sanitized the passage in 1 Corinthians about apostles and their wives to say that the apostles traveled with their sisters or pious women, not wives. The Council of Elvira allowed marriage, but neither sexuality nor children, to priests. The council at Trullo allowed sexual activity but not before the celebration of the Eucharist. This council imposed conditions that no apostle would have countenanced. Priests could not marry a widow, a servant, or an actress.

Married popes reigned until late in the ninth century (Adrian II, who died in 872, was married). In 1139, Lateran II imposed mandatory celibacy on all the Latin-rite clergy. Observance of the rule was not uniform until the Reformation. The major dioceses of England — Ely, London, Salisbury, Durham, Winchester — persisted in choosing married bishops *after* Lateran II.

The impetus to enact mandatory celibacy came from negative attitudes toward sexuality, corruption among the clergy (simony, the bequeathing of church assets and property to priests' families), and the church's desire for the property and inheritance of celibate priests.

Intriguing changes occurred in doctrine. As we have seen, neither biblical teaching nor apostolic practice supported mandatory celibacy. The reasons given for it became increasingly unconvincing, even to church leaders. And so the church invented new reasons: celibacy imitates Jesus; the celibate priest is more available to people. These new reasons presuppose that marriage is a less committed way to be a disciple of Jesus, and that married apostles or married Eastern Catholic priests are less wholehearted in availability and service. The truth of the matter is that availability has little to do with marital status and everything to do with priorities.

The church enforced mandatory celibacy most rigidly after the Reformation, partly because it became a defining difference for Catholic priests and partly because the reformers criticized it so sharply. Mandatory celibacy became less tenable in the twentieth century, precisely when ecumenism became valued and pastors modeled themselves increasingly on the gospel and apostolic practice, rather than official church documents and institutional policy.

It is clear that church reunion cannot occur with a celibate priesthood. At present, the Eucharist has become vulnerable to the Vatican's insistence on maintaining celibacy because of the severe shortage of male celibate priests to celebrate it. Genuine vocations to priesthood for women and men are increasingly discounted, not on the basis of charism, but because of marital status or gender. The New Testament does not support such hierarchies or exclusions.

A mandatory celibate, male-only priesthood violates biblical values, apostolic practice, human rights, and spiritual norms. It tells the Christian community that men are preferable to women, celibates to the married, church policy to the gospel.

As an option, married priesthood is necessary for the church not because of a shortage of priests but because we suffer from a deficiency of vision. The Spirit has summoned the church to honor all the gifts in the community.

> I will pour out my Spirit
>   On all humankind.
> Your daughters and sons will prophesy,
>   Your young people will see visions,
>   And your elders will dream dreams. (Acts 2:17)

A church with visions and dreams does not exclude married men and women from ministerial service.

Discussion Questions
MARRIED CLERGY

1. What has been your experience with married clergy in other religious denominations? What is your experience with married deacons in the Catholic Church? Does marriage hinder or enhance ministry? In what ways?

2. How do you respond to statements of early popes and councils claiming that sexual activity is incompatible with celebrating the Eucharist? Is it? Why or why not?

3. What do the "signs of the times" say to you: should the Roman Catholic Church return to its earlier practice of permitting married clergy or not? Why do you think that?

4. What are the advantages and disadvantages of returning to a married clergy today?

5. Imagine how a parish would function with a married priest and his or her family in the rectory. How would parish life be different? Would you like to participate in such a parish? Why or why not?

Chapter 12

SEXUAL INTIMACY AND PLEASURE

Changes in church teaching on sexual intimacy have been slow, but they have become more apparent in the last half of the twentieth century. Early teaching drew from a philosophical tradition that equated the body with evil and the spirit with good, treated sex as an evil, and sexual pleasure as justifiable only if procreation were intended. In the twentieth century, especially with the Second Vatican Council, the church has begun to reclaim the biblical tradition that celebrates the goodness of sexuality in itself. But even now, church officials find it hard to break from older, negative attitudes.

SCRIPTURE

Canticle of Canticles 7:7–13:

"How beautiful you are, how pleasing, my love, my delight!
Your very figure is like a palm tree; your breasts are like clusters.
I said: I will climb the palm tree, I will take hold of its branches.
Now let your breasts be like clusters of the vine and the fragrance of
   your breath like apples.
And your mouth like an excellent wine — that flows smoothly for my
   lover, spreading over the lips and the teeth.
I belong to my love and my beloved desires only me.
Come, my lover, let us go forth to the fields and spend the night among
   the villages.
Let us go early to the vineyard, and see if the vines are in bloom,
If the buds have opened, if the pomegranates have blossomed;
There I will give you my love."

Context: This celebration of sexual love is from the Hebrew Scriptures. The Second Vatican Council cited it as part of the biblical tradition on sexuality in its Pastoral Constitution on the Church in the Modern World, *49.*

Ephesians 5:25–32:

"Love one another as Christ loved the church.... Love one another as you love your own bodies. Those who love their partners love themselves. No one ever hates one's own flesh; one nourishes it and takes care of it as Christ cares for the church — for we are members of Christ's body. This is why one person leaves home and clings to another, and the two become one flesh."

THE EARLY CHURCH

Augustine, fourth century:

"Love your wives then, but love them chastely. In your intercourse with them keep yourselves within the bounds necessary for the procreation of children. And inasmuch as you cannot otherwise have them, descend to it with regret. For this necessity is the punishment of that Adam from whom we are sprung."

Context: Though never a pope, Augustine was a theologian and philosopher who influenced church attitudes toward sexuality for centuries.

Leo I, *Sermon 22*, c. 450:

"In all mothers conception does not take place without sin."

Gregory I, Letter to the English Bishop Augustine, Tenth Answer, c. 600:

- "As for sleeping with his wife, the husband must not do this until the baby is weaned. For the depraved custom has grown up among couples: the mothers disdain to nurse the babies that they brought into the world and pass them to other women to nurse. And this seems to come from one cause only: incontinence. Not wanting to be continent, they disdain to nurse their infants."

    Context: This was probably a letter in response to the bishop's inquiry. Here, "incontinence" means uncontrolled sexual behavior for the sake of physical self-gratification. "Continence" means abstinence from sexual intercourse. Apparently it was believed that women should abstain from intercourse in order to guarantee the production of breast milk.

- "When they have their menstrual period, it is forbidden for them to have intercourse with their husband; so that the sacred law punishes with death he who approaches a menstruating woman."

Gregory I, *Pastoral Rule*, c. 600:

"Husbands and wives are to be admonished to remember that they are joined together for the sake of producing offspring, and, when giving themselves to immoderate intercourse, they transfer the occasion of procreation to the service of pleasure.... Though they go not outside wedlock yet in wedlock they exceed the just dues of wedlock. Whence it is needful that, by frequent supplications, they do away [sic] their having fouled with the admixture of pleasure, the fair form of conjugal union."

Nicholas I, Letter to the Bulgarians, c. 860:

"If we must abstain from worldly labor on Sunday, how much the more must we be on our guard against fleshly lust and every bodily defilement [on Sunday]."

Context: This was later incorporated into canon law, in which sexual activity was banned on about 150 days of the year, including Sundays, feast days, and holy days.

Leo IX, 1054:

"Masturbators should not be admitted to sacred orders."

HIGH MIDDLE AGES AND RENAISSANCE

Innocent II, Synod of Clermont, 1130:

"Since priests are supposed to be God's temples, vessels of the Lord and sanctuaries of the Holy Spirit... it offends their dignity to lie in the conjugal bed and live in impurity."

Context: This is part of the church's crusade to enforce clerical celibacy, which gained intensity from the mid-eleventh century onward (see chapter 11, "Married Clergy").

Decretum, 1140:

- "At the time of prayer it is not lawful for anyone to engage in conjugal activity."
- "As often as the birthday of the Lord or the other feasts occur, we should abstain not only from the fellowship of infidel concubines but also from our own wives."
- "It is necessary on fast days to abstain even from our wives."
- [Quoting Gregory I] "A man sleeping with his wife ought to refrain from entering church."
- "It is not lawful to celebrate marriage on the days of Lent."

Innocent III, *De Miseria Humane Conditionis,* 1195 (as Cardinal Segni, before he became pope):

- "Everyone knows that intercourse, even between married persons, is never performed without the itch of the flesh, the heat of passion, and the stench of lust. Whence the seed conceived is fouled, smirched, corrupted, and the soul infused into it inherits the guilt of sin, the stain of evil-doing, that primeval taint. Just as drink is polluted by a soiled vessel, anything that touches something polluted becomes polluted."

- "Hear now on what food the child is fed in the womb: actually on menstrual blood which ceases in the female after conception so that the child in her womb will be nourished by it. And this blood is reckoned so detestable and impure that on contact with it fruits will fail to sprout, orchards go dry, herbs wither, the very trees let go their fruit; if a dog eats it, he goes mad. When a child is conceived, he contracts the defect of the seed, so that lepers and monsters are born of this corruption. Wherefore according to the Mosaic law, a woman during her monthly period is considered unclean, and if anyone approach a menstruating woman it is commanded that he be put to death. Because of this uncleanness it is further commanded that a woman keep away from the entrance to the temple for forty days if she bear a male child but for eighty days if she bear a female."

  Context: This book was a medieval bestseller, and is thought to have influenced Geoffrey Chaucer in writing The Canterbury Tales. *It is typically medieval in its deep pessimism, condemnation of anything new, and horror of sexuality.*

Innocent IV, *Apparatus super Libros Decretalium,* c. 1250:

"We do not believe that for the sodomitic vice there can be a separation of beds" [but divorce is allowed if] "the husband wants to draw [the wife] into that sin."

Context: It was taboo even to name "unnatural" sexual practices such as anal intercourse, intercourse not in the "missionary" position, or intercourse at times forbidden by the church; therefore, euphemisms were often used in church documents.

Eugene IV, *Exultate Deo,* 1439:

"Through order the church is indeed governed and multiplied spiritually; through matrimony it is corporally increased."

Context: The population of Europe was decimated in the mid-fourteenth century by the Black Death. "The church suffered a heavy, though uneven, mortality among the clergy.... The mortality of bishops from 1347 to 1350 seems to have been around 35 percent, and careful study of some English dioceses suggests a loss of clergy approaching 40 percent in those years. The effort to replace the deceased in both the secular and the regular clergy led inevitably to less rigid standards of ordination and profession, with unhappy results" (New Catholic Encyclopedia, *vol. 2, p. 598).*

Council of Trent, 1563:

"If anyone says that the married state excels the state of virginity or celibacy, and that it is better and happier to be united in matrimony than to remain in virginity or celibacy, let him be anathema."

THE MODERN PERIOD

Pius XI, *Casti Connubii*, 1930:

- [Quoting canon law] "The primary end of marriage is the procreation and the education of children."

- "This mutual molding of husband and wife, this determined effort to perfect each other, can in a very real sense, as the Roman Catechism teaches, be said to be the chief reason and purpose of matrimony, provided matrimony be looked at not in the restricted sense as instituted for the proper conception and education of the child, but more widely as the blending of life as a whole and the mutual interchange and sharing thereof."

- "Since... the conjugal act is destined primarily by nature for the begetting of children, those who in exercising it deliberately frustrate its natural power and purpose sin against nature and commit a deed which is shameful and intrinsically vicious."

- [Permission to use "rhythm" method of birth control] "Nor are those considered as acting against nature who in the married state use their right in the proper manner although on account of natural reasons either of time or of certain defects, new life cannot be brought forth. For in matrimony as well as in the use of the matrimonial rights there are also secondary ends, such as mutual aid, the cultivating of mutual love, and the quieting of concupiscence which husband and wife are not forbidden to consider so long as they are subordinated to the primary end and so long as the intrinsic nature of the act is preserved."

  Editors' Note: The successive paragraphs above seem to contradict one another.

Pius XII, Address to Italian Catholic Midwives, 1951:

- "To save the life of the mother is a most noble end, but the direct killing of the child as a means to this end is not licit."

- "The Creator who in His goodness and wisdom has willed to conserve and propagate the human race through the instrumentality of man and woman by uniting them in marriage has ordained also that, in performing this function, husband and wife should experience pleasure and happiness in body and spirit. In seeking and enjoying this pleasure, therefore, couples do nothing wrong."

- "And the very labor which, after original sin, the mother must suffer to bring her child into the world is nothing but another bond drawing mother and child even closer. The more pain it cost her, the more a mother loves her child."

- "To embrace the married state, continuously to make use of the faculty proper to it and lawful in it alone, and, on the other hand, to withdraw always and deliberately with no serious reason from its primary obligation [procreation], would be a sin against the very meaning of conjugal life.... Observing the nonfertile periods alone can be lawful only under a moral aspect.... The determination to avoid habitually the fecundity of the union, while at the same time to continue fully satisfying their sensuality, can be derived only from a false appreciation of life and from reasons having nothing to do with proper ethical laws.... God obliges married people to abstain, if their union cannot be fulfilled according to the laws of nature. Therefore, in this case abstinence is possible."

- "The truth is that matrimony as a natural institution, by virtue of the will of the Creator, does not have as its primary, intimate end the personal improvement of the couples concerned but the procreation and the education of new life. The other ends, though also connected with nature, are not in the same rank as the first, still less are they superior to it.... Enjoyment is subordinated to the law of action from which it derives and not the other way about, the action to the law of enjoyment."

Second Vatican Council, *Pastoral Constitution on the Church in the Modern World*, 1965:

- "[Marital] love is uniquely expressed and perfected through the marital act. The actions within marriage by which the couple are united intimately and chastely are noble and worthy ones. Expressed in a manner which is truly human, these actions signify and promote that mutual self-giving by which spouses enrich each other with a joyful and a thankful will."

  Context: "Here, as elsewhere, when the question arises, the council sedulously avoids the terminology of primary and secondary ends of marriage. It insists on the natural ordering of marriage and conjugal love to procreation but without recourse to such formulations" (Flannery [1992], footnote, p. 252). Also see CDF 1979, below.

- "The biblical Word of God several times urges the betrothed and the married to nourish and develop their wedlock by pure conjugal love and undivided affection.... This love is an eminently human one.... It involves the good of the whole person. Therefore it can enrich the expressions of body and mind with a unique dignity.... This love our God has judged worthy of special gifts, healing, perfecting, and exalting gifts of grace and charity.... This love is uniquely expressed and perfected through the marital act."

Paul VI, *Humanae Vitae,* 1968:

- "The church ... teaches that each and every marital act must of necessity retain its intrinsic relationship to the procreation of human life."

- "We are obliged once more to declare that the direct interruption of the generative process already begun and, above all, all direct abortion, even for therapeutic reasons, are to be absolutely excluded as lawful means of regulating the number of children. Equally condemned ... is direct sterilization, whether of the man or of the woman, whether permanent or temporary. Similarly excluded is any action which either before, at the moment of, or after sexual intercourse, is specifically intended to prevent procreation — whether as an end or as a means.... It is a serious error to think that a whole married life of otherwise normal relations can justify sexual intercourse which is deliberately contraceptive and so intrinsically wrong."

Congregation for the Doctrine of the Faith, *Declaration on Certain Questions Concerning Sexual Ethics,* 1975:

"Both the magisterium of the church — in the course of a constant tradition — and the moral sense of the faithful have declared without hesitation that masturbation is an intrinsically and seriously disordered act.... For it lacks the sexual relationship called for by the moral order, namely, the relationship which realizes the full sense of mutual self-giving and human procreation in the context of mutual love. All deliberate exercise of sexuality must be reserved to this regular relationship."

Congregation for the Doctrine of the Faith, *Ruling on Sterilization, Impotence, and Valid Marriage,* 1977:

"Decreed the following responses to the questions posed to them:

1. Whether the impotence which prohibits marriage consists in the prior and permanent inability — either absolute or relative — of accomplishing conjugal intercourse.

2. If so, whether there is necessarily required for conjugal intercourse the ejaculation of semen produced in the testicles.

To the first question: Yes.
To the second question: No."

Congregation for the Doctrine of the Faith, Statement on *Human Sexuality, New Directions in American Catholic Thought,* 1979:

"Admitting that procreation is only one possible form of creativity, but not essential to sexuality, with a gratuitous change in the accepted terms... [is] a change which contradicts the formulation used in Vatican II."

Context: According to Flannery, on the contrary, Vatican II carefully avoided the idea that the primary end of sexual intercourse is procreation and its secondary end is expression of love and commitment. See Second Vatican Council, above.

John Paul II, Audience, 1980:

"Man can commit this adultery 'in the heart' also with regard to his own wife, if he treats her only as an object to satisfy instinct."

John Paul II, *Familiaris Consortio,* 1981:

- "When marriage is not esteemed, neither can consecrated virginity or celibate existence; when human sexuality is not regarded as a great value given by the creator, the renunciation of it for the sake of the Kingdom of Heaven loses its meaning."

- "A very valuable witness can and should be given by those husbands and wives who through the joint exercise of periodic continence have reached a more mature personal responsibility with regard to love and life."

John Paul II, *Love and Responsibility,* 1981:

"The union of persons in love does not necessarily have to be realized by way of sexual relations. But when it does take this form the personalistic value of the sexual relationship cannot be assured without willingness for parenthood."

Code of Canon Law, 1983:

"Antecedent and perpetual impotence to have intercourse, whether on the part of the man or of the woman, which is either absolute or relative in its very nature, invalidates marriage."

Context: Sixtus V first made this pronouncement in 1587, in order to keep castrated choirboys (castrati) from marrying. Pius XII reaffirmed the policy in 1941, and the Vatican revoked it in 1977, only to reintroduce it in 1983.

Congregation for the Doctrine of the Faith, *Instruction on Artificial Insemination,* 1986:

"After natural sexual intercourse, the husband's sperm could be collected by a syringe and aspirated toward the egg. Church officials let it be known that a particular method was approvable for expediting this procedure: use of a perforated condom that would allow some sperm to escape, in keeping with the requirements of the 'natural' act, while retaining by far the greater measure" (Briggs, p. 225).

Congregation for the Doctrine of the Faith, Letter to the Bishops and the Catholic Church on the Pastoral Care of Homosexual Persons, 1986:

"Although the particular inclination of the homosexual person is not a sin, it is a more or less strong tendency ordered toward an intrinsic moral evil... an objective disorder.... Homosexual activity is not a complementary union able to transmit life; and so it thwarts the call to a life of that form of self-giving which the Gospel says is the essence of Christian living."

Congregation for the Doctrine of the Faith, *Some Considerations Concerning the Catholic Response to Legislative Proposals on the Nondiscrimination of Homosexual Persons*, 1992:

"Homosexual persons, as human persons, have the same rights as all persons.... Among other rights, all persons have the right to work, to housing, etc. Nevertheless, these rights are not absolute. They can be legitimately limited for objectively disordered external conduct.... There is no right to homosexuality, which therefore should not form the basis for judicial claims."

SEXUALITY: PROFANE OR SACRED?
Christine Gudorf

Historically, Christian teaching on sexuality has been negative, reflecting and influencing sexual attitudes in the larger culture. The church spread from a Jewish milieu in which marital reproductive sexual activity was regarded as good — within rigid patriarchal controls on women and sexuality — into a Greco-Roman milieu pervaded by mind-body dualism and Stoic distrust of the nonrational aspect of sexuality.

Clerical celibacy is often cited as a cause of negative church attitudes toward sexual activity, sexual pleasure, and women, and of church teaching on the superiority of virginity over marriage. But mandatory clerical celibacy was finally enforced only after the end of the first millennium, after a long struggle over sexuality.

According to historian Peter Brown, the early church experienced an internal struggle between radicals and traditionalists.[1] The radicals wanted to resist the oppressive structures and institutions of the Roman Empire, including the patriarchal family, the class structure, and patterns of wealth

---

1. See Peter Brown, *The Body and Society: Men, Women, and Sexual Renunciation in Early Christianity* (New York: Columbia University Press, 1988), and Rosemary Ruether, "Virginal Feminism in the Fathers of the Church," in Ruether, ed., *Religion and Sexism* (New York: Simon and Schuster, 1974).

accumulation and distribution. So they supported ministry by men and women of all classes who pledged themselves to a freeing celibacy associated with a simple, ascetic lifestyle. The traditionalists were elite married house-holders, often patrons of the local churches as well as leaders in the larger society, among whom patriarchal norms prevailed. Leadership by women, slaves, and the poor was pitted against respect for sex and marriage. Celi-bacy may seem to many people today a severe, unnecessary restriction on the human potential for relationship. But it appeared to many second- and third-century Christians in the Roman Empire as an escape from restrictive control by extended families that dominated all aspects of marriage, divorce, and reproduction in the interests of maximizing family wealth and power.

Virginity or, after a spouse's death, celibate widowhood was the primary vehicle for women's empowerment in the early church. Women could as-sert power over their lives and leadership within the Christian community only when freed from the confines of wifely convention. The earliest Chris-tian communities provided for widows. This practice discouraged the need for remarriage after widowhood and provided local examples of the benefits to women of freedom from spousal and child-rearing responsibilities.[2] On the other hand, the defenders of marriage were, for the most part, defenders of social and familial hierarchy and custom.

Another contextual support for celibacy was the situation of many Chris-tians in these early centuries. They lived in small Christian communities with few potential spouses, with intense pressure not to marry pagans, and with still-powerful prejudice against marrying below one's social rank. During this period celibacy was a mark of Christian freedom that parents chose for children as the best option from both religious and worldly perspectives.

In this battle between the radical ascetics and the patriarchal house-holders, the radicals depended so much on the wealth and the children contributed by married lay people that they were unable to make celibacy normative. But eventually they successfully established the superiority of the monastic model of spirituality and reserved the priesthood for celibates. Later defenses of vowed virginity and ongoing attempts to distinguish leadership in the Christian community from corrupt leadership in the world resulted in much church negativity about sex.

Gnostic attitudes toward sexuality in the ancient world pressured Chris-tians to view the spiritual soul as opposed to the material body, requiring submission to the spiritual soul. Roman stoicism also encouraged discipline over the passions, though it was not associated with virginity but with familial duty.

Modern fastidiousness should also help us understand why sex might ap-pear degraded in an age when many men and women did not choose their

2. Ibid., 148.

own spouses, and when bathing was rare, disease rampant, pregnancies, infant and maternal mortality frequent, and scientific medicine unknown. Emphasis on the spirit and the wisdom imparted by the spirit offered opportunities to transcend the everyday world.

Thus, until the late modern era, even the most progressive Catholics shared the views expressed in these papal statements, because they shared the context that helped shape the statements. For example, until the invention of reliable contraception in the late modern era, the church interpreted God's will, as written in creation, as intending that procreation result from sexual intercourse. This interpretation was not specific to the church. Sexual intercourse was known to be necessary for procreation, and biological analogies with other species seemed to support procreation as the purpose of sex. Furthermore, common wisdom held that population increase was generally good, since it produced greater family and group security and specialization of labor, which generated technology and civilization.

It was not odd, then, when sex became suspect and virginity was exalted, that those who sought to defend marriage, beginning with Clement of Alexandria, focused on reproduction as the primary good of marriage and restricted sex to begetting children.[3] Mutual attraction was not seen as the common basis of marriage and long had been regarded with suspicion, as likely to counter parental wishes, which generally determined marriage choices. Marital love was understood to develop after marriage, and to consist largely of respect, cooperation, and willingness to do one's duty for the spouse, even when it required sacrifice. How could any premodern society understand the formation of a primary, intimate bond between the spouses as the foremost end of marriage, when such bonds were so rare as to seem both exceptional and eccentric?

Vatican II's pronouncement on the mutual molding of husband and wife as a primary reason and purpose of marriage and similar changes in Western understandings of marriage resulted from socioeconomic developments and the technology associated with them.

From the premodern to the modern period, increased partnership between men and women in marriage has become more common in the West, altering general perceptions about possibilities for friendship and intimacy in marriage. Before the modern period, male and female roles in the family and agricultural production were very different. Intimate relationships were not sexual, but were primarily between persons of the same sex, who shared the same training, work, and role. The roles of masters' wives among the medieval guilds and shopkeepers' wives in the early Reformation were unusual in their time, but became the models for a new age. These middle-class women worked in partnership with their husbands, usually under their lead,

---

3. Ibid., 132–34.

but sometimes as widows able to carry on in their place. Sharing work with men raised women's status and sometimes produced more emotional intimacy in marriage as well.

The Industrial Revolution of the eighteenth and nineteenth centuries helped end the extended agricultural family as an ideal and produced nuclear urban families that wanted fewer children because they were expensive to raise. This pressure for smaller families led to Pius XII's approval of birth regulation through abstinence (rhythm). Combined with increasingly efficient contraceptive technologies and the recent perception of a vast overpopulation crisis endangering the health of the biosphere, antinatal economic sentiment pressures a still-resistant Vatican to repeal the church ban on artificial contraception.

The Industrial Revolution also removed women from home production, moved production to factories, and segregated male workers there. But eventually women — first unmarried, later married — entered factory work and demonstrated their ability to do similar work and provide for the family.

As more and more women have entered the workforce in the past fifty years, the common view of women has changed. At the turn of the twentieth century, most people might have agreed with Aquinas that what God meant in designating Eve as "Adam's helpmate" was to help in reproduction, "because in any other task a man would be better aided by another man."[4] But contemporary society rejects this judgment. As the status of women has risen through their increased share in production, social (as opposed to domestic) maintenance and decision-making, so has the possibility of men accepting women as intimates.[5]

From these historical transformations arises an increasingly common perception among Catholics, other Christians, and non-Christians that God's gratuitous love is mediated to us through the mutually enriching and sexually pleasurable, sometimes sacrificial, intimate, and sacramental love we experience in marriage.[6] This dramatic change in attitude has been reflected in official church pronouncements, especially those from Vatican II. More and more Christians are realizing that abstaining from sex to be better able to pray is not necessitated by the nature of sex itself.

Sex is not inherently polluting, distracting, or selfish. Sex is not conducive to communion with God when it enacts relations of pain, dominance, manipulation, commoditization, or other forms of exploitation. But when

---

4. St. Thomas Aquinas, *Summa Theologiae* I, 92, 1.

5. This is not to deny that this increase in the status and power of women in our society has not also unleashed a backlash of violence against them and, some would insist, against children, by men who feel threatened by a loss of control. See Constance A. Bean, *Women Murdered by the Men They Loved* (Harrington Park Press, 1992), chapter 5.

6. See, for example, Charles A. Gallagher et al., *Embodied in Love: Sacramental Spirituality and Sexual Intimacy* (New York: Crossroad, 1986).

human sexual interaction enacts relations of mutually pleasurable, committed self-giving love, it connects us with God at the heart of the universe, and therefore is a form of prayer. Perhaps we could not experience sex as sacred in Christianity until sexual egalitarianism had developed to the point that we could see and reject the eroticization of dominance that has prevailed in Western history. Certainly it is not accidental that the discovery of the possible presence of God in sexual love historically accompanies a contemporary understanding of sexual partnership as grounded in mutuality.[7]

Discussion Questions
SEXUAL INTIMACY AND PLEASURE

1. What is your own experience of sexuality? Have you found it positive or negative in your own life? How do you perceive it in the lives of your family members or close friends?

2. What is your belief about intimate expressions of human sexuality? Do you understand sexual pleasure as essentially negative or positive? Do you understand it as negative in some circumstances and positive in others? If so, what are the circumstances? Why do you see it this way?

3. How do you react to the Canticle of Canticles from the Hebrew Scriptures? To the passage from Ephesians?

4. How do you respond to statements by church authorities whose view of sexuality is negative? How do you react when you read official condemnations of artificial contraception?

5. Commentator Christine Gudorf provides some unique historical insights about celibacy and sexuality throughout the ages. What new insights did you gain from her essay?

6. Do you see any positive values in celibacy? If so, what?

7. How would you talk about intimacy when you explain sex to children? How do you think it should be discussed in the context of religious education?

---

7. Christine E. Gudorf, *Body, Sex and Pleasure: Reconstructing Christian Sexual Ethics* (Cleveland: Pilgrim, 1994), chapter 7.

Chapter 13

CONTRACEPTION

The teaching on contraception has shifted with the sands of time. At various times, condemnations have been rooted in negative views of sex, a fear of potions associated with sorcery, the imperative to procreate the human race, and an unwillingness to decouple the sex act from procreation. At times, church pronouncements associated contraception with abortion. For many centuries, the church banned any method that prevented conception, even periodic abstinence or "rhythm." Today, the hierarchy promotes this method, distinguishing it from condemned "artificial" methods such as condoms or pills. In the 1960s, Pope Paul VI rejected the recommendations of the Papal Birth Control Commission that urged him to approve artificial methods. The very fact that such a commission was established, and its ideas considered, suggests that further changes in this teaching are possible.

CHURCH FATHERS

Augustine, *Marriage and Concupiscence,* fourth century:

"Sometimes this lustful cruelty, or cruel lust, comes to this, that they even procure poisons of sterility, and, if these do not work, extinguish and destroy the fetus in some way in the womb, preferring that their offspring die before it lives, or if it was already alive in the womb to kill it before it was born.... The wife is in a fashion the harlot of her husband or he is an adulterer with his own wife."

Context: "Poisons of sterility" are a form of contraception. Most of the rest of the statement refers to abortion, although it levels an equal judgment against those who use either. Contraception and abortion were often linked in church history because many early writers saw both as results of sorcery or witchcraft. This statement is the basis of the church's later anticontraception policies.

MEDIEVAL CHURCH

Gregory IX, *Decretals,* 1230:

"He who does magic or gives poisons of sterility is a [person who commits] homicide. If anyone to satisfy his lust or in meditated hatred does something

149

to a man or woman or gives something to drink so that he cannot generate, or she conceive, or offspring be born, let him be held a homicide."

Innocent VIII, *Summis Desiderantes* ["Witches' Bull"], 1484:

"It has recently come to our ears... that many persons of both sexes, heedless of their own salvation and forsaking their Catholic faith, give themselves over to devils male and female, and by their incantations, charms, and conjurings, and by other abominable superstitions and sortileges, offenses, crimes and misdeeds, ruin and cause to perish the offspring of women, the foal of animals, the products of the earth, the grapes of vines, and the fruits of trees, as well as men and women, cattle and flocks and herds and animals, and hinder men from begetting and women from conceiving, and prevent all consummation of marriage."

Sixtus V, *Effraenatam*, 1588:

- "Who, then, would not condemn with the most severe punishments the crimes of those who by poisons, potions, and *maleficia* induce sterility in women, or impede by cursed medicines their conceiving or bearing?"
- "Moreover, we decree that they should by the same penalties [for homicide] be wholly bound who proffer potions and poisons of sterility to women and offer an impediment to the conception of a fetus, and who take pains to perform and execute such acts or in any way counsel them, and the women themselves who knowingly and voluntarily take the same potions."

Gregory XIV, *Sedes Apostolica*, 1591:

"Where no homicide or no animated fetus is involved, [the church is] not to punish more strictly than the sacred canons or civil legislation does."

Context: Sixtus's successor, Gregory XIV, revoked Effraenatam, *except for the parts "applying to abortion of an ensouled, forty-day-old fetus" (Noonan, 1986, p. 363).*

MODERN ERA

Pius XI, *Casti Connubii*, 1930:

- "Since... the conjugal act is destined primarily by nature for the begetting of children, those who in exercising it deliberately frustrate its natural power and purpose sin against nature and commit a deed which is shameful and intrinsically vicious."
- "But Christian parents must also understand that they are destined not only to propagate and preserve the human race on earth... but children who are to become members of the church of Christ... that the worshipers of God and Our Savior may daily increase."

- But: "Nor are those considered as acting against nature who in the married state use their right in the proper manner although on account of natural reasons either of time or of certain defects, new life cannot be brought forth.... There are also secondary ends, such as ... the quieting of concupiscence which husband and wife are not forbidden to consider so long as they are subordinated to the primary end and so long as the intrinsic nature of the act is preserved."

    Context: This is the first positive papal acknowledgment of the "rhythm" method of birth control. The final phrase means that use of a condom, other "barrier method," or coitus interruptus is still forbidden.

Pius XII, Address to Italian Catholic Midwives, 1951:

"To withdraw always and deliberately with no serious reason from its primary obligation [procreation], would be a sin against the very meaning of conjugal life.... Observing the nonfertile periods alone can be lawful only under a moral aspect.... The determination to avoid habitually the fecundity of the union, while at the same time to continue fully satisfying their sensuality, can be derived only from a false appreciation of life and from reasons having nothing to do with proper ethical laws.... God obliges married people to abstain, if their union cannot be fulfilled according to the laws of nature."

Pius XII, Address to National Congress of the Family Front and Association of Large Families, 1951:

"The church knows how to consider with sympathy and understanding the real difficulties of the married state in our day. Therefore, in Our last allocution on conjugal morality, We affirmed the legitimacy and, at the same time, the limits — in truth very wide — of a regulation of offspring which, unlike so-called 'birth control,' is compatible with the law of God. One may even hope ... that science will succeed in providing this licit method with a sufficiently secure basis."

Second Vatican Council, *Pastoral Constitution on the Church in the Modern World*, 1965:

"In questions of birth regulation the daughters and sons of the church ... are forbidden to use methods disapproved of by the teaching authority of the church in its interpretation of the divine law."

Papal Commission for the Study of Population, Family and Births, 1966: "The morality of sexual acts between married people takes its meaning first of all specifically from the ordering of their actions in a fruitful married life, that is, one which is practiced with responsible, generous, and prudent parenthood. It does not then depend upon the direct fecundity of each and every particular act. Moreover the morality

of every marital act depends upon the requirements of mutual love in all its aspects."

Editors' Note: Paul VI disregarded this commission's recommendations.

Paul VI, *Humanae Vitae*, 1968:

• "The church . . . teaches that each and every marital act must of necessity retain its intrinsic relationship to the procreation of human life."

• "Equally condemned . . . is direct sterilization, whether of the man or of the woman, whether permanent or temporary. Similarly excluded is any action which either before, at the moment of, or after sexual intercourse, is specifically intended to prevent procreation. . . . It is a serious error to think that a whole married life of otherwise normal relations can justify sexual intercourse which is deliberately contraceptive and so intrinsically wrong."

John Paul II, *Evangelium Vitae*, 1995:

"From the moral point of view contraception and abortion are *specifically different* [emphasis in original] evils: the former contradicts the full truth of the sexual act as the proper expression of conjugal love, while the latter destroys the life of a human being; the former is opposed to the virtue of chastity in marriage, the latter is opposed to the virtue of justice and directly violates the divine commandment 'You shall not kill.'

"But despite their differences of nature and moral gravity, contraception and abortion are often closely connected. . . . It is true that in many cases contraception and even abortion are practiced under the pressure of real-life difficulties, which nonetheless can never exonerate from striving to observe God's law fully. Still, in very many other instances such practices are rooted in a hedonistic mentality unwilling to accept responsibility in matters of sexuality, and they imply a self-centered concept of freedom, which regards procreation as an obstacle to personal fulfillment."

THE SHIFTING GROUND OF CONTRACEPTION
Maggie Hume

A paradox frames Catholic teachings against contraception: sixteen centuries ago, St. Augustine fired his first salvo at birth control, singling out periodic abstinence. Today, the Vatican quotes Augustine in opposing contraception — but distinguishes periodic abstinence from all other methods and sings its praises.

Teachings on contraception flow from beliefs about sexuality. Loathing of sexuality shaped the notions of the "fathers" of Christianity, who took refuge in Stoicism. Stoic hyper-rationalism demanded that the exercise of sex be justified by the "sane" purpose of procreation. "To have coition other than to procreate children is to do injury to nature," Clement of Alexandria said. "Our ideal is not to experience desire at all." This approach set Christians apart from Roman pagans who indulged male promiscuity, and from the Gnostics, Christian-like groups who advocated either sexual asceticism or contraception because they believed that procreation perpetuated the evil of the material world.

Augustine may have done more than anyone to institutionalize antisexual attitudes. He reduced sexuality to lust, interpreted lust as the conduit of original sin, and condemned contraception as a tool of the sin of lust. Sexual acts unredeemed by the goal of begetting a child, Augustine wrote, reduce the couple to "harlot" and "adulterer."

Augustine directed his diatribe against periodic abstinence at the Manichees, a sect to which he had belonged as a young man. In an insidious threat to Christianity, the Manichees blended Christian thinking with ideas the church fathers considered heretical. According to Augustine, the sect's leaders urged abstinence at the time "when a woman is likely to conceive . . . lest a soul be implicated in the flesh." He said this proves that they "consider marriage is not to procreate children, but to satiate lust."

In fact, Augustine said, sex would be irredeemably sinful if it were not necessary: "If there was any other way to have children, then every act of sexual intercourse would quite obviously be a surrender to lust and hence a bad use of this evil." In this century, there is a way — artificial insemination — but the Vatican forbids it. Whereas Augustine opposed contraception and dreamed of asexual reproduction because of sexual pleasure's evil, the Vatican now says both violate an intrinsic link between love and reproduction. The shift in rationales belies any claim to an unchanging teaching.

For many church fathers and medieval church lawmakers, contraception was as heinous as murder. This severity reflected the importance they placed upon procreation as the purpose of marriage, the rejection of sex for any other purpose, the scientific difficulty at that time of telling contraceptives from abortifacients, the association of contraceptive potions with sorcery, the vulnerability of life in an age of barbarity and no medical resources. They saw contraception as an attack on the principle of life. Authors such as Jerome, Augustine's contemporary, explained that early abortion is not killing because the fetus has not yet taken human form, but then turned to contraception and hotly branded it "murder." The fear of contraceptive potions secretly slipped to a sexual partner or a hated neighbor sharpened this criticism.

And so the authors of medieval codes of penance came to treat contraception as murder. From these codes, the idea entered the first compilation of canons issued under a papal stamp: the *Decretals* of Gregory IX. If anyone administers a contraceptive spell or potion, for lust or for malice, "let him be held a homicide," said the *Decretals*. It bears noting that Gregory, a promoter of the Inquisition, took this position as part of his campaign to stamp out "heretics" such as the Cathars. Like the Gnostics and Manichees, the Cathars opposed all procreation. For them, Gregory set the penalty of death by fire.

Treated as murder, contraception warranted harsher penalties than early abortion. Gregory's *Decretals* quoted the judgment of Pope Innocent III on a monk who had caused his mistress to abort. Innocent had said the action should not be treated as murder if the fetus was not "vivified," that is, animated, formed, or ensouled. This text probably indicates that church authorities did not take literally the treatment of contraception as murder. The rhetoric of murder, however, struck fear into believers and made contraception a priority for the confessional.

Fear and demonization of the unknown fueled the fire. In the thirteenth century, St. Thomas Aquinas treated sorcery and the notion of sex with the devil as serious concerns. Thomas also wrote that sexual sins are mortal because they attack potential life. Pope Innocent VIII fused all these ideas in the 1484 "Witches' Bull" (*Summis desiderantes*), which ordered inquisitors to investigate "sorcerers" who prevented married couples from conceiving and thus promoted carnal sin. This led to the hunting and killing of "witches" — midwives who really or allegedly provided contraceptives — as agents of the devil.

The condemnation of contraception as murder was mainly a matter of penance, but it became criminal law briefly under the 1588 bull *Effraenatam*. The bull was part of a crackdown on poor morals in Rome by the rather intense Pope Sixtus V. Sixtus was especially concerned about wayward clerics and about the depletion of Rome's population by bouts of plague and famine. In *Effraenatam* he threatened excommunication and the death penalty for contraception and abortion at any stage. Three years later, Gregory XIV repealed *Effraenatam*. The condemnation of contraception as murder fell away by the mid-eighteenth century.

A nineteenth-century shift in the treatment of abortion, however, set the stage for additional Vatican arguments against certain contraceptives during the twentieth century. For nearly two millennia, standard theology held that the soul was infused into a fetus forty to eighty days after conception. The church did not treat as homicide abortion of a fetus before it was ensouled (*fetus inanimatus*). In 1854, however, Pope Pius IX declared the dogma of Mary's Immaculate Conception, or freedom from original sin at conception. The implication was that Mary's soul was present at conception. Pius went on to imply that every soul is infused at conception. In the 1869 constitution *Apostolicae sedis*, he revised the existing penalty of excommunication for abortion, omitting the reference to the "ensouled fetus." He considered abortions the same at any stage, implying immediate ensoulment.

A century later, this implied position reinforces Vatican opposition to contraception because of the way in which certain contraceptives work — specifically, the intrauterine device (IUD) and some hormonal contraceptives. These methods may not always prevent the union of sperm and egg; sometimes, they prevent the implantation of a fertilized egg in the uterine lining. In some cases, that is, they prevent pregnancy, but not conception. For this reason, the Vatican condemns these methods as "abortifacients."

In the early twentieth century, the growing birth control movement, wars that had depleted European populations, and the Anglican Church's approval of birth control in 1930 galvanized Vatican opposition to contraception. At the same time, these factors may have driven the church to give Catholics some relief by endorsing the rhythm method of birth control.

Pius XI's letter *Casti connubii* invoked couples' duty to "raise up... members of God's household, that the worshipers of God and Our Saviour may daily increase." Pius denounced "those wicked parents who seek to remain childless" but permitted intercourse that the couple expected to produce no children. This would include sex during menopause or the infertile phase of the menstrual cycle, which scientists had recently charted accurately. Pius justified predictably sterile sex by saying that the secondary ends of marriage included the cultivation of mutual love and "the quieting of concupiscence."

Casti connubii did not endorse the rhythm method of birth control — theologians debated the status of rhythm after the encyclical — but it paved the way for approving periodic abstinence. In 1951, rhythm received papal endorsement — as long as couples did not use it "habitually" or "without serious reason." Pope Pius XII said married couples who have sex are virtually obligated to have some children. "On partners who make use of matrimony by the specific act of their state, nature and the Creator impose the function of providing for the continuance of the human race," he said in a speech to Catholic midwives. But because a couple may forgo sex altogether for "serious motives" — whether "medical, eugenic, economic, [or] social" — it is also acceptable, for "grave reasons," to suspend sex during fertile periods only, said the pope. He went a little further a month later, in an address to family groups. Citing "the real difficulties of the married state in our day," he confirmed the "legitimacy and, at the same time, the limits" of rhythm and looked forward to the method's improvement through greater scientific knowledge.

Pius XII also made it clear that the principle of "double effect" permitted sterilizing operations, such as castration to treat prostate cancer or medicines with contraceptive side effects. The pill was licit to treat endometriosis, excessive bleeding, or severe menstrual pain — but not to prevent pregnancy, even when it threatened a woman's life.

During the 1960s, the Second Vatican Council reiterated the prohibition against contraception but acknowledged "serious and alarming problems" caused by population growth. While enjoining married couples to have children — and praising large families — the council endorsed "responsible" parenthood. Parents' responsibility entails "a consideration of their own good and the good of their children already born or yet to come, an ability to read the signs of the times and of their own situation on the material and spiritual level, and, finally, an estimation of the good of the family, of society, and of the church." These practical considerations had not troubled the early church fathers who established procreation as the measure of marriage.

Meanwhile, in a far cry from the days when the church called contraception murder, Pope John XXIII and Paul VI sponsored a commission to consider permitting birth control. The majority of this commission — theologians and bishops as well as lay scientists, demographers, and married couples — recommended that the pope permit contraception. A minority worried that if the church said it had been wrong about contraception, its "authority... in moral matters would be thrown into question."

The conservative view won out in 1968, when Paul VI issued his long-awaited encyclical on contraception. "Each and every marriage act must remain open to the transmission of life," Paul wrote in *Humanae Vitae*. He cited old texts but gave a new reason: "the inseparable connection, willed by God and unable to be broken by man on his own initiative, between the two meanings of the conjugal act: the unitive meaning and the procreative meaning." This "nexus" was plainly absent from all the teachings that had said sexual pleasure tainted sex and marriage. The main evil alleged against contraception was not that it frustrated nature — although Paul claimed that, too — but that it broke this newfound nexus of love and procreation. The pope also suggested that rhythm is better because abstinence requires self-denial. In effect, couples "pay" for the infertile sex they do have. At the same time, he encouraged scientists to improve the method — that is, make it work better for people who want to have sex and intentionally avoid procreation.

Pope John Paul II's contribution to arguments against contraception has been his attack on the "contraceptive mentality." In his 1995 encyclical, *Evangelium Vitae*, he noted the difference between abortion and contraception — an obvious rejection of Jerome, Gregory IX, and Sixtus V — but asserted that they are kindred sins at the level of motivation. Both, he said, may arise from "real-life difficulties" but too often come from "a hedonistic mentality," sexual irresponsibility, and self-centeredness.

The Vatican sometimes says of the rule against contraception, "This authoritative teaching will not change," but no pope or council of bishops ever has declared it to be dogma. Nor is the ban infallible by virtue of unanimity: many bishops do not believe in it, and huge numbers of Catholics do not "receive" the teaching. In the United States, Catholic women use contraception at the same rate as non-Catholics: three out of five do. In Ireland, half of all Catholics reject the Vatican's opposition to contraception; in the Philippines, seven out of ten do. In developing countries, contraceptive use among Catholics corresponds to its availability. In Brazil, 70 percent of Catholic women have used methods forbidden by the Vatican; in Botswana, 64 percent; in Indonesia, 61 percent.

In the sixteen centuries separating Augustine from Pope John Paul II, teaching against contraception has shifted with social factors and the personalities of popes and prominent theologians. Judgments of contraception have varied in harshness, from a crime as evil as murder to a practice whose possible morality popes later considered. Reasons advanced for the prohibition have varied: popes have cited the need to increase the population of Christians on earth and souls in heaven at some times, but not at others. Population growth and recognition of socioeconomic pressures led popes to permit the rhythm method of birth control.

The ground beneath the prohibition — that is, teaching on sexuality — also has shifted. Augustine said that to "seek the pleasure of the flesh" with a spouse was a venial sin; but since the Second Vatican Council, the church says sex within marriage is "noble and honorable" and "enriches the spouses in joy and gratitude." Now popes make an argument against contraception that was impossible when they saw sex only in terms of lust, not love. They say contraception breaks the symbolic connection between the two "meanings" of sexuality: love and procreation. In this way, the Vatican has turned a theological advance in relation to marriage and sexuality into a practical setback for married couples.

Discussion Questions
CONTRACEPTION

1. What has been your experience with contraception — in your own life, in your family, among your friends? If you, or others you know, use it, has it been positive or negative for marriage and the family?

2. Do the Catholics you know accept the church's ban on artificial contraception, or do they use these methods themselves? If so, do they (as far as you know) use contraception in good conscience, or do they feel guilt as a result?

3. Commentator Maggie Hume shows how the grounds for condemning contraception have shifted throughout the centuries. How do you respond to this history?

4. Church teaching today says that every marital act must be open to procreation. Do you agree with that? Why or why not?

5. Surveys show that the vast majority of Catholics want the teaching on contraception to change. What are possible reasons for desiring such a change? Are there any reasons for keeping the teaching as it is?

6. If you were to write a new church teaching on contraception, what would it say?

7. What relationship do you see, if any, between contraception and abortion? Would promoting contraceptive use help lower the incidence of abortion?

8. What relationship do you see, if any, between the availability of contraceptive methods and the rights of women?

Chapter 14

DIVORCE AND REMARRIAGE

In the first three centuries, "consensual divorce," or the dissolution of marriage by mutual consent of the spouses, was not uncommon. Until the eleventh century, divorce and remarriage were allowed under certain circumstances, including adultery, desertion, and a spouse's entering religious life. After the twelfth century, remarriage after divorce was forbidden. Today, those who divorce and remarry without obtaining an annulment are not permitted to receive the Eucharist. Many point to the widespread use of annulments in the U.S. church today as a way around the ban on divorce and remarriage. Some suggest that more change may be in the offing.

SCRIPTURE

Matthew 5:31–32:

"It was also said, 'Whenever a couple divorces, each partner must get a decree of divorce.' But I tell you that everyone who divorces — except because of adultery — forces the spouse to commit adultery. Those who marry the divorced also commit adultery."

1 Corinthians 7:12–15:

"I have this to say to you who are in relationships — and this is not from me but from God: you are not to leave your partners. But if you do separate, you must either remain single or be reconciled to each other; you are not to divorce each other. To the rest of you, I say — this is not from God but from me: if one of you has a mate who is not a believer, and if the believer is willing to live with the unbeliever, then there must not be a divorce. For the unbelieving member of the relationship is sanctified through the believing member. If this were not so, any children of the relationship would be unclean; as it is, they are holy. Now if the unbeliever leaves, let it be. For the believing partner is not bound to the relationship in such circumstances. God has called us to live in peace. For how do you know, wife, whether you will save your husband or not? And how do you know, husband, whether you will save your wife or not?"

Editors' Note: Today this is interpreted as the "Pauline Privilege."

159

CHURCH FATHERS

Tertullian, *Against Marcion,* c. 200:

"Since, therefore, his [Jesus'] prohibition of divorce was a conditional one, he did not prohibit [it] absolutely; and what he did not absolutely forbid, that he permitted on some occasions, when there is an absence of the cause why he gave his prohibition.... If however, you deny that divorce is in any way permitted by Christ, how is it that you on your side destroy marriage, not uniting man and woman, not admitting to the sacrament of baptism and of the Eucharist those who have been united in marriage anywhere else, unless they should agree together to repudiate the fruit of the marriage, and so the very Creator himself? Well, then, what is a husband to do in your sect, if his wife commit adultery? Shall he keep her? But your own apostle, you know, does not permit 'the members of Christ to be joined to a harlot.' Divorce, therefore, when justly deserved, has even in Christ a defender."

MEDIEVAL CHURCH

Council of Toledo, 681:

"It is the command of the Lord that a wife must not be dismissed by her husband except because of fornication."

Gregory II, 726:

"You have asked what is a husband to do if his wife, having been afflicted with an infirmity, cannot have sexual intercourse with the husband. It would be good if he could remain as he is and practice abstinence. But since this requires great virtue, if he cannot live chastely, it is better if he marry. Let him, however, not stop supporting her, since she is kept from married life by her infirmity and not by a detestable fault."

Council of Compiègne, 756:

"If a wife committed incest with her brother-in-law, her husband must separate from her, and with the right to remarry.... If one spouse permitted the other to pronounce the vows of monastic life, he or she could remarry."

Synod of Bourges, 1031:

The Synod of Bourges allowed remarriage after separation in the case of adultery.

Alexander III, *Decretals,* c. 1170:

"If between the man and the woman legitimate consent... occurs in the present, so indeed that one expressly receives another by mutual consent with the accustomed words... whether an oath is introduced or not, it is not permissible for the woman to marry another. And if she should marry, even if carnal intercourse has taken place, she should be separated from him, and forced by ecclesiastical order to return to the first, although some think otherwise and also judgement has been rendered in another way by certain of our predecessors."

Context: "Betrothal could become a marriage without further ado, if the parties had intercourse with each other subsequent to their betrothal. . . . Only unconsummated marriages could be dissolved. . . . Indissolubility, then, was a consequence of sexual relations within marriage" (Brundage, pp. 67f.). Alexander III's Decretals became part of canon law.

Alexander III, Letter to King Canute of Sweden, 1171:

"It is forbidden to a husband to dismiss his wife except for her adultery. And if, after dismissing her, he takes another while she still lives, he will be called an adulterer, and so too will the woman he takes."

Innocent IV, *Apparatus super Libros Decretalium,* c. 1245:

"We do not believe that for the sodomitic vice there can be a separation of beds" . . . [but divorce is allowed when] "the husband wants to draw [the wife] to that sin."

Context: "Sodomitic vice" probably means any form of sexual behavior that the church considered "unnatural" because it would not lead to conception.

Council of Trent, 1563:

"If anyone says that the bond of marriage can be dissolved on account of heresy, difficulties in cohabitation, or malicious absence from the spouse, let him be anathema."

MODERN ERA

Code of Canon Law, 1917:

- "Valid, ratified, and consummated marriage cannot be dissolved by any human power or for any reason, apart from death."

- "A nonconsummated marriage between baptized persons or between a baptized and a nonbaptized party is dissolved either by the law itself as a result of solemn religious profession or by a dispensation granted for just cause by the Apostolic See, at the request of either party, even if the other is unwilling."

- "A legitimate marriage between nonbaptized persons, even if consummated [, may be] dissolved in favor of the faith, in virtue of the Pauline privilege" (see 1 Corinthians 7:10–16, above).
  Context: The second canon cited above is the "Petrine Privilege."

John Paul II, *Familiaris Consortio,* 1981:

"The church affirms the practice which is based on Sacred Scripture, of not admitting to Eucharist communion divorced persons who have remarried.... If these people were admitted to Eucharist the faithful would be led into error and confusion regarding the church's teaching about the indissolubility of marriage."

Catechism of the Catholic Church, 1994:

- "Between the baptized, 'a ratified and consummated marriage cannot be dissolved by any human power or for any reason other than death.'"

- "If civil divorce remains the only possible way of ensuring certain legal rights, the care of the children, or the protection of inheritance, it can be tolerated and does not constitute a moral offense."

- "Divorce is a grave offense against the natural law.... Contracting a new union, even if it is recognized by civil law, adds to the gravity of the rupture: the remarried spouse is then in a situation of public and permanent adultery."

- "Divorce is immoral also because it introduces disorder into the family and into society."

- "It can happen that one of the spouses is the innocent victim of a divorce decreed by civil law; this spouse therefore has not contravened the moral law."

Pontifical Council on the Family, 1997:

Remarried Catholics without annulment should be refused "any sign, public or private, that could appear to be a legitimization of the new union."

John Paul II, 1997:

"While Catholics who are divorced and civilly remarried cannot participate in the Eucharist, they must be welcomed as members of the church and encouraged to participate in parish life."

THE SENSE OF THE FAITHFUL
Charles N. Davis

Church teaching on divorce and remarriage has changed significantly over the centuries. In the early church, Paul's words, "that you are called to live in peace," seem to have resonated well beyond the bounds of the so-called "Pauline Privilege," which permitted Christians to remarry if partners who were nonbelievers deserted them (1 Cor. 7:12–15).

The faithful were not required to maintain fidelity to a spouse who was unfaithful to a marriage or abandoned it. Bishops and popes — some of whom were married themselves — allowed those with failed marriages to continue the vocation of marriage with another. According to Theodore Mackin, SJ, a recognized expert on this subject, in the first three centuries, consensual divorce — the dissolution of marriage by mutual consent of the spouses — "hardly caused the Christians any anguish of indecision" (Mackin, p. 116).

As the quotations from the Council of Toledo (641) and Gregory II (726) show, the early medieval church made no absolute prohibition on divorce and remarriage. Adultery, and even a spouse's infirmity that prevented the possibility of sexual intercourse, were seen as legitimate reasons for remarrying. Early church authorities seem to have assumed that the wife would usually be the one to commit adultery or experience infirmity and the husband would have the right to remarry. This, of course, was a reflection of male dominance in marriage and the attitudes of the male hierarchy.

In the twelfth century, the teaching changed. The church declared marriages indissoluble except on the death of one of the partners. Divorce and remarriage were forbidden. A number of factors overcame the earlier, compassionate approach that allowed some remarriage after divorce.

According to historian Joseph Martos, Augustine misinterpreted Paul, and his resulting concept of "indissolubility" became very influential over time. In Ephesians 5:32, St. Paul spoke metaphorically about the mysterious union of Christ and the church, not literally about the marriage bond between men and women. This was Paul's concept of *mysterion,* which was mistranslated in Latin as *sacramentum.* Augustine understood *sacramentum* to mean that marriage was a visible sign of the invisible union between Christ and his spouse the church — a sacred bond between husband and wife that could be dissolved only by the death of one of the partners. In short, this meant marriage was indissoluble. Augustine, and later the official church, argued that Christians should be faithful to an original marriage, even if the other partner were not.

The efforts of Pope Gregory VII (1073–85) to enforce clerical celibacy culminated in strict legislation against married clergy at the Second Lateran Council in 1139, making any marriage of clerics not only unlawful but invalid. This cut the clergy off from the direct experience of marriage and laid the groundwork for a new and rigid approach to divorce and remarriage that became the official teaching for many centuries. Alexander III pronounced marriage indissoluble and subsequent papal decrees reinforced this teaching. But Jesuit historian Theodore Mackin observed,

> ... in the twelfth and thirteenth centuries the Western Catholic authorities invented a prescriptive definition of marriage that had indissolubility as one of its parts. They did not intend by this to say that marriages were really indissoluble.... What they apparently intended was only to strengthen marriages' resistance to dissolution by writing this invented indissolubility into marriage's abstract definition, and thereby to deny civil authorities' power to dissolve, and reserve this power to ecclesiastical authority. (Mackin, p. 543)

In addition, practices and regulations about divorce and remarriage varied somewhat in different places. Consequently, the papacy's growing and more centralized power in the second millennium contributed to the change to a single standard teaching. In 1074, for example, Pope Gregory VII said that the pope alone can depose or absolve bishops, and he maintained the pope can be judged by no one. These enhanced papal claims of authority ultimately reinforced pronouncements on the indissolubility of marriage.

Nonetheless, the early Christian approach of allowing divorce and remarriage lives on in the Orthodox Church. Remarriage is permitted for specified reasons and the second marriage is recognized as real, although not sacramental. As Martos points out, a second marriage for the Orthodox does not symbolize the union between Christ and the church, but those in such marriages are not considered "adulterers" living in sin. Unlike their counterparts in the Catholic Church, they are allowed to receive the sacraments (Martos, pp. 414–15). Interestingly, the Roman Catholic Church recognizes this Orthodox practice as valid and does not require a divorced member of the Orthodox Church to obtain an annulment in order to marry a Catholic. But the Catholic Church requires Protestants who are in the same situation to obtain an annulment.

It is instructive to note that Orthodox priests (but not bishops) are allowed to marry. Thus there is still a direct connection between the experience of marriage and those responsible for formulating and implementing church teachings.

In contemporary times, Catholic Church officials may even have altered Scripture translations to bolster the official position against divorce and remarriage. For example, the Jerusalem Bible, approved in 1966 by the Catholic archbishop of Westminster, England, says that everyone who divorces a spouse "except for the case of fornication," makes that person an adulterer (Matt. 5:31–32). The 1971 edition of the New American Bible, sponsored by the U.S. Bishops' Committee of the Confraternity of Christian Doctrine, agrees, saying that "lewd conduct is a separate case." Translations by Priests for Equality, the National Council of Churches, and most others agree with this version.

But the 1988 edition of the New American Bible — now the official Catholic translation of the Bible in the U.S. — says that whoever divorces a spouse "unless the marriage is unlawful" causes that person to commit adultery (Matt. 5:32). This translation seems to deny that Christ allowed divorce for *any* reason, and it fits the Vatican's current requirement for an annulment, namely, that the marriage was never valid from the start.

Thus, the current teaching of the Vatican is that marriages are indissoluble, save for the use of the Petrine and Pauline privileges. The Pauline privilege allows a Catholic to remarry only if he or she originally married a person who was not a Christian and then could not live in peace with that person. The Petrine Privilege is similar; it allows dissolution of a nonsacramental marriage so the baptized party can be free to live the faith.

The Use of Annulments

Hierarchical practice, especially in the United States, implicitly recognizes that the faithful reject absolute indissolubility. Therefore, church officials in the U.S. have tried to ameliorate the situation by easing the requirements for an annulment without changing the nine-hundred-year-old ban on divorce, and remarriage. Divorce recognizes that a marriage existed but it died, and declares it null and void after a certain date. An annulment, on the other hand, says that "no sacramental marriage bond had ever existed, because of a lack of validity traceable to an unknown or concealed impediment, an essential defect in consent, or a condition placed by one or both of the parties against the nature of the sacrament" (Deedy, 1993, p. 192). In the past twenty years, reasons for annulments have expanded to include psychological factors such as gross immaturity or "grave lack of discretionary judgment."

Church leaders deny that annulments are "Catholic divorces," but in effect they are. They allow the hierarchy to change its policy toward married couples without claiming any change in doctrine.

U.S. Catholics account for about 72 percent of the annulments granted worldwide. This percentage has remained fairly constant. According to Vatican statistics for 1994, the number of annulments issued in the entire world totaled almost 51,000. Of that number almost 36,500 — more than 71 percent — were granted to Catholics in the U.S.

While the Vatican tolerates relaxation of the requirements in the U.S., the curia is concerned that the practice is getting out of hand here. As a result, priests and pastoral caregivers reported that by the end of 1997, the process of granting annulments had slowed.

Although the number of U.S. annulments is high compared to those in the rest of the world, it is extremely low compared to the number of U.S. Catholics who simply divorce and remarry without benefit of any church process. Like the rest of the U.S. population, more than 40 percent of Catholics marry, divorce, and remarry. Fr. Ladislas Orsy, SJ, a canon lawyer, reports that 81 percent of these Catholics do not even submit their cases to a diocesan marriage tribunal to apply for an annulment (*America*, October 4, 1997). Officially, the hierarchy forbids these Catholics to receive the Eucharist. In February 1998, Cardinal Mahoney publicly forbade the sacraments to no less a figure than the mayor of Los Angeles because he remarried without seeking an annulment.

Yet the mayor's actions reflect the sense of the faithful. Almost 75 percent of all Catholics disagree with the Vatican's pronouncement that Catholics who remarry without annulment should not receive communion, according to a 1992 Gallup survey. Moreover, a 1993 Gallup survey found that only 23 percent of all Catholics believe that the pope and bishops have "final say" about right and wrong when a divorced Catholic remarries without an annulment.

In short, the Catholic faithful believe that marriages can die. They do not agree with the Catholic *Catechism* that "divorce is immoral." They reject Pope John Paul II's assertion that remarriage is "a state of adultery except for those who practice sexual abstinence." Some see divorce as a necessary relief from ties to an abusive or absent spouse. Many see it as a second chance to continue the vocation of marriage: to live a life of intimacy and grace with another divinely created person, instead of withering away in compulsory celibacy.

Statistics show that fissures are growing within the church on these issues. On the one hand, the doctrinal teaching of the past nine centuries still holds marriage to be indissoluble and rejects divorce. On the other hand, many Catholics ignore the pope and remarry without an annulment, probably because they have problems of conscience in admitting what the annulment process demands, namely, that a former marriage — often with children — never existed sacramentally. Many of these Catholics receive the sacraments, also out of conscience. And many priests ignore Vatican directives and serve communion to the divorced and remarried.

Some bishops and many priests, theologians, and Catholic reform groups are trying to reconcile these contradictions. Bishop Walter Kasper of Germany writes, "It is very painful to meet Christians who perceive their second marriage as a happy one, and thus find themselves with a moral obligation to it, especially if there are children, when they also have a desire for the sacrament. To tell them that they are once and for all excluded unless they break up — we just can't say that. I believe... tradition is more open and broader... than the present disciplinary rule in our church."

Some theologians have suggested the "internal forum" as a solution — going to confession to a priest and having him recognize the second marriage as in good conscience without going through the annulment process. However, at the 1980 Synod of Bishops, Pope John Paul II "effectively ruled out an internal forum solution widely recommended by many priests for those involved in hardship cases. This solution had allowed those who, in sincere conscience, were convinced that their former marriage was truly dead and that their present marriage was right before God to receive the Eucharist" (Kaufman, p. 128).

Ladislas Orsy, SJ, suggests returning to the ancient tradition of "an act of economy." This is "a gracious act from the bishop...intended to heal a wound in the church no law can cure."

In February 1998, John Paul II announced a new commission to review canon law on marriage annulments. The pope said he was aware of

> the anguishing and dramatic problem faced by the faithful whose marriages have become shipwrecked through no fault of their own and, before having obtained a possible ecclesial sentence declaring the nullification of the marriage, have formed new unions which they wish to have blessed and consecrated before a minister of the church. (*National Catholic Reporter*, 2/6/98, p. 10)

This may be a sign that the Spirit is alive and well in the church. The sense of the faithful may yet receive the respect it deserves. The authentic church teaching of the first millennium that recognized divorce and remarriage may well be restored in the third millennium.

Discussion Questions
DIVORCE AND REMARRIAGE

1. What has been your experience with divorce and remarriage among Catholics in your own life, in your family, among your friends, or in your parish? What do you think about Catholics who have divorced and remarried? Do you believe that circumstances justified their actions? Why or why not?

2. What has been your experience, if any, with the annulment process of the Catholic Church? Have you known people who have sought annulments? How did they judge the process? What do you think about the extensive use of annulments in the church today?

3. More than 80 percent of divorced Catholics do not even apply to the church for an annulment. Why do you think that is? What do you think is the significance of this?

4. Commentator Charles N. Davis shows how the church has changed its marriage rules over the centuries. How do you respond to that historical reality?

5. What circumstances justify divorce? If you could design Catholic policy on divorce and remarriage, what would it look like?

Chapter 15

COPERNICAN THEORY AND GALILEO

The church's attitude toward theories of the universe has undergone a complete turnabout since the seventeenth century. At first the church unequivocally condemned Copernican theory — which taught that the sun rather than the earth is the center of the universe — and Galileo, who espoused it, for a "serious and pernicious" error. In the nineteenth century, Pope Leo XIII openly supported Galileo's theories, and in the twentieth century, Pope John Paul II formally reversed the judgment against Galileo. Some of this shift in opinion resulted from changes in permissible forms of biblical interpretation and the movement from a fundamentalist to a critical reading of Genesis (see chapter 3). In addition, the Second Vatican Council emphasized the "legitimate autonomy of science."

Vatican Consultants' *Report on Copernicanism,* February 24, 1616

"Propositions to be assessed:

"(1) The sun is the center of the world and completely devoid of motion.

"*Assessment:* All said that this proposition is foolish and absurd in philosophy and formally heretical since it explicitly contradicts in many places the sense of Holy Scripture, according to the literal meaning of the words and according to the common interpretation and understanding of the Holy Fathers and the doctors of theology.

"(2) The earth is not the center of the world, nor motionless, but it moves as a whole and also with diurnal motion.

"*Assessment:* All said that this proposition receives the same judgment in philosophy and that in regard to theological truth it is at least erroneous in faith."

Sentence of Galileo by Seven Cardinals, Members of the Roman Inquisition, June 22, 1633:

"We say, pronounce, sentence, and declare that you, the above-mentioned Galileo, because of the things deduced in the trial and confessed by you as above, have rendered yourself according to this Holy Office vehemently suspected of heresy, namely, of having held and believed a doctrine which is false and contrary to the divine and Holy Scripture, that the sun is the center of the world and does not move from east to west, and the earth moves and is not the center of the world, and that one may hold and defend as probable an opinion after it has been declared and defined contrary to Holy Scripture.... Furthermore, so that this serious and pernicious error and transgression of yours does not remain completely unpunished, and so that you will be more cautious in the future and an example for others to abstain from similar crimes, we order that the book *Dialogue* by Galileo Galilei be prohibited by public edict."

1642:

Galileo dies while under house arrest.

1757:

Some books supporting Copernican theory are removed from the Index of Forbidden Books, but not Galileo's *Dialogue*. (Cardinal Poupard [see below] says all books supporting Copernicanism were removed from the Index in 1757.)

Editors' Note: the Index of Forbidden Books was a list of books Catholics were forbidden to read or even possess, except under specified circumstances. It existed from 1557 until 1966.

Pius VII, 1822:

The pope ratifies the Holy Office decision to allow publication of books supporting Copernicanism.

1835:

Galileo's *Dialogue* is removed from the Index.

Leo XIII, *Providentissimus Deus*, 1893:

"The Catholic interpreter, although he should show that those facts of natural science which investigators affirm to be now quite certain are not contrary to the Scripture rightly explained, must, nevertheless, always bear in mind that much which has been held and proved as certain has afterwards been called in question and rejected."

Context: This statement essentially endorses Galileo's understanding of the relationship between science and Scripture.

Second Vatican Council, *Pastoral Constitution on the Church in the Modern World*, 1965:

"We cannot but deplore certain attitudes which have existed among Christians themselves, insufficiently attentive to the legitimate autonomy of science."

Editors' Note: John Paul II quoted this in his Address to the Pontifical Academy of Sciences, 1979.

John Paul II, Address to the Pontifical Academy of Sciences, 1979:

- "I wish that theologians, scholars and historians, animated by a spirit of sincere collaboration, might examine more deeply the Galileo case and, in an honest recognition of wrongs on whatever side they occur, might make disappear the obstacles that this affair sets up, in many minds, to a fruitful concord between science and faith, between church and world."

- "Galileo had much to suffer — we could not hide it — from the men and agencies of the church."

John Paul II, Address to the Pontifical Academy of Sciences, 1992:

- "It is a duty for theologians to keep themselves regularly informed of scientific advances in order to examine, if such be necessary, whether or not there are reasons for taking them into account in their reflection or for introducing changes in their teaching."

- "The sentence [against Galileo] of 1633 was not irreformable."

- "In fact, the Bible does not concern itself with the details of the physical world, the understanding of which is the competence of human experience and reasoning."

Cardinal Paul Poupard, "Galileo: Report on Papal Commission Findings," 1992:

- "Certain theologians, Galileo's contemporaries, being heirs of a unitarian concept of the world universally accepted until the dawn of the seventeenth century, failed to grasp the profound, nonliteral meaning of the Scriptures when they described the physical structure of the created universe. This led them unduly to transpose a question of factual observation into the realm of faith."

- "It is in that historical and cultural framework, far removed from our own times, that Galileo's judges, incapable of dissociating faith from an age-old cosmology, believed quite wrongly that the adoption of the Copernican revolution, in fact not yet definitively proven, was such as to undermine Catholic tradition, and that it was their duty to forbid its being taught. This subjective error of judgment, so clear to us today, led them to a disciplinary measure from which Galileo 'had much to suffer.' These mistakes must be frankly recognized, as you, Holy Father, have requested."

COPERNICUS, GALILEO, AND THE CATHOLIC CHURCH, THEN AND NOW

James Orgren

The Catholic Church today faces a crisis of confidence that is not unprecedented. In the seventeenth century, the church's actions in the Galileo Affair
precipitated a near-catastrophe from which recovery has been exceedingly
slow and painful.

The origins of the Galileo Affair go back to ancient Greece. Anaxagoras,
born about 500 B.C.E., was exiled for his impiety in suggesting that the sun
was bigger than the peninsula on which Athens was located. Plato (420–340
B.C.E.) put the earth at the center of an ideal universe, and the heavenly
bodies surrounded by a band of crystalline spheres which held the sun, stars,
and planets in place as they revolved around the earth. Although Aristotle
was aware of a sun-centered explanation for the alternation of day and night
and the seasons, he rejected the heliocentric model. Plato and Aristotle had
a powerful impact on Western thought, and the geocentric model remained
essentially unquestioned for the next sixteen hundred years.

Nicholas Copernicus (1473–1543), a Polish doctor, astronomer, mathematician, and canon lawyer, published De Revolutionibus Orbium Coelestrium
(On the Revolutions of Heavenly Bodies), which set forth a heliocentric model
of the cosmos. Afraid of being branded a heretic, he delayed publication until
he was on his deathbed. The preface suggested that the book merely proposed
a hypothetical model to simplify the calculation of future planetary positions,
which saved the text from instant condemnation by the church.

The Catholic Church began strongly opposing the heliocentric model after
the monk and philosopher Giordano Bruno supported it in the late 1500s.
In 1600 he was burned at the stake for supporting Copernican theory and
preaching that the universe has a soul. Galileo was coming to scientific
maturity at this time.

The Galileo Affair

Galileo Galilei was born in Pisa in 1564. In 1592 he moved from the University of Pisa to the University of Padua, where he remained for eighteen
years. He taught astronomy according to the geocentric model, despite private doubts. In 1609, he built a telescope and with it showed that the
traditional geocentric model was incompatible with his observations of the
moon, Venus, Mars, and Jupiter. By 1611 Galileo had cast serious doubt on
the Aristotelian model.

After publishing "The Starry Messenger" in 1610, Galileo returned to the

University of Pisa as chief mathematician, determined to speak and teach openly about the Copernican universe. New professors at Pisa were forbidden to teach that the earth might move, or even to discuss the possibility among themselves. A philosophy professor there declared that it was sheer heresy to suggest that the sun might be the center of the universe. Galileo, however, was on excellent terms with the Grand Duke Cosimo (whom he had tutored as a youth) and Cardinal Matteo Barberini, later Pope Urban VIII. In 1611 he was invited to join the recently formed Lincean Academy, the world's first scientific society.

All was not calm, however. At the end of 1611, a friend told Galileo that regular meetings were taking place at the house of the archbishop of Florence to plot against him. In late 1614, a Dominican friar preached a fiery sermon against Galileo and other Copernicans because he thought their beliefs contradicted the Bible and were heretical. A few months later, another Dominican filed formal charges against him with the Roman Inquisition. Also in 1615, Galileo wrote the "Letter to Grand Duchess Christina," defending his views and attempting to reconcile them with Scripture.

On February 24, 1616, eleven theologians reported to the Holy Office that the Copernican theory was "formally heretical." There is no evidence that any of them understood (or perhaps had even read about) the Copernican theory, Galileo's observations, or his arguments in its favor. The next day Pope Paul V endorsed their finding and ordered the powerful Cardinal Bellarmine to warn Galileo to abandon his Copernican views.

In March 1616, Galileo was reassured by a friendly meeting with the pope. At about the same time, the Congregation for the Index of Forbidden Books published its first formal condemnation of Copernicus's works and "all other books which teach the same," but did not name any of Galileo's books.

In 1620 the Index published its "corrections" of Copernicus's book; they made it appear that Copernicus had intended the work merely as a calculating aid. Galileo apparently concluded that "hypothetical" treatment of Copernican theory was still acceptable to the church.

In 1623, Galileo's friend and admirer, Cardinal Barberini, was elected Pope Urban VIII. In 1616, Barberini had been instrumental in preventing condemnation of Galileo and Copernicanism for heresy. Galileo dedicated one of his books to Urban VIII, who was greatly pleased and welcomed him to weekly meetings when Galileo was in Rome. Furthermore, Urban VIII reportedly told a cardinal that the church had not condemned Copernicanism, nor was about to condemn it as heretical, "but only as temerarious, and that one should not fear that it could ever be proved to be necessarily true." Such a statement from the pope, his friend, did little to discourage Galileo from continuing to work on Copernican theory. He began writing what was to become the *Dialogue on the Two Great World Systems*.

In the *Dialogue*'s preface, Galileo said he would present only observational and rational arguments against the Aristotelian worldview and in favor of Copernican theory, and that his silence since 1616 was based on religious, rather than rational, considerations. He cast the work in the form of a discussion among Salviati, who holds strong Copernican views; Sagredo, an intelligent onlooker and inquirer; and Simplicio, who clings doggedly to Aristotelian doctrines, accepting them without question.

One of the censor's conditions for publishing the *Dialogue* was that the debate should conclude with the pope's favorite response to questions about the cosmos: "It would be excessively bold if someone should want to limit and compel divine power and wisdom to a particular fancy of his." Unfortunately, Galileo put the papal speech in the mouth of Simplicio, who had lost virtually every other argument in the *Dialogue*. Many who read the book before it was banned identified Simplicio (which sounds in Italian like the word for "simpleton") with Urban VIII. This miscalculation probably explains the pope's sudden and vehement anger against Galileo. The pope prohibited the printer from further distributing the book and appointed a special commission to investigate the matter.

The commission consisted entirely of clerics unfriendly to Galileo. Its report in September 1632 said that the *Dialogue* supported the heretical doctrine of Copernicanism. Galileo was summoned to Rome for trial before the Inquisition in early 1633. When a friend sought an opportunity for Galileo to justify himself, Pope Urban VIII told him, "In these matters of the Holy Office, the procedure is simply to arrive at a censure and then call the defendant to recant" (Finocchiaro, p. 229).

When under "rigorous examination" to tell the truth, Galileo denied four times that he had held the Copernican doctrine to be valid after Cardinal Bellarmine's warning in 1616. On June 22, 1633, he was called before the ten members of the Roman Inquisition (all cardinals) to hear his sentence.

We say, pronounce, sentence, and declare that you ... have rendered yourself according to this Holy Office vehemently suspected of heresy, namely, of having held and believed a doctrine which is false and contrary to the divine and Holy Scripture: that the sun is the center of the world and does not move from east to west, and the earth moves and is not the center of the world, and that one may hold and defend as probable an opinion after it has been declared and defined contrary to Holy Scripture.

On his knees before his accusers, Galileo then performed his ultimate act of humiliation by abjuring, cursing, and detesting the very truths to whose discovery and defense he had dedicated the greater portion of his life. Thus his public career was ended. He continued his research under house arrest. *Dialogues on the New Sciences,* considered his greatest work, was published in

1638 in Protestant Amsterdam. He died on January 8, 1642, at age seventy-eight, after receiving the last rites and Urban VIII's benediction.

Preparations were made for a public funeral, and a marble monument was ordered to mark Galileo's grave. The pope declared that any such observance would be inappropriate for "someone who had...caused the greatest scandal to all Christendom" and might "offend the reputation of the Holy Office." Consequently his remains were hidden away, without epitaph, in a corridor under the Church of Santa Croce. In 1737 Galileo's remains were finally moved to a mausoleum inside the church.

Results and Implications of the Galileo Affair

Scientific developments from the sixteenth to the eighteenth centuries were too powerful to be ignored. Astronomy developed on heliocentric assumptions, and it was applied to navigation. As a result, the church was forced to relent. In 1757 all works formerly prohibited because they taught the mobility of the earth were removed from the Index. But it was only in 1822 that the works of Galileo, Copernicus, and Kepler were removed.

Another 170 years went by before John Paul II finally acknowledged, in a speech to the Pontifical Academy of Sciences in October 1992, that the Catholic Church had erred in condemning Galileo for holding that the earth was not the center of the universe. The pope said that seventeenth-century theologians had erred in assuming that the "literal sense of Sacred Scripture" explained the physical world. He acknowledged that Galileo had developed better rules for scriptural interpretation than the theologians of the time. He also said it was an important matter to understand in case of future conflicts between religion and science. Finally, he acknowledged that the Inquisition had wronged Galileo.

In the short term, the seventeenth-century church hierarchy considered it had won its battle to keep thinking channeled within the confines it defined as orthodox. Its theologians maintained their position at the top of the disciplinary ladder, keeping the upstart "natural philosophers" (scientists) in their proper place at the bottom. The authority of the church had triumphed, thanks to the fear that the Holy Office and the Inquisition had instilled with a stunning exercise of raw power.

The long-term balance sheet tells a much different story. By silencing Galileo, the pope closed off the evolution of science in Italy and deprived Italian commerce of potentially valuable innovations. Italy was not the only Catholic region thus affected. The Paris Observatory in Catholic France also used the Aristotelian model. Thus Italy and France lost their chance to significantly influence the scientific revolution. It was Newton, born in Protestant England in the year Galileo died, who completed the grand theoretical framework for which Copernicus, Kepler, and Galileo had provided the foundation.

By seeking to silence any discussion of ideas at variance with entrenched religious doctrines, the church set itself up to be perceived as the enemy of intellectual freedom and progress. We will never know how science might have developed if the church had acted more moderately.

Culture has greatly influenced Christianity from the very beginning. In his "Letter to the Grand Duchess Christina," Galileo points out that the idea of an unmoving earth was essentially unquestioned by the culture in which Christianity began and developed. Since it fit with commonsense notions and literal reading of the Scriptures, geocentrism remained unchallenged until Copernicus. Galileo asserts that since the church never seriously questioned this culturally biased assumption and did not debate it, geocentrism was not legitimately accepted or presented as an article of faith. Yet the church of Galileo's time used its considerable spiritual and political power to prematurely silence all dialogue on this crucial issue.

In the church today, dialogue on several issues has been stifled by edict well before they have been subjected to serious, open discussion.

The Vatican today no longer has the political power to physically enforce its edicts. It is, however, able to effectively employ spiritual and psychological intimidation, and it does. But silencing dialogue on women's ordination, priestly celibacy, or contraception does not resolve those issues. Instead, it threatens serious harm to the church as a whole and to the credibility of its leaders in particular, just as it did in the Galileo affair.

It took 350 years for the official church to recognize publicly that it had made a grievous error in the Galileo Affair. It must be asked whether those in charge have taken a hard look at the factors that led to that mistake, and whether they have considered their responses to today's questions in light of that history. We cannot afford any more Galileo Affairs.

Discussion Questions
COPERNICAN THEORY AND GALILEO

1. What, in your experience, has been the church's attitude toward science and new scientific developments?

2. What, in your view, *should* be the church's relationship to the physical and natural sciences?

3. Many observers have expressed views on what Galileo ought to have done with his theory of the universe:

   a. Some say he should have remained completely silent after the warning from Cardinal Bellarmine in 1616.

   b. Some say he should have restricted himself to speaking of Copernican theory merely as a useful tool for planetary calculations, without any connection to reality.

    c. Some say that he should have restricted himself to discussing his theory only with his academic peers, instead of writing a book in the vernacular and making it available to the general public.

    d. Others think he was right in publishing his theory for general discussion.

    e. And still others believe that he was right and should not have recanted.

Galileo's decision was not unlike those faced by theologians under Vatican scrutiny today. Which of these various decisions would have been better for the church in the long run? What do you think he should have done? Why?

4. Why do you think that church authorities in Galileo's day forbade discussion of Copernican theory? What does the church have to gain by forbidding dialogue on an issue? What does it have to lose? How do you respond when church authorities say that a topic may not be discussed?

5. James Orgren's essay draws parallels between the situation of Galileo and issues in the contemporary church, such as women's ordination. Do you agree with him that there are parallels? If so, what lessons does Galileo's treatment have to offer the church today?

Chapter 16

EVOLUTION

Teaching about the scientific evolution of species has undergone rapid change. After Charles Darwin put forward the theory of evolution in the nineteenth century, Pope Pius IX condemned it strongly. A papal biblical commission in 1909 worried that evolution contradicted the creation story in the Book of Genesis. In 1950, however, Pius XII acknowledged that the church "did not forbid" belief in evolution. More than forty years later, in 1996, Pope John Paul II recognized its wide acceptance in the scientific world as "more than a hypothesis."

Alexander III, 1163:

Alexander III forbade ecclesiastics to study physics "or the laws of the world." Penalty: excommunication.

Pius IX, Letter, 1877:

"A system which is repugnant at once to history, to the tradition of all peoples, to exact science, to observed facts, and even to Reason herself, [Darwinism] would seem to need no refutation, did not alienation from God and the leaning toward materialism due to depravity, eagerly seek a support in all this tissue of fables.... And, in fact, ... after rejecting the Creator of all things and proclaiming man independent, wishing him to be his own king, his own priest, and his own God, pride goes so far as to degrade man himself to the level of the unreasoning brutes, perhaps even of lifeless matter, thus unconsciously confirming the Divine declaration, when pride cometh, then cometh shame. But the corruption of this age, the machinations of the perverse, the danger of the simple, demand that such fancies, altogether absurd though they are, should — since they borrow the mask of science — be refuted by true science."

Pontifical Biblical Commission, *On the Historical Character of the First Three Chapters of Genesis*, 1909:

"May, in particular, the literal historical sense be called in doubt in the case of facts narrated in these chapters, which concern the foundations of the Christian religion: amongst which are, the creation of all things by God at the beginning of time; the peculiar creation of man; the formation of the first woman from the first man; the unity of the human race; the original happiness of our first parents in a state of justice, integrity, and immortality; the precept given by God to man to test his obedience; the transgression of the Divine precept and the persuasion of the devil under the form of a serpent; the fall of our first parents from that primeval state of innocence; and the promise of a future Redeemer?

"No."

Context: The commission affirmed a literal, fundamentalist reading of Scripture in this decree.

Pius XII, *Humani Generis,* 1950:

- "Some imprudently and indiscreetly hold that evolution, which has not been fully proved, even in the domain of natural sciences, explains the origin of all this, and audaciously support the monistic and pantheistic opinion that the world is in continual evolution. Communists gladly subscribed to this opinion so that, when the souls of men have been deprived of every idea of a personal God, they may the more efficaciously defend and propagate their dialectical materialism."

- But: "The Teaching Authority of the church does not forbid that, in conformity with the present state of human sciences and sacred theology, research, and discussions, on the part of men experienced in both fields, take place with regard to the doctrine of evolution, in as far as it inquires into the origin of the human body as coming from preexistent and living matter — for the Catholic faith obliges us to hold that souls are immediately created by God. However this must be done in such a way that the reasons for both opinions, that is, those favorable and those unfavorable to evolution, be weighed and judged with the necessary seriousness, moderation, and measure, and provided that all are prepared to submit to the judgment of the church, to whom Christ has given the mission of interpreting authentically the Sacred Scriptures and of defending the dogmas of faith. Some however rashly transgress this liberty of discussion, when they act as if the origin of the human body from preexisting and living matter were already completely certain and proved by the facts which have been discovered up to now and by reasoning on those facts, and as if there were nothing in the sources of divine revelation which demands the greatest moderation and caution in this question."

- "The first eleven chapters of Genesis ... do nevertheless pertain to history in a true sense; the same chapters ... both state the principal truths which are fundamental for our salvation, and also give a popular description of the origin of the human race and the chosen people. If however, the ancient sacred writers have taken anything from popular narrations (and this may be conceded), it must never be forgotten that they did so with the help of divine inspiration, through which they were rendered immune from any error in selecting and evaluating those documents."

Context: This limited acceptance of evolution may have been in response to Pierre Teilhard de Chardin, theologian and scientist. His superiors forbade him to publish or publicly discuss his ideas on philosophy and theology during his lifetime.

Paul VI, Address to Theologians at the Symposium on Original Sin, 1966:

"As to the theory of evolutionism, you will not consider it acceptable if it is not clearly in agreement with the immediate creation of human souls by God and does not regard the disobedience of Adam, the first universal parent, as of decisive importance for the destiny of mankind."

John Paul II, *Magisterium and Evolution,* Message to the Pontifical Academy of Sciences, 1996:

- "In order to delineate the field of their own study, the exegete and the theologian must keep informed about the results achieved by the natural sciences.... New knowledge leads to recognition of the theory of evolution as more than a hypothesis.... The convergence, neither sought nor provoked, of the results of work that was conducted independently is in itself a significant argument in favor of this theory."

- But: "Theories of evolution which, in accordance with the philosophies inspiring them, consider the spirit as emerging from the forces of living matter or as a mere epiphenomenon of this matter are incompatible with the truth about man."

EVOLUTION, IN NATURE AND CATHOLIC THOUGHT
John F. Haught

Evolution has to do with change and development over the course of time. Placing our religious lives and traditions inside the evolutionary scheme — as the Darwinian paradigm appears to demand of all truly living systems — threatens the notion of the timelessness and integrity of religious doctrine. Failure to come to grips with evolution parallels, and in a sense quietly legitimates, understanding of official church statements as immune to the transformations that the passage of time brings to every other facet of life, and indeed the entire universe.

Until Pope John Paul II admitted that the evidence for biological evolution is compelling, papal statements have been notably lacking in both force and clarity on this issue. They seem to have condemned, ignored, or given only grudging acceptance to the ideas made famous by Charles Darwin's *On the Origin of Species*, first published in 1859.

Compared to the vehement hostility to evolutionary science so obvious in some other sectors of Christianity, however, Catholicism has been remarkably tolerant of the Darwinian revolution. Few contemporary Catholic theologians appear to have serious difficulties with "neo-Darwinism" (the modern synthesis of Darwin's theory of natural selection and more recent developments in genetics and molecular biology). It is worth noting that Catholic theologians show very little of the explicit resistance to evolution that occurs among the so-called "scientific creationists" and other conservative Christians, such as the outspoken and influential Berkeley law professor Phillip Johnson.[1] Only a minority has integrated Darwinian science into systematic theology, however.

Surprisingly large numbers of American Christians continue to think of Darwinian theory as inimical to belief in God. For some, the evolutionary picture of nature obviously conflicts with a literal reading of Scripture. Prominent evolutionary scientists present Darwinism to the public in a manner that makes it appear antithetical to theistic religion. The fact that some of our most renowned scientists and philosophers still think of Darwinism as inherently atheistic does not make it any easier for Christians to embrace it. Despite internecine squabbles, scientists such as Richard Dawkins, Stephen Jay Gould, Richard Lewontin, and E. O. Wilson, along with many other neo-Darwinians, maintain that evolutionary science is inseparable from materialist metaphysics.[2]

In addition, various philosophers, most notably Daniel Dennett, proclaim that Darwinian science is nothing less than a radically naturalistic vision of life, logically incompatible with any form of theism.[3] If this interpretation of Darwin were correct, then all theists would have to spurn it on logical as well as theological grounds.

It is instructive to take note of the obstacles these contemporary interpretations of Darwinism still present to believers. They may help us understand the misgivings expressed in Pius IX's 1877 letter, in which — not entirely without reason — he observed that some Darwinists were using the "mask of science" to propagate a fundamentally materialist interpretation of nature. By 1877, Karl Marx and Ernst Haeckel (the main European promoter of Darwinism) had already found in Darwin's ideas decisive confirmation of

---

1. See Phillip Johnson, *Darwin on Trial* (Downers Grove, Ill.: InterVarsity Press, 1993).

2. Probably the best examples are Richard Dawkins's books, *The Blind Watchmaker* (New York: Norton, 1986) and *River Out of Eden* (New York: Basic Books, 1995).

3. Daniel C. Dennett, *Darwin's Dangerous Idea: Evolution and the Meaning of Life* (New York: Simon & Schuster, 1995), p. 266.

the doctrine that "matter is all there is." Even today — when we are supposed to have become more sensitive to the role of ideology in allegedly
objective discourse — some of our most respected biologists and scientific
writers continue to embed evolutionary ideas in materialist belief systems,
making their brand of "Darwinism" religiously unpalatable. Hence we should
not be entirely surprised that religious leaders in the late nineteenth and
early twentieth centuries, including popes, remained suspicious of Darwin's
revolutionary ideas.

If we look carefully at the papal statements about evolution, up to and
including John Paul II's recent statement, we can see that an underlying
concern has been the specter of philosophical naturalism or scientific materialism, which almost from the beginning has accompanied the ideas of
common descent and natural selection. However, long before Pope John
Paul II formally acknowledged the scientific evidence for evolution, Catholic
theologians, along with many evolutionary scientists, had already distinguished between the science of evolution and various philosophical systems,
including materialist naturalism. So in principle, the recent papal clarification
could have been issued decades ago, and the benefit to theology would have
been enormous.

While Catholic theology has long held that there can be no real conflict
between scientific and religious truth, it has also recognized that there is an
inevitable conflict between the philosophy of scientific materialism and theistic faith. The elementary distinction between scientific method on the one
hand and materialist ideology on the other — a distinction that even today
both scientific skeptics and influential Christian authors like Phillip Johnson
refuse to accept when it comes to evolutionary ideas — has long allowed
Catholic theologians to reject the notion that evolutionary science and theistic religion conflict. This has given them the freedom, perhaps too seldom
exercised until recently, to reinterpret the doctrines of creation, redemption,
revelation, eschatology, and grace in evolutionary terms.[4]

It should not be forgotten, however, that Pope Leo XIII — perhaps un-

---

4. For a good recent example of this kind of reinterpretation, see Elizabeth Johnson's "Does
God Play Dice? Divine Providence and Chance," *Theological Studies* 57 (March 1996): 3–18.
The most notable rethinking of Christianity in evolutionary terms is that of the Jesuit paleon-
tologist Teilhard de Chardin. One of the most accessible of his numerous works is the collection
The Future of Man, trans. N. Denny (New York: Harper Colophon Books, 1969). His superiors
heavily censored Teilhard's works until after his death, when his executors published them without church authorization. As a result, even today few Catholic works deeply integrate evolution
into theology. The church's suspicion about Darwinism, reflected in the sparse history of papal
statements on it, has meant that those who have formulated evolutionary theologies have done
so in an atmosphere of fear and suspicion, rather than one of enthusiastic ecclesial support. Consequently, their efforts still seem marginal to many Catholics rather than central to the substance
of theology. In view of this suspicion, Pope John Paul II's recent clarifications may constitute a
very significant change, though for many theologians and scientists they have appeared too late
to make a great deal of difference.

intentionally — might have helped spare a whole generation of Catholics the anguish about evolution that many non-Catholic Christians continue to experience. In his encyclical *Providentissimus Deus* (1893), he felicitously pointed out the inappropriateness of looking to biblical texts for information of a purely scientific nature. He thereby discouraged any efforts — which biblical literalists undertake as fervently today as ever — to situate the biblical creation accounts alongside Darwinian science, as if they were a competing set of scientific ideas about the natural world. The pope's sophisticated hermeneutical caution not only prevented much unnecessary hostility to science; it also served to protect the sacred texts from the implicit desacralization that occurs whenever we place them in the same mundane informational context as scientific treatises. The whole issue of the relevance of Catholic teaching to evolution is inseparable from the modern developments concerning the interpretation of Scripture. And so the changes that have occurred in official church statements on scriptural exegesis and interpretation are reflected in gradual acceptance of Darwinian science.

Nevertheless, Catholic systematic theologians and ethicists still show little enthusiasm for the Darwinian revolution or the theology of nature. It is only in very recent years that a number of writers have begun to publish serious explorations of a theology of ecology. Most seminaries still lack a solid curriculum in this area. Catholic religious scholars are typically more at home with personal spirituality or historical, political, and social issues than the natural world. This indifference seems to me to impoverish Catholic thought, which, with its rich sacramental tradition, could have focused more on God's relationship to nature than it has throughout the late modern period. One cannot help wondering how much of this contemporary neglect of the natural world results from the church's reluctance since the middle of the nineteenth century to embrace the science of evolution, much less to encourage the development of evolutionary theology.

In any case, evolution has now become the integrating concept, not only among the natural sciences, but increasingly in the human sciences. Every educated person knows today that

- the universe is not eternal and changeless;
- it began about 15 billion years ago;
- life on earth has unfolded in its enormous diversity only gradually and experimentally over a period of 3.8 billion years;
- humans share with other primates a common ancestry going back five or six million years;
- our genetic heritage overlaps that of other species;
- human behavior and culture are in some sense "constrained" (though not fully determined) by our evolutionary and genetic prehistory;

- conscious self-awareness, ethical aspiration, and religious sensitivity also evolved gradually over time.

The evidence for all of this is so overwhelming as not to require any defense. And yet, evolution has not dramatically shaped much of our theology, nor has it deeply affected religious education. The negative consequences of theology's self-distancing from evolutionary science are apparent in some theologians' unreadiness to undertake the radical rethinking of humanity's relationship to nature that the current ecological crisis demands.[5] Authors such as Thomas Berry (1988), Brian Swimme (1992), Leonardo Boff (1995), and Elizabeth Johnson (1993) are making breakthroughs, but this school of theology is still in its infancy.

Theologians have more reason than ever to undertake this revision, now that Pope John Paul II has formally enunciated the church's acknowledgment of the evidence for biological and cosmic evolution. His recent statement clearly reverses previous condemnations, and it advances considerably beyond earlier, lukewarm concessions. Although it is possible to make a less dualistic reading of humanity's relationship to the rest of nature than his formulation offers, this statement still marks a major readjustment in papal teaching. Nothing provides more dramatic evidence of evolutionary change in the history of papal teaching than papal statements concerning evolution itself.

Discussion Questions
EVOLUTION

1. What were you taught in school about evolution and the creation and development of the universe and animal species, including human beings? Were you educated in a Catholic school or public school?

2. Does it surprise you to discover that official Catholic teaching is open to the theory of evolution? Why or why not?

3. In some localities in the U.S., the religious right — inspired largely by Protestant fundamentalism — has tried to force public schools to teach "scientific creationism." How do you respond to the demand that evolution and creationism must have equal time in classrooms?

4. In light of the current acceptance of evolution as the explanation of how our universe and our species developed, how does one teach the

---

5. Many recent studies have established a close link between patriarchal religion and the ecologically questionable distancing of religious life from nature. See, for example, Mary Heather MacKinnon and Moni McIntyre, eds., *Readings in Ecology and Feminist Theology* (Kansas City: Sheed & Ward, 1995), and Rosemary Radford Ruether, *Gaia and God* (San Francisco: Harper, 1992).

first chapters of Genesis (that God created the world in seven days, and human beings were created directly from the dust of the earth)? How does one understand that account? Was it meant to be a scientific explanation, or is it something else?

5. Does the theory of evolution have any implications for the study of theology in the church? Can official teachings "evolve" over time? Should they evolve? Why or why not?

Chapter 17

WAR AND PEACE

The early church embraced Jesus' nonviolence and rejected war. With the Edict of Milan (313) and later acceptance of Augustine's just-war principles, the church recognized the state's responsibility for public order and accommodated itself to war. Gospel nonviolence became a minority tradition. At the time of the Crusades, church leaders even initiated wars. In the twentieth century, with its unrestrained, total warfare, church pronouncements have begun to change again. The Second Vatican Council condemned nuclear war, church leaders have increasingly opposed war itself, especially the targeting of civilians, and official statements have emphasized justice as a prerequisite for peace.

SCRIPTURE

Matthew's Gospel:

- "Blessed are those who work for peace: they will be called children of God" (5:9).

- "You've heard the commandment, 'An eye for an eye and a tooth for a tooth.' But I tell you, don't resist an evil person. When someone strikes you on the right cheek, turn and offer the other" (5:38–39).

- "Therefore treat others as you would have them treat you" (7:12).

- "Those who live by the sword die by the sword" (26:52).

CHURCH FATHERS

Justin Martyr, *Dialogue with Trypho*, c. 160:

"We who used to kill one another, do not make war on our enemies.... We who were filled with war and mutual slaughter, and all wickedness, have each and all of us throughout the earth changed our instruments of war, our swords into plowshares, our spears into farming tools; and cultivate piety, justice, and love of humanity."

Tertullian, *On Idolatry*, c. 200:

"The Lord in disarming Peter ungirdled every soldier."

Origen, *Contra Celsum,* c. 250:

"We do not brandish the sword against any people, nor do we learn to make war, because we have become children of peace through Jesus, whom we follow as our leader."

Didascalia and *Apostolic Constitutions,* fourth century:

The *Didascalia* and the *Apostolic Constitutions* "expressly forbade bishops from doing violence" (Musto, p. 59).

Council of Sirmium, 378:

The Council of Sirmium enforced "the rule keeping former soldiers or civil magistrates from entering holy orders. Innocent I repeated this prohibition (404)" (Musto, p. 59).

   Editors' Note: This was repeated by Councils of Chalcedon (451), Angers (453), Agda (453), Lerida (524), Macon (585), Toledo (633/635), Bordeaux (after 650), Ratisbon (742), and Mainz (813).

Augustine, Letter to Boniface, 417:

"Peace should be the object of your desire. War should be waged only as a necessity and waged only that through it God may deliver men from that necessity and preserve them in peace. For peace is not to be sought in order to kindle war, but war is to be waged in order to obtain peace. Therefore, even in the course of war you should cherish the spirit of a peacemaker."

Augustine, *City of God,* 426:

* "Waging war seems happiness to the wicked, but for the good it is a necessity" (XV).

* The peace of a just war "seeks to impose its own domination of fellow men in place of God's rule" (XIX, 12).

   Context: The statements above show Augustine's ambivalence toward even "just" war.

MEDIEVAL CHURCH

Nicholas I, d. 867:

War is "the devil's work."

Council of Narbonne, 1045:

"A Christian who kills another Christian spills the blood of Christ."

Urban II, Sermon Proclaiming the First Crusade, 1095:

"Oh race of the Franks,...Let us then reenact the law of our ancestors known as the Truce of God. And now that you have promised to maintain the peace among yourselves you are obligated to succor your brethren in the East, menaced by an accursed race, utterly alienated from God. The Holy Sepulchre of our Lord is polluted by the filthiness of an unclean nation. ...Start upon the road to the Holy Sepulchre to wrest that land from the wicked race and subject it to yourselves."

Context: The Truce of God tried to limit warfare between Christians. See below, Second Lateran Council.

Second Lateran Council, 1139:

"We decree that the truce is to be inviolably observed by all from sunset on Wednesday until sunrise on Monday, and from Advent until the octave of the Epiphany and from Quinquagesima until the octave of Easter."

Editors' Note: In his Decretals (c. 1230), Gregory IX extended this "Truce of God" to feast days of Jesus, Mary, the apostles, St. Lawrence, St. Michael, and principal patron saints, and to fast days and vigils.

Decretum, 1140:

Criteria for just war: "It should be waged by proper authority and there should be a clear legal wrong or injustice and the intention to correct it" (Musto, p. 104).

Innocent III, Letter to Peter Capuano, 1204:

"These warriors of Christ, who should have wielded their weapons only against infidels, have bathed in Christian blood....Even virgins vowed to God were subject to their ignominious brutality."

Context: This was written after crusaders sacked Constantinople.

Innocent III, Letter to King Philip II of France, 1207:

"Since wounds that do not respond to the healing of poultice must be lanced with a blade and those who have little regard for ecclesiastical correction must be suppressed by the arm of secular power, we have considered that we ought to call on your aid, most beloved son, to vindicate the injury to Jesus Christ and to seize *the little foxes* who, influencing the simple, are forever destroying the vineyard of the Lord of Hosts....We...enjoin you for the remission of sins to arm yourself strongly and powerfully to root out such degenerate shoots which after putting down roots into the depths of the soil, produce suckers and not grapes. You must eliminate such harmful filth, so that the purity of your faith...may be revealed in deeds by vigorous action and also so that the perfidious heretical sectaries, worn out by the force of your power, may be brought back amid the sufferings of war at least to a knowledge of the truth."

Context: With this letter, Innocent III authorized a crusade against the Albigensians of southern France, whom he considered "worse than Muslims."

Martin V, 1424:

"In 1424 papal troops...defeated Braccione de Montone, the dominant ruler of central Italy, in the battle of L'Aguila, and in 1429 they crushed by force a revolt by Bologna" (McBrien, p. 255).

Julius II, 1506:

"In full armor and in the lead, [Julius II] captured Perugia and Bologna from their tyrannical rulers" (McBrien, p. 270).

Paul III, *Sublimis Deus*, 1537:

Indians "are by no means to be deprived of their liberty or the possession of their property, even though they may be outside the faith of Jesus Christ...nor should they be in any way enslaved; should the contrary happen, it shall be null and of no effect.... The said Indians and other peoples shall be converted to the faith of Jesus Christ by preaching the word of God and by example of good and holy living."

First Latin American Bishops' Synod, *Declaration of the Rights of the Indians*, 1546:

"War against unbelievers for the purpose of subjecting them to Christian control, and to compel them by this means to accept the Christian faith and religion, or to remove obstacles to this end that may exist, is reckless, unjust, perverse, and tyrannical."

MODERN ERA

Leo XIII, *Quod Apostolici Muneris*, 1878:

"And if at any time it happen that the power of the state is rashly and tyrannically wielded by Princes, the teaching of the Catholic Church does not allow an insurrection on private authority against them, lest public order be only the more disturbed, and lest society take greater hurt therefrom. And when affairs come to such a pass that there is no other hope of safety, she teaches that relief may be hastened by the merits of Christian patience and by earnest prayers to God."

Leo XIII, *Notis Errorem,* 1889:

"Since peace is based upon good order, it follows that, for empires as well as individuals, concord should have her principal foundation in justice and charity."

Benedict XV, *Ad Beatissimi Apostolorum,* 1914:

"On every side the dread phantom of war holds sway; there is scarce room for another thought in the minds of men.... There is no limit to the measure of men and of slaughter; day by day the earth is drenched with newly shed blood and is covered with the bodies of the wounded and the slain.... We implore those in whose hands are placed the fortunes of nations to harken to Our voice. Surely there are other ways and means whereby violated rights can be rectified. Let them be tried honestly and with good will, and let arms meanwhile be laid aside."

Benedict XV, *Pacem Dei Munus,* 1920:

"All States, putting aside mutual suspicion, should unite in one league, or rather a sort of family of peoples, calculated both to maintain their own independence and safeguard the order of human society. What specially, amongst other reasons, calls for such an association of nations, is the need generally recognized of making every effort to abolish or reduce the enormous burden of the military expenditure which States can no longer bear, in order to prevent these disastrous wars or at least to remove the danger of them as far as possible."

Pius XI, *Ubi Arcano Dei,* 1922:

"The nations of today live in a state of armed peace which is scarcely better than war itself, a condition that tends to exhaust national finances, to waste the flower of youth, to muddy and poison the very fountainheads of life, physical, intellectual, religious, and moral."

Pius XII, *Un'Ora Grave,* 1939:

"It is by force of reason, and not by force of arms, that justice makes progress, and empires which are not founded on justice are not blessed by God."

Pius XII

1954: "When the harm [war] does is not comparable with that caused by the injustice being suffered... one can be obliged to suffer the injustice."

1955: "Annihilation pure and simple of all human life within the war zone ... is not permitted for any reason whatsoever."

1957: "A Catholic citizen may not make appeal to his own conscience as ground for refusing to give his service to the State, and to fulfill duties affixed by law."

1959: "Since human freedom is able to touch off an unjust conflict hurtful to a nation, it is certain that such a nation can under certain conditions, rise up in arms and defend itself."

John XXIII, *Pacem in Terris*, 1963:

"In this age, which boasts of atomic power, it is senseless to think of war as a tool for redressing the violation of rights."

Second Vatican Council, *Pastoral Constitution on the Church in the Modern World*, 1965:

- "Peace is more than the absence of war: it cannot be reduced to the maintenance of a balance of power between opposing forces nor does it arise out of despotic dominion, but it is appropriately called 'the effect of righteousness' (Isa. 32:17)."

- "Peace cannot be achieved on earth unless people's welfare is safe-guarded and people freely and in a spirit of mutual trust share with one another the riches of their minds and their talents."

- "The council wishes to remind people that the natural law of peoples and its universal principles still retain their binding force. The conscience of humanity firmly and ever more emphatically proclaims these principles. Any action which deliberately violates these principles and any order which commands such actions is criminal, and blind obedience cannot excuse those who carry them out. The most infamous among such ac-tivities is the rationalized and methodical extermination of an entire race, nation, or ethnic minority. These must be condemned as frightful crimes."

- "Every act of war directed to the indiscriminate destruction of whole cities or vast areas with their inhabitants is a crime of God and humanity, which merits firm and unequivocal condemnation."

- "The arms race is one of the greatest curses on the human race and the harm it inflicts on the poor is more than can be endured.... Warned by the possibility of the catastrophes which humanity has created, let us profit by the respite we now enjoy, thanks to the divine favor, to take stock of our responsibilities and find ways of resolving controversies in a manner worthy of human beings. Providence urgently demands of us that we free ourselves from the age-old bondage of war."

John Paul II, *Centesimus Annus*, 1991:

"No war ever again! War destroys the lives of the innocent; it teaches killing and throws even the lives of the killers into confusion. It leaves behind it a trail of rancor and hate, making it harder to achieve a just solution of the problems that provoked it. Just as within the individual states the time has finally come when the system of private revenge and reprisals has been replaced by the rule of law, so it is urgent now that the same sort of progress take place in the international community."

THE PEACE OF CHRIST
AND JUST VIOLENCE
William H. Slavick

Radical shifts in the church's view of war since World War II can only unsettle those who insist that church teaching is fixed.

In the Second World War, German bishops urged their flocks to fight and die in the Führer's unjust war. Just-war assumptions resulted in American Catholics being routinely denied conscientious objector status. Few raised moral objections to total war, even to the use of atomic weapons. In 1957, Pius XII found conscientious objection an unacceptable moral posture. In the late 1960s, New York's Cardinal Francis Spellman defended our Vietnam involvement with, "My country, right or wrong."

But even before Spellman spoke, John XXIII had called for substituting mutual trust for nuclear terror, and the Second Vatican Council had condemned the use of nuclear weapons and affirmed primacy of conscience, the foundation for conscientious objection. Soon after, Catholics were at the forefront of civil disobedience in protesting the Vietnam war, which the U.S. bishops then condemned. By the 1980s, the bishops had recognized the ancient Christian pacifist tradition that had been dismissed for so long and had all but disallowed possession of nuclear weapons. In 1995, the Vatican's UN ambassador declared that nuclear weapons are immoral and must be destroyed. In 1997, New York's Cardinal John O'Connor gave his support for the canonization of Dorothy Day, the leading American pacifist and mentor of Thomas Merton and Daniel and Philip Berrigan.

How can church authorities be so unequivocal about abortion, about which the gospel says nothing, but so divided, changeable, and tolerant about war, which has taken well over a hundred million lives in this century, when the gospel clearly rejected violence and the early church consistently rejected war?

Gospel Nonviolence

Today scholars generally agree that Jesus' message is an unqualified call to nonviolence.[1] He calls us to love our fellow human beings, even our enemies — to pray for those who persecute us. He accepted death on the cross and rejected the sword. His message is reconciliation, forgiveness, and love. The gospel identifies Jesus as "the Prince of Peace" and "the way to peace." The Sermon on the Mount is a blueprint of nonviolent peacemaking. We should trust in God ("See the lilies of the field...") without regard for consequences or expectation of recompense.

Jesus and his disciples championed nonviolent resistance: Turn the other cheek, walk the second mile, give your tunic as well. Christians should employ "the gospel of peace" and "the shield of faith" as weapons against the power system of the day, "against the principalities, against the powers, against the world rulers of this present darkness" (Eph. 4:1–3).

For Paul, resistance to violence must be nonviolent, an understanding that Justin Martyr, Clement of Alexandria, and others echoed over three centuries, as Christians went, without resistance, to be martyred. Christians saw themselves called, through the gift of the Holy Spirit and by God's grace, to be one with the crucified Christ. Trusting in God, they were called to treat all as Christ, to reject violence. That love was an expression of the reign of God.

The Legacy of Constantine

After a period of intense persecution, the Edict of Milan gave the church security and power. The many opportunistic converts who moved easily from government posts to positions of church authority (the first full-time bishops) already recognized the state's responsibility to serve the common good and protect its citizenry. Now the church followed suit, supporting the Roman Empire's wars. But for the faithful, nothing in Jesus' words, the gospels, early Christian experience, or early commentaries supported abandonment of pacifism for justifiable violence.

The popular view is that the church simply recognized defense of the innocent as legitimizing war and cast aside gospel nonviolence. The dissenting view is that, with Constantine, the church rendered unto Caesar that which is God's and sold its soul — like the pact Dostoyevsky's Grand Inquisitor makes with the devil to substitute security for the heavy burden of God's gift of freedom.

The story is more complex. Many compromised, but thousands fled Rome and other empire cities, retiring to the desert, founding pacifist monasteries, settling agricultural communities. Others, such as the former soldier and

---

1. See John L. McKenzie, *Commonweal* review, September 22, 1972; James Douglass, *The Non-violent Cross* (New York: Macmillan, 1968); and Hans Küng, *On Being a Christian* (New York: Doubleday, 1984).

monk Martin, bishop of Tours, Patrick, the apostle of Ireland, and Pope Gregory the Great, put nonviolent Christian peacemaking principles into effect in society.

Ambrose (330–c. 397), an imperial governor who became bishop of Milan, and his protégé, Augustine of Hippo (354–430), set the dominant course. Augustine distinguished between the coexistent cities of God and of the world. The individual must be faithful to the gospel, even to martyrdom, but force is the way of the world and may be necessary to achieve "the tranquility of order."

Spurred by the danger of invasion from the north, Augustine applied Ciceronian as well as Stoic, Neoplatonic, and Manichean thought to argue that one can love the enemy one wars against. And, in the hope of limiting war, he set forth Ciceronian just-war principles. Just war required a clear wrong, proper intention, and legitimate authority. Augustine recognized the shortcomings of the just war as "seeking to impose its own domination" on other humans "instead of God's rule," but, as Thomas Merton observes, his position made him "the father of all modern Christian thought on war."

Thomas Aquinas, highly influential in developing the church's moral norms, was also pessimistic in arguing that the love the gospels ask for is humanly impossible. He, Spanish scholastics, and others added to and refined the just-war principles. They sought to require fair means and certainty of victory, to make war a last resort when diplomacy fails, to measure anticipated redress against the cost, to require a proportionality of means to end, and to prohibit killing noncombatants. Centuries later, Pius XII limited "cause" to defense against attack.

The just use of force — as the lesser evil — buttressed efforts to serve the common good and bring order to society. But those trying to follow Jesus were never comfortable with killing other humans they were supposed to love.

In application, however, just-war principles did not work. Applied unilaterally by combatants, they were honored more in the breach than the observance. The enemy was demonized; righteousness distorted reality, and concern for justice and life disappeared. In 1204, Christians massacred Christians in Constantinople.

Once the church had legitimized violence in the service of the state, the Crusades were inevitable. Killing the infidel was an act of piety. The zeal to purify Christendom justified the Inquisition's tortures, executions, and wars. Colonial power justified violent expansion into the New World and the East and wars of nationalism, imperialism, racial and ethnic hatred, and for economic power. The cross the crusaders and conquistadores carried was a sword.

In this century, World War I lacked just cause and quickly failed the test of proportionality. Most saw stopping Hitler as just cause for World War II, but both sides bombed civilians indiscriminately, which led to firestorm raids and

U.S. use of atomic weapons. Millions of civilians were targeted in Vietnam; civilians were primary targets in the Contra War in Nicaragua. Operation Just Cause in Panama took thousands of civilian lives. The proportion of noncombatant war victims has doubled in a century to 90 percent. Despite United Nations' efforts to curb violence, today's wars are likely to be total.

The world wars and the nuclear arms race have prompted the church to reconsider the morality of war. John XXIII challenged the legitimacy of modern warfare and proposed a program for political, economic, and social peacemaking. The Second Vatican Council condemned the arms race and its cost to the poor, calling for an "entirely new attitude" toward war. Paul VI saw the need to transform social structures to promote peace. John Paul II has repeatedly condemned war. But the Vatican's lack of the trust and de-tachment from the world that marked apostolic times and its concern for the state's responsibilities still outweigh the gospel's unqualified call to non-violence. Rome still legitimizes just wars. Obedient to the state, Christians still kill and are killed.

The Ancient Pacifist Tradition Sustained

Before Vatican II, just-war principles so dominated church teaching that one would think that there had never been a tradition of gospel nonviolence. Yet the ancient tradition of pacifism lived on among the People of God.

In the Middle Ages, Christians were still considered other Christs, and Christians were not to kill Christians. The eleventh century Peace of God, a consequence of popular calls for peace, protected almost everyone, except rulers and soldiers, from war. In the thirteenth century, Francis of Assisi divested himself of possessions that had to be defended, and Franciscans be-came peacemakers everywhere they went. A thirteenth-century peace march called the "Great Alleluia" gathered four hundred thousand near Verona, Italy, to call for an end to war, for reconciliation and peace. More partic-ipated in medieval peace movements than in the Crusades. Bartolomé de las Casas and the mendicants in Mexico urged nonviolence in Indian rela-tions. During the Counter-Reformation, Catholic pacifists took refuge in the Protestant peace churches.

In this century, Mohandas Gandhi, Martin Luther King, and Dorothy Day's Catholic Worker movement renewed the Catholic pacifist tradition. Franz Jagerstatter's World War II martyrdom and the nonviolent witnesses of Archbishop Oscar Romero and the many martyrs of Central America have watered and nurtured it. In the 1980s, successful nonviolent resistance to oppression affected a huge proportion of the world's population, from eastern Europe to the Philippines.

A renewed interest in Scripture has stimulated rediscovery of the non-violent Jesus, who, in giving his life, calls us to transcend violence with love. Just-war advocates cannot answer the question, "What would Jesus do?" In recent years, church leaders have moved closer to the ancient gospel tradition, frequently condemning war and emphasizing the building of justice. Interest in nonviolent conflict resolution — in families, institutions, and between nations — grows.

Still, despite the Vatican's reservations with the just-war theory and the difficulty in applying it, that theory remains dominant. For most Catholics, the right to self-defense and national defense (as in opposing Hitler) remains an unquestioned tradition.

Seventeen centuries have not resolved the contradiction between gospel nonviolence and the legitimization of warfare. The tension between the two traditions continues.

Peace: Realizing the Reign of God

Today peace means, for most, an absence of large-scale armed hostilities. The early Christian understanding of peace went far beyond that: "See these Christians, how they love one another." Peace meant a dynamic oriented to order, tranquility, and harmony rooted in love of God and neighbor, from which justice flows in realizing the reign of God.

Even as early Christians thought the end of the world imminent, that broader understanding of peace permeated their communities. It is reflected even in the medieval hierarchy of societal roles — "order and degree"; the responsibilities of sovereigns; the continuity of institutions serving the orphaned, widowed, poor, ill, and aged. More recently, church social encyclicals have promoted laws governing working conditions and wages, human rights, state social programs, and international efforts to create a just world order.

In recent years, John Paul II and others have called, in eloquent words, for the peace that justice brings, but the challenge grows ever larger as wealth becomes more concentrated, poverty increases, arms proliferate, and war and repression continue to be commonplace. In the U.S., the pursuit of social justice seems a lower priority for the church than concern about sexual morality. When Latin Americans began to emphasize living the beatitudes in response to Vatican II's call for Christians to engage the world, Rome showed more concern with nineteenth-century philosophical issues than with the Latin American bishops' call at Medellín for a preferential option for the poor. The Vatican sought to curb base communities without offering anything as a substitute and appointed bishops ill-qualified to practice what Rome preaches. It would appear that peace, the reign of God, can wait.

Discussion Questions
WAR AND PEACE

1. What has been your personal experience with war or physical violence? Did you serve in the armed forces in a combat role? Did a member of your family or a close friend serve and share the experience with you? How did you (or a person close to you) find the experience of doing violence? Do you believe it is a violation of gospel norms and values? If so, why? If not, why not?

2. Were you ever a victim of violence (in any circumstance) yourself? What was that like? Having been a victim, do you believe that doing violence is contrary to gospel norms? In your view, is war governed by different norms than violent street crime or domestic violence? If so, how? If not, why not?

3. Why do you think the early Catholic tradition of gospel nonviolence is so little known? Why is it so little preached?

4. Do you think that the just-war principles can be made to work in an age of total warfare? If so, how? What recent wars, if any, satisfy just-war principles? Why or why not?

5. How do you understand the gospel call to nonviolence? Are we called to trust completely in God and abandon the use of force, including self-defense and attempts to right injustices? Is a nation or group of people ever justified in using force? If you believe it is, how do you reconcile this position with the gospel?

6. There is a famous bumper sticker that quotes Pope Paul VI: "If you want peace, work for justice." What does this mean to you? How is work for social justice a part of peacemaking? Is it necessary to twenty-first-century peacemaking? Why or why not? If so, what social injustices must be corrected to achieve lasting peace in the world?

7. Most people believe, theoretically at least, that the nations of the world should reduce armaments, abolish nuclear, chemical, and biological weapons, and solve conflicts through diplomacy or other nonviolent means.

   • What new steps could the church take to move the world closer to that ideal?
   • What new steps could your parish take?
   • What new steps could you personally take?

Chapter 18

USURY

The church unequivocally condemned usury, the lending of money at interest, until capitalism began developing in Europe in the late Middle Ages. At first, church officials implicitly recognized the practice by permitting secular officials to allow Jews to lend money at interest. Gradually, they created loopholes for interest-taking in limited circumstances. By the mid-nineteenth century, the church itself was borrowing money at interest. Since then, the issue has quietly disappeared from official pronouncements, and church administrators are now required to do what was once forbidden: invest church assets at interest.

EARLY CHURCH

Council of Nicaea, 345:

"Many clerics, motivated by greed and a desire for gain, have forgotten the scriptural injunction, 'he gave not his money to usury' and instead demand a monthly rate of one percent on loans they make; therefore this holy and great council decrees that in future anyone taking interest or in any way whatsoever dealing in usury and demanding his 50 percent profit or seeking some similar way of earning money is to be deposed and removed from his order."

Council of Aix, 789:

It is "reprehensible even for laymen to make money by lending at interest."

MEDIEVAL CHURCH

Second Lateran Council, 1139:

"We condemn that detestable, shameful, and insatiable rapacity of moneylenders, which has been denounced by divine and human laws and throughout the Old and New Testaments, and we deprive them of all ecclesiastical consolation, commanding that no archbishop, no bishop, no abbot of any order, nor anyone in clerical orders, shall, except with the utmost caution, dare receive usurers; but throughout their life let them be stigmatized with the mark of infamy, and unless they repent let them be deprived of Christian burial."

Third Lateran Council, 1179:

"Seeing that almost everywhere the crime of usury has taken such hold that many pass over other professions to devote themselves to the business of usury, as if it were lawful, and thus disregard the strict scriptural prohibition, we decree that notorious usurers are not to be admitted to the communion of the altar, nor, if they die in that sin, to receive Christian burial. Neither shall anyone accept their offering. Anyone taking such an offering or giving them Christian burial, shall be condemned to return what he has taken. Furthermore, till he has satisfied the wishes of the bishop, let him remain suspended from office."

Fourth Lateran Council, 1215:

"The more Christians are restrained from the practice of usury, the more are they oppressed in this matter by the treachery of the Jews, so that in a short time they exhaust the resources of the Christians. Wishing, therefore, in this matter to protect the Christians against cruel oppression by the Jews, we ordain in this decree that if in future, under any pretext, Jews extort from Christians oppressive and excessive interest, the society of Christians shall be denied them until they have made suitable satisfaction for their excesses. Christians shall also, if necessary, be compelled by ecclesiastical censure, from which there shall be no appeal, to abstain from all business dealings with them.... Lastly, we decree that the Jews be compelled by the same penalty to compensate churches for the tithes and offerings owing to them, which the Christians were accustomed to supply from their houses and other properties before they fell into the hands of the Jews under some title or other. In this way the churches will be protected against loss."

Context: Jews were forbidden to enter most occupations but were permitted to practice usury, and the church's attitude toward moneylending became permeated with anti-Semitism.

Clement V, Council of Vienne, 1311:

"If anyone falls into the error of believing and affirming that it is not a sin to practice usury, we decree that he be punished as a heretic, and we strictly command the ordinaries of the localities and the inquisitors to proceed against those suspected of such errors in the same way as they would proceed against those accused publicly or suspected or heresy."

CAPITALIST ERA

Nicholas V, 1452,

Nicholas V "acceded to the request of Emperor Frederic III and permitted the Jews of Nuremberg to act as usurers... [and] approved a similar re-

quest of the city of Lucca to keep Jewish usurers 'for the public benefit'"
(Lapide, p. 56).

*Context: Jews were tolerated as usurers when their activities were in the church's
and secular rulers' economic interest. Sixtus IV (1478) and Innocent VIII (1489)
gave similar absolutions to Frankfurt and Siena.*

Fifth Lateran Council, 1512–17:

- "Usury means nothing else than gain or profit drawn from the use of a
  thing that is by its nature sterile, a profit that is acquired without labor,
  cost, or risk."

- "We declare and define... that... credit organizations established by
  states and hitherto approved and confirmed by the authority of the apostolic see, do not introduce any kind of evil or provide any incentive
  to sin if they receive, in addition to the capital, a moderate sum for
  their expenses and by way of compensation, provided it is intended exclusively to defray the expenses of those employed and of other things
  pertaining... to the upkeep of the organizations, and provided that no
  profit is made therefrom."

Innocent XI, 1679

Innocent XI "ruled that interest could not be taken on the grounds that a
greater value is to be put on money actually possessed than on that to be
received in the future; and that interest exacted in virtue of gratitude (not
justice) was equally usurious" (Hulme, p. 51).

Benedict XIV, *Vix Pervenit*, 1745:

- "We do not deny that at times together with the loan contract certain
  other titles — which are not at all intrinsic to the contract — may run
  parallel with it. From these other titles, entirely just and legitimate reasons arise to demand something over and above the amount due on
  the contract. Nor is it denied that it is very often possible for someone,
  by means of contracts differing entirely from loans, to spend and invest
  money legitimately, either to provide oneself with an annual income or
  to engage in legitimate trade and business.... We decide nothing for the
  present; we also shall not decide now about the other contracts in which
  the theologians and canonists lack agreement."

- "Those who desire to keep themselves free and untouched by the contamination of usury and to give their money to another in such a manner
  that they may receive only legitimate gain should be admonished to
  make a contract beforehand. In the contract they should explain the
  conditions and what gain they expect from their money."

- "Christian minds should not think that gainful commerce can flourish by usuries or other similar injustices."

Holy Office, Letter, 1821:

This letter "includes the statement that usury is against the natural law, that it is wrong in its essence" (Hulme, p. 57).

Pius VIII, Audience, 1830:

Pius VIII "gave a reply to the Bishop of Rennes, allowing some who were taking interest to be left in peace...provided that they were willing to be guided by any future official decision [of the church]" (Hulme, p. 55).

Pius IX, mid-nineteenth century:

Pius IX borrowed 50 million francs in 1850 from Rothschilds. In 1873 he "delivered a vehement anti-Jewish address to the dignitaries of the Roman curia in which he branded all Jews as 'money-lusting enemies of Christ and Christianity'" (Lapide, p. 57).

Code of Canon Law, 1917:

The 1917 Code of Canon Law "gives the punishment, exclusion from an office held in the church and from any share in the government of the church, of one who is justly convicted of various crimes, one of which is usury."

Pius XII, *Citorna Particolarmente*, 1950:

"Does not the social function of the bank consist in making it possible for the individual to render his money fruitful, even if only in a small degree, instead of dissipating it, or leaving it sleep without any profit, either to himself or to others?"

Context: "Today then, there is general agreement [in the church] that interest is lawful. This does not mean that usury is allowed or tolerated....It does mean that a just right to interest is recognized widely under modern conditions" (Hulme, p. 56).

Code of Canon Law, 1983:

"All administrators are bound to fulfill their office with the diligence of a good householder....For this reason they must...with the consent of the ordinary invest the money which is left over after expenses and which can be profitably allocated for the goals of the juridic person."

ONCE A SIN,
NOW GOOD STEWARDSHIP
Amata Miller, IHM

People who live in an economy built on credit are understandably mystified that the morality of charging interest on money lent was bitterly contested over many centuries. "Usury" today means charging *excessive* interest, above the legal maximum. Until charging interest became legal in Europe in the sixteenth century, however, *any* fee for using money was called "usury." Official church condemnation of "usury" — all interest-taking — continued until the early nineteenth century. At that time differences of opinion among moralists became so severe as to cause confusion among confessors, denial of absolution to some of the faithful, and "much spiritual unrest."

In 1822, a priest denied absolution to Mlle. de Saint Marcel of Lyons because she had received legal interest on an investment, and she appealed to the Holy Office. The Holy Office ruled against her confessor, on condition that she would abide by future decisions of the Holy See. Subsequently the Holy Office granted other appeals on the same grounds. These judgments settled the practical question, though not the theoretical issues. Since that time, theologians have almost unanimously agreed that anyone may take interest on money as long as it is not excessive or does not cause hardship to the poor. The topic was on the agenda of Vatican Council I, but the Franco-Prussian War of 1870 ended proceedings before the council could discuss it. Since 1917, canon law has *required* interest-taking, previously forbidden, as a *mandatory* responsibility for those administering church assets.

But why the long centuries of condemnation? And what led to the differences among moralists that finally changed the church's attitude toward interest-taking? Acceptance of changed economic realities and a new understanding of the functions of money finally broke through centuries-old philosophical constructs and moral precepts that had once, but no longer, fit the situations being judged.

The church's condemnation of interest-taking was rooted in Old Testament prohibitions. In the ancient Jews' agricultural economy, lending was primarily an obligation of charity among members of the community, to enable satisfaction of basic needs. Simple commutative justice governed such transactions: there must be equality in the exchange; the lender was to receive back only what he or she had lent and no more. All loans were to be canceled every seventh year as part of the sabbatical observance. Usurers were condemned as exploiters who enriched themselves at the expense of less fortunate neighbors. However, traders in the Mediterranean area did business with foreigners, such as Phoenicians, who recognized interest-taking as part of commerce, so the Jews were allowed to charge interest. This was an acknowledgment that the practice was not inherently evil.

In pre-Christian Greece and Rome, capital was scarce; interest-taking was legal, and rates were regulated to protect the poor and farmers. Aristotle, however, saw money as barren and unproductive, intended to serve only as a medium of exchange. As long as a person returned what was borrowed, justice had been done. Roman philosophers and the public condemned taking interest. Historians believe, however, that moneylending at interest went on throughout Roman history, with the interest rate fluctuating according to economic conditions.

Jesus acknowledged Roman realities in the parable of the servant who did not invest the master's money at interest and was punished because he failed to act as a good steward (Matt. 25:14–30). But in Luke's Gospel, Jesus exhorted the people to lend without expecting repayment, and he called them to be compassionate, as God is compassionate (Luke 6:34–35). The gospel attitude toward lending is based on the obligations of charity and mercy toward the needy. For Christians these must always supersede the obligation for commutative justice.

The early church fathers reiterated scriptural teachings, condemning interest-taking because it was rooted in avarice and resulted in exploitation of the poor. In an era of wars and famine and the sweeping socioeconomic changes accompanying the Roman Empire's breakdown, interest-taking meant taking advantage of another's misfortune, an offense against charity and mercy. By the sixth century, however, a few texts of the fathers seemed to condone taking interest on commercial loans. Nevertheless, ecclesiastical legislation and early councils prohibited interest-taking by clerics and called it contrary to church teaching for the laity. By the twelfth century, councils forbade it for all.

The economy of early medieval Europe was feudal and agricultural. The Saracen triumph in the Mediterranean ended most trading. Closing the channels of international trade also diminished trade between town and country. Great estates became self-contained economic units, providing for all the needs of the feudal lord or lady and his or her dependents. They were bound together by a structure of mutual obligations and privileges designed to provide order and mutual security. People borrowed only in times of famine. These circumstances validated the church's traditional prohibition against interest-taking as exploitative of another's need.

By the beginning of the twelfth century, a commercial revival had begun in northern Europe and Italy. Maritime and overland trading routes were established; agriculture became an export industry; new industries served distant markets. New towns grew up to service huge international fairs for wholesale traders. The use of money and credit expanded, prices rose, borrowing increased, and banking developed. Yet the bulk of borrowing was still in the form of consumption loans to individuals (aristocrats whose fixed revenues were no longer adequate), to public authorities, and to churches and monasteries that borrowed in emergencies rather than sell their land. Every loan was still a private contract between lender and borrower; *commercial* loans were not yet differentiated from *consumption* loans. Obviously, the new circumstances called for a new approach to the morality of interest-taking.

Accepting Aristotle's view of money as intrinsically barren, Scholastic theologians continued to condemn interest-taking. However, they developed some exceptions, using "extrinsic titles," which recognized the increasingly monetized economy and justified taking payment for the use of money under certain conditions.

These "extrinsic titles" allowed interest-taking

- as a penalty for a debtor's late payment;

- as compensation for an actual loss suffered because of late payment;

- as compensation for certain profit forgone;

- as a premium for risking the loss of part or all of the capital.

Investments in enterprises were, on the basis of the risk, distinguished from mere loans. Pope Innocent III (1198–1216) declared investments immune from the usury prohibition.

Still, popes and councils condemned usury vehemently. In the 1180s, Alexander III and Urban II decreed that usurers were bound to make restitution, in addition to other penalties. For a considerable period, the Jews, as non-Christians outside the prescriptions of canon law, were immune from the prohibitions. In the late Middle Ages, as the sway of church law extended to all of civil society, Urban II and the Fourth Lateran Council withdrew their immunity. In 1311, Clement V at the Council of Vienne decreed excommunication of civil authorities who enacted laws requiring debtors to pay interest or declaring that interest-takers did not have to make restitution. The council also said it was heretical for anyone to claim that interest was not a sin.

Fifteenth-century papal decrees made exceptions to the prohibition on usury by declaring licit the profit from certain types of investments. During the next two centuries, the church tempered the severity of the practical legislation as the times warranted, by dropping some of the conditions for an "extrinsic title," such as proof of actual loss. The "extrinsic titles" approach had suited the period when increased borrowing was still predominantly in the form of contracts between individuals for consumption purposes. But in practice, these modifications broke down the prohibition of usury over time.

From the sixteenth century on, as commercial borrowing increased and a competitive market for capital emerged, opinions on the morality of usury divided. Some Protestant reformers (Luther, Zwingli, and the English) retained the Catholic prohibitions against interest-taking. Others, such as Calvin, began to develop an intrinsic moral justification for interest-taking.

Living in the prosperous commercial city of Geneva, Calvin preached that condemning interest-taking as intrinsically evil was foolish. Under the new conditions, in which both lender and borrower gained from a loan with interest, capital and credit were normal and indispensable. With its highly developed commerce, the Netherlands embraced the new doctrine and legalized lending at interest in 1658.

A few Catholic writers also began to question the official church position against usury. They distinguished between consumption and production loans. They found that interest-taking was against natural and divine law only if it involved avarice, dishonesty, or cruelty, or placed an intolerable burden on one's neighbor. Some scholars believed interest-taking was not absolutely prohibited as long as these negative conditions were not present and it conformed to local laws and customs.

The usury controversy re-ignited in the Netherlands in the early eighteenth century, when Jansenist exiles migrated there from France. At the same time, a debate arose in Verona over floating a public loan at 4 percent. Benedict XIV appointed a commission of cardinals and theologians to study the morality of interest-taking. The conclusions were published in an encyclical letter, *Vix pervenit*, which reiterated the traditional doctrine that interest-taking is sinful, but allowed compensation if one of the "extrinsic titles" existed. The letter went to the bishops of Italy in 1745 and to the universal church in 1836. Controversy spread throughout the whole Catholic world. Catholic jurists had begun to accept interest-taking as justified, but theologians still debated its morality throughout the nineteenth century. This confusion troubled the consciences of the faithful. The replies of Roman congregations to individual appeals ultimately resolved the practical moral question.

Interest-taking is now morally acceptable as long as it is moderate and does not violate charity and overburden the individual. In fact, administrators of church property *must* make interest-bearing investments as part of responsible stewardship. In modern Catholic social teaching, however, references to interest-taking are few. The 1917 Code of Canon Law still listed usury — *excessive* interest — as a sin, but the 1983 Code did not. Teachings now focus, as in the early church, on the effects of debt burdens on the poor. Recent papal encyclicals and episcopal pastoral letters have called for liberal lending terms and cancellation of poor nations' debts.

This saga reveals how changes in the meaning and purpose of money and lending resulted in changed moral teaching. In agricultural societies, money served only as a medium of exchange, and justice required the return of only the original amount lent. Lending went on primarily among members of a community for consumption purposes; the obligations of charity toward

those in need superseded those of justice. But in complex commercial, industrial, and postindustrial societies, people borrow for production purposes. The
value of money received in the future is less than that of money today, since
one sacrifices opportunities by forgoing its use for the period of the loan. The
existence of organized money markets, in which interest rates are determined,
and of a variety of investment vehicles, means that the sacrifice is real and
can be quantified. Commutative justice now requires some compensation for
the sacrifice of opportunities.

The official church responded slowly to internal and external changes. At
first Christians were a minority, and they emphasized sharing material things
with one another and the poor. In the Middle Ages, the church prescribed
for all aspects of society, ecclesiastical and civil; its philosophical, theological,
and legal principles reigned largely unchallenged. As it became wealthy and
then corrupt, it developed exceptions that would allow it to participate in
the new opportunities without denying traditional principles. Officially prohibited moneylending became the monopoly of the Jews, whom the church
and the state used but despised and taxed. Reformers exposed the hypocrisies
and divided the church. In reaction, counter-reformers preached return to
traditional orthodoxies even when economic realities were changing. For several centuries the church's official position, based on Scholasticism rooted in
Aristotelian thought, denied modernity and reflected a desire to restore the
socioeconomic order of medieval Christendom. Only with Vatican II's *Pastoral Constitution on the Church in the Modern World* did the church come to
terms with its role in this world, sharing the "joys and hopes, the griefs and
anxieties" of the people of this time, "especially those who are poor or in
any way afflicted." Now administrators must invest church funds at interest,
preferably to attend to the needs of the poor.

This is a story of how rigid doctrine can lead to victimization of marginalized social groups, such as the Jews of the Middle Ages. Rigidity later required
"exceptions" to accommodate changed social circumstances. Failure to come
to grips with social changes engendered successive struggles and controversies, until the church finally recognized that new moral approaches were
needed. It is also a story of the ultimate triumph of respect for individual
conscience. For change ultimately came from an appeal by a woman who believed in the rightness of her own action and from the response of Roman
officials to the truth of her belief.[1]

---

1. For a very thorough and careful treatment of usury, see Thomas F. Divine, SJ, *Interest: An
Historical and Analytical Study in Economics and Modern Ethics* (Milwaukee: Marquette University
Press, 1959).

Discussion Questions
USURY

1. What is your own experience with borrowing or lending money? Do you believe that interest-taking is morally justified? If so, at what level? What principles should determine what is *excessive* interest?

2. Have you ever heard a homily on excessive interest-taking? Should church officials speak out on that issue or economic issues in general? Why or why not? If so, what themes would you like to see emphasized?

3. Interest-taking today is a major issue in economic relations between the developed world, largely international creditors, and underdeveloped debtor nations. Some people involved in social justice advocate that international lending institutions should forgive the debts of undeveloped nations because the burden of debt repayment falls on the poorest of the poor. In light of Amata Miller's essay, what do you think of this idea?

4. Some theologians and church officials claim that the church's moral teaching never changes. Yet Amata Miller shows how the moral teaching on usury changed dramatically in response to changing economic conditions. How do you respond to that historical development?

5. Does this change in the usury policy suggest that the church needs to take notice of other changes (education of the laity, new roles of women, democratization of the world, etc.) and alter its policy and teaching in other areas as well? Why or why not?

THE CASE IS
NEVER CLOSED

Linda Rabben

The ceilings are low, the lights shine rather dimly, and the air smells of dust in the stacks of the Catholic University Library. The sacred precincts of the canon law reading room are kept locked; I'd hold my breath on the rare occasions when I entered. I spent most of my time in the more welcoming theological studies library. There I searched for Pope Nicholas I's Letter to the Bulgarians (866), Innocent IV's authorization to inquisitors to use torture (1252), a prayer by John XXIII that reversed two thousand years of Catholic theology, and hundreds of other papal statements. What seemed at first to be obscure, pedantic rummaging through the leavings of the dead became a joyful, if sometimes frustrating, hunt for rough diamonds, begrimed by time but precious nonetheless.

Although I loved studying history in college, I specialized in anthropology and was writing a book about Brazilian Indians when Catholics Speak Out commissioned me to work on the papal statements project. So I spent many mornings of 1997 in the Amazon and afternoons in Rome, looking for traces of a world where some of my ancestors had lived and died in misery, violence, and obloquy. I never felt more Jewish than when I was searching the stacks for bulls and encyclicals.

This research aroused many conflicting emotions: joy of discovery, indignation, ironical glee, disgust, compassion, horror, pity, disbelief, awe. My Catholic colleagues at the Quixote Center found my enjoyment of the task more than a little odd. I explained it as a result of my necessary detachment as a non-Catholic. But on certain gloomy afternoons, while reading the long history of Christian anti-Semitism, I didn't feel at all detached. It was too easy to imagine my ancestors in twelfth-century England, fifteenth-century Spain, eighteenth-century Poland, or twentieth-century Ukraine being martyred for their faith. The sentence I found in one book, "In the past thousand years one out of every two Jews born into the world has been murdered," haunted me. It pushed me to search unrelentingly for Innocent IV's torture authorization, which took a month to find. After that, I could no longer contemplate pictures of the Sistine Chapel or portraits of popes with aesthetic appreciation; their beauty was obscured by the bloody handprints of count-less tragedies. As I treaded the library's cloistered corridors, I kept pondering what miracle had saved my family and brought me to that particular place in the late twentieth century. At such moments, the study and recovery of history seemed very important indeed, not just for me but for everybody. To understand where we are going, we need to understand where we have come from.

Despite its claim that it never changes and never errs, the church is an all-too-human institution with a rich, often contradictory history. Some of the changes have had good consequences, both for Catholics and for people of other religions. Some of the papal and conciliar statements quoted in this book do not, however, show the institutional church and its very fallible lead-ers in a positive light. Nonetheless, they have many valuable lessons to teach us, if not always the ones they intended.

Among the lessons I learned was the value of persistence. In doing the re-search, I encountered many frustrating obstacles. Language was one of the most obvious. Most papal statements made before the twentieth century, and many since, have not been translated into English. As recently as 1917, the Code of Canon Law was deliberately not translated from Latin into any other language — except Chinese. Consequently, church historians do much of their research in Latin-language, primary sources, and they often don't see the necessity of translating or directly quoting papal statements. Apparently assuming that few others read their work, they are content to paraphrase or merely refer to the original documents.

With limited time and resources, I had to depend mainly on English-language, secondary sources. To reacquaint myself with events unstudied since high school and college, I had to cover broad areas very quickly. Ex-cellent works by scholars of skill and rigor helped me. I came away with great admiration for John Noonan (sexuality, usury), Brian Tierney (papal infallibility), David Kertzer (the Mortara case), John Maxwell (slavery), Cynthia Carlen (papal pronouncements and encyclicals), Solomon Grayzel (thirteenth-century Jews), and the commentators in this book.

One of them, Kenneth Stow, demanded that I find the original sources of all the statements on Jews on which he would comment. But many of the quotations came from secondary sources whose authors did not al-ways provide complete (or correct) citations. Writers as varied as Thomas Bokenkotter, Richard McBrien, and Peter de Rosa provided few or no cita-tions. Although I had encountered errors, misquotations, mistranslations, and miscitations in the works of scholars with excellent reputations, I was still ir-ritated by Stow's demand. With the budget and time allotted for the research dwindling, I started checking sources, grumbling as I went.

Stow particularly questioned the authenticity of a prayer by John XXIII, which he said reversed two thousand years of Catholic theology on Jews. I had found it in de Rosa's *Vicars of Christ: The Dark Side of the Papacy*, a polemic whose reliability I frankly doubted. So I searched elsewhere for the prayer, wishing it were genuine because I liked its sentiments so much:

> The mark of Cain is stamped upon our foreheads. Across the centuries, our brother Abel has lain in blood which we drew, and shed tears we caused by forgetting Thy love. Forgive us, Lord [sic], for the curse we falsely attributed to their name as Jews. Forgive us for crucifying Thee a second time in the flesh. For we knew not what we did.

If John XXIII didn't say it, he should have, I thought. But I couldn't find the prayer in any of the biographies of John XXIII on the library's shelves, in official Vatican publications, or in the English-language books about his papacy. I finally found it as the epigraph of a book Stow didn't much like or trust. The author had provided a citation, however, to the *Catholic Herald* of May 14, 1965. Stow was willing to put aside his doubts, but I thought I'd better look up the quote. There are half-a-dozen *Catholic Heralds* in the world, published in London, Milwaukee, Philadelphia, and other places. Catholic University and Georgetown University libraries keep them for a year and then discard them. The Library of Congress had a *Catholic Herald* on microfilm but couldn't say which *Herald* it was or what years were available. And I wondered why the prayer wasn't published until almost two years after John XXIII's death.

I called Eugene Fisher, associate director of the Secretariat for Ecumenical and Interreligious Affairs of the National Conference of Catholic Bishops. "That prayer is a hoax," he said. "It was written by Malachi Martin, around the time of Vatican II." Why Martin would have invented the prayer, he couldn't say. A mystery was apparently solved but another mystery was created. Stow sent me an e-mail message: "You see why I have been somewhat old-maidish about the sources." Let that be a lesson to researchers!

In his new *Lives of the Popes*, Richard McBrien observes,

> What a nonhistorian like myself was startled to discover as he rummaged his way through these diverse secondary sources is the vast number of discrepancies, inconsistencies and outright errors regarding dates and names and sometimes even regarding the details of significant historical events, such as papal elections. One appreciates more fully how original sin is transmitted from generation to generation. Analogously, the transmission of factual error happens in historical studies all the time. One author relies on another, who has relied, in turn, on another, and that one on another — and on and on it goes. (McBrien, 1997, p. 3)

The popes themselves made selective use of institutional history. In some cases, forged documents passed as genuine for centuries, and popes based their claims to primacy on them. To justify repressive measures against Polish Jews, an eighteenth-century pope, Benedict XIV, cited a 1253 letter from Innocent IV to the king of France, authorizing the expulsion of the Jews, well before the Jews were actually forced to leave the country. But the original letter is "lost"; nor can scholars find any other reference to it besides Benedict XIV's.

And whenever the Vatican does change its position on an issue, it invariably prefaces the announcement with the phrase, "As we have always maintained." Or it uses the most baroque obfuscation imaginable to avoid admitting error.

Errors of wishful thinking are as interesting as factual errors, discrepancies, and distortions. Some authors want so much to believe that one or another pope said something they could agree with that they misinterpret or mistranslate papal statements, "accidentally on purpose," as my mother would say.

For example, in his landmark study *Infallible?* no less a scholar than Hans Küng read Pope John XXII's condemnation of irreformability as a condemnation of infallibility. Irreformability is the rule that one pope may not reformulate, overrule, or contradict the decisions of his predecessors. Although it is related to infallibility, the two concepts are not the same. When John XXII condemned irreformability in the fourteenth century, the doctrine of papal infallibility was still inchoate.

I discovered Küng's error of wishful thinking on reading Tierney's magisterial work, *Origins of Papal Infallibility, 1150–1350.* Unlike Küng, Tierney is a professional historian with no theological perspective to defend. He does not hesitate to declare:

> Whatever divine guidance the church may have enjoyed through the course of the centuries, that guidance has not been such as to prevent the church as a whole from falling into grievous errors. To present [Vatican II's statement on religious freedom] as a "development of a single unchanging Catholic truth..." is surely to strain human credulity too far. A man [*sic*] who believes that will believe anything.... Some scholars seem to imagine that to explain by historical analysis why the church has contradicted itself is to demonstrate that the contradictions are nonexistent. And this is nonsense of course. (Tierney, 1988, p. 277)

One could hardly imagine Küng calling any theological exercise nonsense. To maintain his standing as a Catholic theologian, he had to operate within the constraints of the discipline and state his conclusions in language acceptable to the Vatican's thought police. Even so, he lost his status as an officially approved Catholic theologian. Just the question mark in *Infallible?*'s title was enough to guarantee such an outcome.

Perhaps, however, this sanction freed Küng, as it liberated the modernist theologian Alfred Loisy (1857–1940), whose first reaction to excommunication was

> inexpressible relief. The church restored to me — after no end of fracas, in the guise of disgrace and condemnation, by way of ostracism, and so far as possible by means of my extermination — nevertheless at last she restored to me the liberty which I had been so ill-advised as to alienate to her thirty years before. Despite herself, but effectually, she gave me back into my own keeping, and I was almost ready to bless her for it. (Kurtz, 1986, p. 160)

Loisy is one of many memorable figures whose acquaintance I had the honor to make through this project. Nor can I forget Jan Hus, granted a safe-conduct to travel from Prague to the Council of Constance in 1415 — but no safe-conduct back. Accused of heresy, he refused to recant and was burned at the stake, right there at the council. Then there were the four Franciscans who burned in the 1320s for insisting that Jesus and the apostles lived in absolute poverty and owned nothing. I also remember Galileo, old, blind, and ill, imprisoned at home, his favorite daughter dead, continuing to do astronomy and managing to publish his final book in Protestant Amsterdam.

Prohibited from publishing his works before Vatican II, Teilhard de Chardin wisely gave them to a friend so they would not be "lost" in the Vatican labyrinth after his death. And in our own time, Tissa Balasuriya, excommunicated in 1997 for refusing to sign an oath that included a statement against women's ordination, kept speaking out. The church has had no shortage of heroic "heretics," men and women ahead of their times, who risked everything to bear witness to their deepest convictions.

For me, these women and men exemplify the highest development of Catholic thought and action. (And they remind me of Spinoza, whom the local Jewish community excommunicated for freethinking.) These saints of resistance hover in the wings, offering the enforcers of orthodoxy the divine and redemptory blessing of forgiveness. Remember them as you read, as you consult your conscience, and as you act, in accordance with its "certain judgment."

CITATIONS

1. Infallibility

Irenaeus, Ambrose, Hormisdas: Cheetham, p. 47.

Boniface I: McBrien (1997), p. 68.

Constantinople II: Sullivan, pp. 62–63.

Constantinople III: Sullivan, p. 64.

Gregory VII: Comby, vol. 1, p. 137.

Decretum: Tierney (1971), p. 158; McClory (1997), p. 22.

Innocent III, c. 1200: Granfield, p. 32.

Innocent III, *Etsi:* Cheney and Semple, p. 216.

Boniface VIII: Mann, vol. 18, p. 350.

John XXII: Tierney (1971), p. 861; Tierney (1988), p. 171.

Clement VI: Granfield, p. 36.

Constance: Sullivan, p. 72.

Pius II: Bokenkotter (1979), p. 198.

Pius IX, *Infallabilis:* McBrien (1994), p. 1102.

Pius IX, *Tuas:* Gaillardetz, p. 25.

Vatican I: Deedy (1990), p. 259.

Pius XII: p. 5.

Vatican II, *Dogmatic Constitution:* Flannery (1996), p. 34.

Vatican II, *Pastoral Constitution:* Maguire, p. 49.

CDF, *Mysterium Ecclesiae:* NCR, p. 24.

Catechism, p. 28.

John Paul II, *Tertio: Origins* 24, no. 24, 11/24/94, pp. 410–11.

CDF, *Dubium:* Ratzinger, p. 1.

CDF, 1996: *Tablet* (1997), p. 561

2. Primacy of Conscience

Innocent III: Küng (1994), p. 39.

Aquinas: Aquinas, vol. 2, pp. 674–75, 1004–5, 1008.

Pius VI: Comby and MacCulloch, vol. 2, p. 113.

Pius IX: Carlen, PE, vol. 2, p. 381.

Leo XIII: Leo XIII, pp. 155, 161.

Pius XII: Rudin, p. 157.

John XXIII: Carlen, PE, vol. 5, p. 108.

Vatican II, *Dogmatic Constitution:* Flannery (1996), p. 22.

Vatican II, *Pastoral Constitution:* Flannery (1996), pp. 178, 212.

Vatican II, *Religious Liberty:* Flannery (1996), p. 554.

Paul VI: Carlen, PE, vol. 5, p. 190.

John Paul II, Audience: McClory (1997), p. 155.

John Paul II, *Veritatis:* Miller, p. 763.

Catechism: p. 442.

3. Scriptural Interpretation

Leo I: Megivern, p. 143.

Gregory I: Megivern, pp. 148–49.

Toulouse: Peters (1980), p. 195.

Clement V: Megivern, pp. 172–73.

Leo X: Megivern, p. 178.

Trent: Schroeder, pp. 18–19.

Clement XI: Megivern, p. 186.

Pius VII: Megivern, pp. 187–88.

Pius IX: Megivern, p. 190.

Vatican I: Megivern, p. 192.

Leo XIII, *Providentissimus:* Carlen, PE, vol. 2, p. 332.

Leo XIII, *Vigilantiae:* Megivern, p. 222.

Inquisition: Megivern, p. 258.

Pius X: Megivern, p. 266.

Biblical Commission: Megivern, pp. 234–35, 237.

Canon Law: Brown et al., p. 1111.

Benedict XV: Carlen, PE, vol. 3, p. 181.

Pius XII, *Divino:* Carlen, PE, vol. 4, pp. 70–71, 73, 75.

Biblical Commission, 1943: Megivern, p. 315.

Biblical Commission, 1948: Megivern, p. 351.

Pius XII: Megivern, p. 368; Carlen, PE, vol. 4, pp. 179, 182.

Vatican II: Abbott, pp. 119–20, 125–26, 128.

Paul VI: Megivern, p. 424.

Biblical Commission, 1993: *Origins* 23, no. 29, 1/6/94, pp. 510–11, 517.

John Paul II: *Origins* 26, no. 25, 12/5/96, p. 415.

4. Religious Freedom

Augustine: Coste, p. 288.

Theodosian Code: Peters (1980), p. 45.

Lucius III: Burman, p. 25

Innocent III, *Vergentis:* Peters (1988), p. 48.

Innocent III, *Cum ex officii:* Peters (1988), p. 50.

Lateran IV: Tierney (1988), p. 277.

Gregory IX: Peters (1988), p. 56.

Innocent IV: Vacandard, p. 108.

Leo X, *Exsurge* and Letter: Bainton (1950), pp. 147–48.

Pius VI: Comby and MacCulloch, vol. 2, p. 113.

Gregory XVI: Carlen, PE, vol. 1, p. 237.

Pius IX: Carlen, PE, vol. 2, p. 381.

Leo XIII: Leo XIII, pp. 150f.

Pius X: Carlen, PE, vol. 3, p. 46.

Pius XI: Comby, vol. 2, p. 208

Pius XII: Rudin, p. 157.

John XXIII: Carlen, PE, vol. 5, p. 108.

Vatican II, *Religious Liberty:* Flannery (1996), pp. 552, 557, 563.

Vatican Secretariat of State: Bernstein and Politi, p. 536.

John Paul II: *Origins* 24, no. 24, 11/24/94, p. 411.

5. Ecumenism

Leo IX: Fouyas, p. 12.

Boniface VIII: Mann, vol. 18, p. 350.

Florence: Minus, p. 48.

Pius IX, 1863: Fremantle, pp. 131–32.

Holy Office, 1864: Fremantle, p. 131.

Leo XIII, *Amantissimae:* Tavard (1960), p. 61.

Leo XIII, *Provida:* Tavard (1960), p. 85.

Leo XIII, *Satis:* Carlen, PP, vol. 1, p. 403.

Leo XIII, *Apostolicae:* Leo XIII, p. 405.

Pius X: Carlen, PE, vol. 3, p. 117.

Code of Canon Law (1917): Tavard, personal communication.

Pius XI, *Discorsi:* Minus, p. 59; Tavard (1960), pp. 120–21.

Pius XI, *Mortalium Animos:* Carlen, PE, vol. 3, p. 313.

Pius XI, *Caritate Christi:* Minus, p. 50.

Holy Office (1948): Minus, p. 166.

Holy Office (1950): Minus, p. 168.

Pius XII, *Sempiternus:* Tavard (1960), p. 225.

Pius XII, Allocution: Tavard (1960), p. 227.

John XXIII: *Pope Speaks,* vol. 5, no. 4, p. 372.

Vatican II, *Decree on Ecumenism:* Abbott, pp. 348, 352; Flannery (1996), p. 508.

Vatican II, *Dogmatic Constitution:* Flannery (1996), pp. 17, 22.

Paul VI: *L'Osservatore Romano,* 12/3/70.

Code of Canon Law (1983), p. 319.

John Paul II, *Ut unum sint:* Miller, pp. 933, 944, 973.

John Paul II, Vespers: *Origins* 26, no. 27, p. 439.

John Paul II, *Tertio: Origins* 24, no. 24, 11/24/94, p. 410.

6. The Jewish People

Church fathers: Lapide, p. 25.

Gregory I: Schweitzer, p. 132.

Calixtus II: Schweitzer, p. 135.

Decretum: Noonan (1982), p. 94.

Innocent III, *Licet:* Grayzel (1933), p. 93.

Innocent III, 1201: Grayzel (1966), p. 103.

Innocent III, 1205: Grayzel (1966), p. 115.

Innocent III, 1208: Grayzel (1966), p. 127.

Arles: Grayzel (1966), p. 327.

Gregory IX, no punishment enough: Cohen (1982), p. 66.

Gregory IX, letter: Grayzel (1933), p. 243.

Innocent IV: Grayzel (1966), p. 269.

Alexander IV: Chazan, p. 177.

Clement IV: Grayzel (1989), p. 15.

Nicholas III: Cohen (1982), p. 83.

Clement VI: Synan, p. 133.

Basel: Gilchrist, p. 217.

Innocent VIII: Lapide, p. 56.

Paul IV: Stow, pp. 5–6.

Benedict XIV: Carlen, PE, vol. 1, p. 43.

Pius IX: Kertzer, p. 260.

Holy Office: Passelecq and Suchecky, p. 98

Pius XI: Passelecq and Suchecky, pp. 138–39.

Paul VI: Riegner in Perry and Schweitzer, p. 301.

Conversion Prayer: Lefebvre, p. 497.

John XXIII, meeting: Lapide, p. 323.

John XXIII, prayer: Lapide, overleaf.

Vatican II, *Non-Christian Religions:* Flannery (1996), p. 573.

John Paul II, 1986: Bernstein and Politi, pp. 443–44.

John Paul II, 1990: Fisher in Perry and Schweitzer, p. 415.

John Paul II, 1994: *Origins* 23, no. 45, 4/28/94, p. 784.

John Paul II, 1995: *Origins* 24, no. 34, 2/9/95, p. 562.

Commission: USCC, pp. 7, 11–12.

7. Slavery

Gangra: Maxwell, p. 30.

Gregory I, manumission: Maxwell, p. 41.

Gregory I, *Pastoral Rule:* Schaff, vol. 12, Pt. 2, p. 28.

Gregory I, *Expositio:* Maxwell, p. 36; *Morals,* p. 534.

Toledo: Maxwell, p. 37.

Urban II: Somerville and Kuttner, p. 261.

Decretum: Deedy (1972), p. 28.

Alexander III: Maxwell, p. 34.

Lateran III and IV: Maxwell, p. 48; Tanner, p. 270.

Nicholas V: Maxwell, p. 53.

Pius II: Maxwell, p. 52.

Paul III, *Sublimis:* Maxwell, p. 70.

Paul III, *Motu:* Maxwell, p. 75.

Pius V: Maxwell, p. 76.

Gregory XIV: Maxwell, p. 71.

Urban VIII: Maxwell, p. 72.

Urban VIII et al.: Maxwell, pp. 76–77.

Holy Office: Maxwell, p. 78.

Benedict XIV: Maxwell, p. 73.

Index: Maxwell, p. 99.

Gregory XVI: Davis, pp. 39–40.

Holy Office: Maxwell, pp. 78–79; context: Morris, p. 78.

Pius IX: Maxwell, p. 20.

Leo XIII: Maxwell, p. 117.

Leo XIII, *Rerum:* Maxwell, p. 120.

Canon Law: Maxwell, p. 122.

Vatican II: Maxwell, p. 12.

8. Democracy in the Church

Celestine: Küng in Bianchi and Ruether, p. 89.

Leo I: Letter 10, no. 6, Schaff, vol. XII, p. 11.

Toledo: Benson, p. 56.

Leo IX: Küng in Bianchi and Ruether, p. 90.

Nicholas II: Pullen, p. 54.

Gregory VII: Comby, vol. 1, p. 137.

Lateran II: Tanner, vol. 1, p. 203.

Boniface VIII, *Unam sanctam:* Comby, Vol. I, p. 173.

Clement VI: Granfield, p. 36.

Constance: Bokenkotter (1979), p. 200; Bianchi and Ruether, p. 58; Crowder, pp. 128–29.

Pius II: Crowder, p. 180.

Vatican I: Deedy (1990), p. 259.

Pius X: Comby and MacCulloch, vol. 2, p. 161.

Pius XI: Coleman in Bianchi and Ruether, p. 232.

Pius XII: Carlen, PE, vol. 4, p. 178.

Vatican II: Flannery (1996), pp. 12, 50, 28–30.

Paul VI: Coleman in Bianchi and Ruether, p. 227.

Synod: NCCB, p. 44.

John Paul II: Swidler and O'Brien, p. 116.

Code of Canon Law, no. 377, p. 139; no. 208, p. 71.

John Paul II, *Veritatis splendor:* Miller, p. 765.

9. Theological Dissent

Augustine: Coste, p. 288.

Theodosian Code: Peters (1980), p. 45.

Decretum: Schatz, p. 95.

Lateran III: Peters (1980), p. 168.

Lucius III: Burman, p. 25.

Innocent III: Peters (1988), p. 50.

Lateran IV: Tierney (1988), p. 277.

Gregory IX: Peters (1988), p. 56.

Innocent IV: Vacandard, p. 108.

Alexander IV: Lea (1888), p. 575.

John XXII, 1317: Burman, p. 65.

John XXII, 1319: Guirard, p. 87.

John XXII, *Cum inter nonnullos:* Peters (1980), p. 247.

Lateran V: Megivern, p. 178.

Leo X, *Exsurge* and Letter: Bainton (1950), pp. 147–48.

Trent: Schroeder, p. 278.

Pius VI: Comby and MacCulloch, vol. 2, p. 113.

Gregory XVI: Carlen, PE, vol. 1, p. 237.

Pius IX: Carlen, PE, vol. 1, p. 382.

Vatican I: Comby and MacCulloch, vol. 2, p. 136.

Leo XIII, *Instructio:* Carlen, PE, vol. 3, p. 96.

Pius X: Carlen, PE, vol. 3, pp. 89, 93f.

Pius XI, 1923: Swidler and O'Brien, p. 59.

Pius XI, *Mortalium:* Comby and MacCulloch, vol. 2, p. 208.

Pius XII, *Mystici:* Rudin, p. 157.

John XXIII: Carlen, PE, vol. 5, p. 108.

Vatican II, *Dogmatic Constitution:* Flannery (1996), p. 56.

Vatican II, *Relation:* Flannery (1996), pp. 570–71.

Vatican II, *Religious Liberty:* Flannery (1996), p. 566.

Vatican II, *Pastoral Constitution:* McCarthy, p. 75.

Paul VI: Catholic Theological Society (1990), p. 84.

CDF, *Professio:* Catholic Theological Society (1990), p. 84.

CDF, Instruction: McCarthy, p. 135.

John Paul II: *Origins* 24, no. 24, 11/24/94, p. 411.

CDF, *Notification: Origins* 26, no. 32, 1/30/97, p. 529.

10. Women in the Church

Tertullian: Young, p. 46.

Cyril, Ambrose, Chrysostom: Ranke-Heinemann, pp. 128ff.

Didascalia: Higgins, p. 90.

Constitutiones: Higgins, pp. 88–89; Moll, p. 127; Ranke-Heinemann, p. 128.

Synod of Laodicea: Ranke-Heinemann, p. 132.

Gelasius: Rossi, p. 81.

Gregory I: Schaff, vol. 13, p. 78.

Synod of Paris: Ranke-Heinemann, p. 133.

Urban II: Higgins, p. 89.

Decretum: Tavard (1977), p. 99.

Hadrian IV: van der Meer, p. 117.

Innocent III: Innocent III, p. 9.

Gregory IX: van der Meer, p. 116.

Boniface VIII: Bernstein, p. 22.

Paul III: van der Meer, p. 118.

Pius X: Hayburn, p. 220.

Canon Law, 1917: Ranke-Heinemann, p. 133.

Pius XII: Carlen, PE, vol. 4, p. 288.

John XXIII: Carlen, PE, vol. 5, p. 109.

Paul VI, E *motivo:* Gudorf, p. 324.

Vatican II: Flannery (1996), p. 194.

Paul VI, *Ministeria: Pope Speaks,* vol. 17, no. 1, p. 261.

Paul VI, *Soyez:* Gudorf, p. 322.

Commentary: *Origins* 6, no. 33, 2/3/77, pp. 529–30.

Congregation for Sacraments: *Origins* 10, no. 2, 5/29/80, p. 43.

John Paul II, *Mulieris: Origins* 18, no. 17, 10/6/99, p. 273.

John Paul II, 1994: Bernstein and Politi, p. 538.

John Paul II, *Ordinatio: Origins* 24, no. 4, 6/9/94, p. 51.

John Paul II, *Christi: Origins* 25, no. 13, 9/14/95, p. 202.

CDF: Ratzinger, p. 1.

11. Married Clergy

Elvira: Prince, p. 15.

Gangra: Schaff, vol. 14, p. 93.

Leo I: Harkx, p. 43.

Hilarius: Harkx, p. 33.

Gregory I: Schaff, vol. 13, p. 75.

Trullo: Schaff, vol. 14, pp. 362–63.

Paiva: Schillebeeckx, p. 43.

Gregory VII: *New Catholic Encyclopedia,* vol. 3, p. 373.

Urban II: Somerville and Kuttner, p. 261.

Innocent II: Ranke-Heinemann, p. 110.

Lateran II: Tanner, p. 198.

Trent: Schroeder, p. 182.

Pius XI: Carlen, PE, vol. 3, p. 505.

Paul VI, *Sacerdotalis:* Carlen, PE, vol. 5, p. 210.

Paul VI, *Abbiamo:* Carlen, PP, vol. 2, p. 469.

John Paul II, 1990: *Origins* 20, no. 21, 11/90, p. 334.

John Paul II, 1993: *L'Osservatore Romano,* 3/18/93.

Popes sons of priests; noncelibate popes: McBrien (1997), passim.

12. Sexual Intimacy

Augustine: Schaff, vol. 6, Sermon 1, p. 254.

Leo I: Schaff, vol. 12, p. 131.

Gregory I, Letter: Schaff, vol. 13, p. 78.

Gregory I, Pastoral Rule: Schaff, vol. 12, p. 57.

Nicholas I: Ranke-Heinemann, p. 140.

Leo IX: Catholic Theological Society (1979), p. 220.

Innocent II: Ranke-Heinemann, p. 110.

Decretum: Noonan (1982), pp. 262f.

Innocent III: Innocent III, pp. 8–9.

Innocent IV: Noonan (1986), pp. 263–64.

Eugene IV: Noonan (1986), p. 276.

Trent: Schroeder, p. 182.

Pius XI, *Casti:* Carlen, PE, vol. 3, pp. 394f.

Pius XII: *Tablet,* 11/10/51, p. 342; Noonan (1986), p. 493.

Vatican II, *Pastoral Constitution:* Flannery (1996), p. 222.

Paul VI: Carlen, PE, vol. 5, pp. 226–27.

CDF, Declaration: *Origins* 5, no. 31, 1/22/76, pp. 489–90.

CDF, Ruling: *Origins* 7, no. 11, 9/1/77, p. 163.

CDF, Statement: *Origins* 8, no. 11, 8/30/79, p. 168.

John Paul II, Audience: *Origins* 10, no. 18, 10/16/80, p. 303.

John Paul II, *Familiaris: Origins* 11, no. 28, p. 443.

John Paul II, Love: Wojtyla, pp. 229–30.

Code of Canon Law, p. 397.

Instruction: Briggs, p. 225.

CDF, Letter: *Origins* 16, no. 21, 11/6/86, p. 379.

CDF, "Some Considerations": *Origins* 22, no. 10, 8/6/92, p. 176.

13. Contraception

Augustine: Noonan (1986), p. 129.

Decretum: Noonan (1982), p. 172.

Gregory IX: Noonan (1986), p. 178.

Innocent VIII: Kors and Peters, p. 108.

Sixtus V: Noonan (1986), pp. 362–63.

Gregory XIV: Hurst, p. 15.

Holy Office: Noonan (1970), pp. 33–34.

Pius XI: Carlen, PE, vol. 3, p. 393.

Pius XII, Address to Midwives: *Tablet* 198, p. 342; Noonan (1986), p. 493.

Pius XII, Address to Association: *Catholic Mind* 49, pp. 310–11.

Vatican II: Flannery (1996), p. 225.

Papal Commission: Callahan in Swidler and O'Brien, p. 153.

Paul VI: Carlen, PE, vol. 5, pp. 226f.

John Paul II: Miller, pp. 802–3.

14. Divorce and Remarriage

Tertullian: Roberts and Donaldson, vol. 3, p. 405.

Toledo: Mackin, p. 234.

Gregory II: Wrenn, p. 138.

Compiègne: Mackin, p. 237.

Bourges: Kaufman, p. 123.

Alexander III, *Decretals:* Denzinger, p. 155.

Alexander III, Letter: Mackin, p. 307.

Innocent IV: Noonan (1970), pp. 263–64.

Trent: Wrenn, p. 140.

Canon Law 1917: Steininger, pp. 117–18; Steininger, p. 44.

John Paul II, *Familiaris: Pope Speaks* 27, 1982, p. 73.

Catechism: pp. 573–74.

Council on Family: *Origins* 26, no. 38, 3/13/97, p. 626.

John Paul II, 1997: *Origins* 26, no. 35, 2/20/97, p. 584.

15. Copernican Theory

Galileo biographical information: Finocchiaro, passim.

Vatican Consultants' Report: Finocchiaro, p. 146.

Sentence of Galileo: Finocchiaro, p. 291.

Leo XIII: Leo XIII, pp. 294–95.

Vatican II: Flannery (1996), p. 201.

John Paul II, Address (1979): *Origins* 9, no. 24, 11/29/79, p. 391.

John Paul II, Address (1992): *Origins* 22, no. 22, 11/12/92, pp. 372–73.

Poupard: *Origins* 22, no. 21, 11/5/92, pp. 574–75.

16. Evolution

Alexander III: White, p. 386.

Pius IX: White, p. 75.

Biblical Commission: Messenger, pp. 227–28.

Pius XII: Carlen, PE, vol. 4, pp. 176, 178, 180, 181.

Paul VI: Neuner and Dupuis, p. 133.

John Paul II: *Pope Speaks* 42, no. 2, pp. 119–20.

17. War and Peace

Justin Martyr: McSorley, pp. 70–71.

Tertullian: Musto (1996), p. 35.

Origen: Decosse, p. 111.

Didascalia: Musto (1986), p. 59.

Sirmium: Musto (1986), p. 59.

Augustine, Letter: Musto (1996), p. 49.

Augustine, *City:* Bainton, pp. 95–96.

Nicholas I: Musto (1986), p. 64.

Narbonne: Decosse, p. 112.

Urban II: Vaux, pp. 109–10.

Lateran II: Tanner, p. 199.

Decretum: Musto (1986), p. 104.

Innocent III, 1204: Godfrey, p. 148.

Innocent III, 1207: Riley-Smith, pp. 79–80.

Martin V: McBrien (1997), p. 255.

Julius II: McBrien (1997), p. 270.

Paul III: Musto (1986), pp. 141–42.

Synod: Musto (1986), p. 143.

Leo XIII, *Quod:* Musto (1996), p. 315.

Leo XIII, *Notis:* Musto (1986), p. 170.

Benedict XV, *Ad Beatissimi:* Carlen, PE, vol. 3, pp. 143–44.

Benedict XV, *Pacem:* Carlen, PE, vol. 3, p. 174.

Pius XI: Carlen, PE, vol. 3, p. 227.

Pius XII, *Un'Ora:* Musto (1986), p. 176.

Pius XII, 1954: Decosse, p. 118.

Pius XII, 1955: Decosse, p. 119.

Pius XII, 1957: *New Catholic Encyclopedia,* vol. 14, p. 804.

Pius XII, 1959: Decosse, p. 118.

John XXIII: Decosse, p. 120.

Vatican II, *Pastoral Constitution:* Flannery, pp. 263–68.

John Paul II: Decosse, p. 122.

18. Usury

Nicaea: Gilchrist, p. 155.

Aix: Hulme, p. 41.

Lateran II, III, IV: Gilchrist, pp. 165, 173, 182–83.

Clement V: Gilchrist, p. 206.

Nicholas V: Lapide, pp. 56–57.

Lateran V: Gilchrist, p. 115; Tanner, p. 627.

Innocent XI: Hulme, p. 51.

Benedict XIV: Carlen, PE, vol. 1, pp. 16–17.

Holy Office: Hulme, p. 57.

Pius VIII: Hulme, p. 55.

Pius IX: Lapide, p. 57.

Code of Canon Law (1917): Hulme, p. 56.

Pius XII: *Catholic Mind* 49, p. 332.

Code of Canon Law (1983), pp. 458–59.

BIBLIOGRAPHY

Abbott, Walter M., SJ, ed. *The Documents of Vatican II.* New York: Guild Press, 1966.

Acta Apostolicae Sedis 38 (Vatican, 1940): p. 141.

Aquinas, Thomas. *Summa Theologica,* Vol. 2. Westminster, Md.: Christian Classics, 1981.

Bainton, Roland H. *Here I Stand: A Life of Martin Luther.* New York: Abingdon Press, 1950.

——. *Christian Attitudes toward War and Peace.* New York: Abingdon Press, 1960.

Bassett, William W. *The Bond of Marriage.* Notre Dame, Ind.: University of Notre Dame Press, 1968.

Benson, Robert L. "Election by Community and Chapter: Reflections on Co-responsibility in the Historical Church." In Coriden, pp. 54–80.

Bernstein, Carl, and Marco Politi. *His Holiness.* New York: Doubleday, 1996.

Bernstein, Marcelle. *The Nuns.* Philadelphia: J. B. Lippincott, 1976.

Berry, Thomas, with Stephen Dunn, Anne Lonergan, and Thomas E. Clarke. *Befriending the Earth: A Theology of Reconciliation between Humans and the Earth.* Mystic, Conn.: Twenty-Third Publications, 1991.

"Beware Murky World of 'Secondary Truth.' " *National Catholic Reporter,* editorial, June 6, 1997, p. 24.

Bianchi, Eugene, and Rosemary Ruether. *A Democratic Catholic Church.* New York: Crossroad, 1992.

Boff, Leonardo. *Ecology and Liberation: A New Paradigm.* Maryknoll, N.Y.: Orbis Books, 1995.

Bokenkotter, Thomas. *A Concise History of the Catholic Church.* New York: Doubleday, 1979.

——. *Essential Catholicism: Dynamics and Belief.* New York: Doubleday, 1985.

Briggs, Kenneth. *Holy Siege: The Year That Shook Catholic America.* San Francisco: Harper, 1992.

Brown, Raymond, Joseph A. Fitzmyer, and Roland E. Murphy, eds. *The New Jerome Biblical Commentary.* Englewood Cliffs, N.J.: Prentice-Hall, 1990.

Brundage, James A. "Marriage and Sexuality in the Decretals of Alexander III." In *Miscellanea Rolando Bandinelli Papa Alessandro III.* Siena: Accademia Senese degli Intronati, 1986, pp. 57–84.

Burman, Edward. *The Inquisition: The Hammer of Heresy.* Wellingborough, Northants, U.K.: Aquarian Press, 1984.

Burr, David. *Olivi and Franciscan Poverty: The Origins of the Usus Pauper Controversy.* Philadelphia: University of Pennsylvania Press, 1989.

Carlen, Claudia, IHM. *The Papal Encyclicals.* Ann Arbor, Mich.: The Pierian Press, 1990.

————. *The Papal Pronouncements.* Ann Arbor, Mich: The Pierian Press, 1990.

Catechism of the Catholic Church. Washington, D.C.: U.S. Catholic Conference, 1994.

Catholic Mind (monthly). New York: America Press.

Catholic Theological Society of America. *Human Sexuality: New Directions in American Catholic Thought.* New York: Paulist Press, 1979.

————. *Report of Committee on the Profession of Faith and Oath of Fidelity.* Washington, D.C., April 1990.

Chamberlain, Gay, and Patrick Howell, eds. *Empowering Authority.* New York: Sheed & Ward, 1990.

Charlesworth, James H., ed. *Overcoming Fear between Jews and Christians.* New York: Crossroad, 1993.

Chazan, Robert, ed. *Church, State and Jew in the Middle Ages.* West Orange, N.J.: Behrman House, 1980.

Cheetham, Nicolas. *Keepers of the Keys: A History of the Popes from Peter to John Paul II.* New York: Scribner, 1986.

Cheney, C. R., and Mary G. Cheney, eds. *Letters of Pope Innocent III Concerning England and Wales.* Oxford, U.K.: Clarendon Press, 1967.

Cheney, C. R., and W. H. Semple. *Selected Letters of Pope Innocent III Concerning England (1198–1216).* London: Nelson, 1953.

Code of Canon Law. Washington, D.C.: Canon Law Society of America, 1983.

Cohen, Jeremy. *The Friars and the Jews: The Evolution of Medieval Anti-Judaism.* Ithaca, N.Y.: Cornell University Press, 1982.

————. "Recent Historiography on the Medieval Church and the Decline of European Jewry." In Sweeney and Chodorow, pp. 251–62.

Coleman, Gerald D. *Divorce and Remarriage in the Catholic Church.* New York: Paulist, 1988.

Coleman, John, SJ. "Not Democracy but Democratization." In Bianchi and Ruether, pp. 226–47.

Comby, Jean. *How to Read Church History,* Vol. 1. New York: Crossroad, 1985.

————, and Diarmaid MacCulloch. *How to Read Church History,* Vol. 2. New York: Crossroad, 1989.

Commission for Religious Relations with Jews. "We Remember: A Reflection on the *Shoah.*" Washington, D.C.: U.S. Catholic Conference, 1998.

Coppa, Frank J. *Pope Pius IX: Crusader in a Secular Age.* Boston: Twayne Publishers, 1979.

Coriden, James, ed. *Who Decides for the Church? Studies in Co-responsibility.* Hartford, Conn.: Canon Law Society, 1971.

Coste, Réné. *Theologie de la liberté réligieuse.* Gembloux, Belgium: Editions J. Duculot, 1969.

Crowder, C. M. D. *Unity, Heresy and Reform, 1378–1460.* New York: St. Martin's Press, 1977.

Curran, Charles E. *New Perspectives in Moral Theology.* University of Notre Dame, Ind.: Notre Dame Press, 1976.

Davis, Cyprian. *Black Catholics in the United States.* New York: Crossroad, 1990.

Decosse, David E., ed. *But Was It Just? Reflections on the Morality of the Persian Gulf War.* New York: Doubleday, 1992.

Deedy, John. *What a Modern Catholic Believes about Conscience, Freedom and Authority.* Chicago: Thomas More Press, 1972.

———. *Retrospect: The Origins of Catholic Beliefs and Practices.* Chicago: Thomas More Press, 1990.

———. *Facts, Myths and Maybes.* Chicago: Thomas More Press, 1993.

Denzinger, Henry. *The Sources of Catholic Dogma.* St. Louis and London: Herder, 1955.

deRosa, Peter. *Vicars of Christ: The Dark Side of the Papacy.* New York: Crown, 1988.

Dulles, Avery, SJ. *Theology and the Magisterium: Proceedings of the Catholic Theological Society* 31 (1976).

Dundes, Alan, ed. *The Blood Libel Legend: A Casebook in Anti-Semitic Folklore.* Madison: University of Wisconsin Press, 1991.

Ellis, John T., ed. *Documents of American Catholic History.* Wilmington, Del.: Michael Glazier, 1987.

Finocchiaro, Maurice A., ed. *The Galileo Affair: A Documentary History.* Berkeley: University of California Press, 1989.

Fisher, Eugene J. "Pope John Paul II's Pilgrimage of Reconciliation." In Perry and Schweitzer, pp. 405–24.

Flannery, Austin, OP, ed. *Vatican Council II: The Conciliar and Post-conciliar Documents.* Dublin: Dominican Publications, 1992.

———, ed. *The Basic Sixteen Documents: Vatican Council II Constitutions, Decrees, Declarations.* Northport, N.Y.: Costello Publishing Co., 1996.

Fouyas, Methodios. *Orthodoxy, Roman Catholicism and Anglicanism.* London: Oxford University Press, 1972.

Fox, Thomas C. *Sexuality and Catholicism.* New York: Braziller, 1995.

Fremantle, Anne. *The Papal Encyclicals in Their Historical Context.* New York: New American Library, 1963.

Gaillardetz, Richard. *Witnesses to the Faith: Community, Infallibility and the Ordinary Magisterium.* New York: Paulist Press, 1992.

Gilchrist, J. *The Church and Economic Activity in the Middle Ages.* London: Macmillan, 1969.

Godfrey, John. *1204, The Unholy Crusade.* New York: Oxford University Press, 1980.

Granfield, Patrick. *The Limits of the Papacy: Authority and Autonomy in the Church.* New York: Crossroad, 1987.

Grayzel, Solomon. *The Church and the Jews in the Thirteenth Century.* Philadelphia: Dropsie College, 1933; rev. ed., vol. 1: 1198–1254, New York: Herman Press, 1966; vol. 2: 1254–1314, Kenneth Stow, ed., New York: Jewish Theological Seminary, 1989.

Gudorf, Christine. *Catholic Social Teaching on Liberation Themes.* Lanham, Md.: University Press of America, 1980.

Guirard, Jean. *The Mediaeval Inquisition.* New York: Benziger, 1930.

Harkx, Peter. *The Fathers on Celibacy.* DePere, Wis.: St. Norbert Abbey Press, 1968.

Hayburn, Robert F. *Papal Legislation on Sacred Music, 95 AD to 1977 AD.* Collegeville, Minn.: Liturgical Press, 1979.

Helgeland, J., R. J. Daly, and P. J. Burns, eds. *Christians and the Military.* London: SCM, 1985.

Higgins, Jean. "Fidelity in History." In L. and A. Swidler, pp. 85–91.

Hulme, Anthony. *Morals and Money.* London: St. Paul, 1957.

Hurst, Jane. *The History of Abortion in the Catholic Church.* Washington, D.C.: Catholics for a Free Choice, 1989.

Innocent III. *On the Misery of the Human Condition,* D. R. Howard, ed. New York: Bobbs-Merrill, 1969.

Jans, Jan. "Freedom of Science and Research." In *Disciples and Discipline: European Debate on Human Rights in the Roman Catholic Church,* C. Van der Stichele et al., eds. Leuven: Peeters, 1993, pp. 113–24.

Johnson, Elizabeth. *Women, Earth and Creator Spirit.* New York: Paulist, 1993.

Johnson, James Turner, and George Weigel. *Just War and the Gulf War.* Lanham, Md.: University Press of America, 1991.

Kaufman, Philip S., OSB. *Why You Can Disagree and Remain a Faithful Catholic.* New York: Crossroad, 1995.

Kertzer, David. *The Kidnapping of Edgardo Mortara.* New York: Knopf, 1997.

King, Geoffrey. "Reception, Consensus and Church Law." In *The Tabu of Democracy within the Church,* James Provost and Knut Wolf, eds. London: SCM Press, 1992.

Kors, Alan, and Edward Peters, eds. *Witchcraft in Europe, 1100–1700: A Documentary History.* Philadelphia: University of Pennsylvania Press, 1972.

Küng, Hans. "Participation of the Laity in Church Leadership and in Church Elections." In Bianchi and Ruether, pp. 80–93.

———. *Infallible?* New York: Continuum, 1994.

Kurtz, Lester R. *The Politics of Heresy: The Modernist Crisis in Roman Catholicism.* Berkeley: University of California Press, 1986.

Lambert, Malcolm. *Medieval Heresy: Popular Movements from the Gregorian Reform to the Reformation.* Oxford: Blackwell, 1992.

Langford, Jerome. *Galileo, Science, and the Church.* New York: Desclée, 1966.

Langmuir, Gavin. *History, Religion, and Anti-Semitism.* Berkeley: University of California Press, 1990.

Lapide, Pinchas. *Three Popes and the Jews.* New York: Hawthorne Books, 1967.

Lea, Henry Charles. *History of the Inquisition of the Middle Ages.* New York: Harper & Bros., 1888.

———. *History of Sacerdotal Celibacy in the Christian Church.* New York: Russell & Russell, 1957.

———. *The Inquisition of the Middle Ages: Its Organization and Operation.* London: Eyre & Spottiswoode, 1963 (abridged version of 1888 edition).

Lefebvre, Gaspar. *The St. Andrew Daily Missal.* St. Paul, Minn.: E. M. Lohmann, 1957.

Legrand, Herve-Marie. "Theology and the Election of Bishops in the Early Church," *Concilium 77* (1972), pp. 31–42.

Leo XIII. *The Great Encyclical Letters of Leo XIII.* New York: Benziger, 1903.

Loisy, Alfred. *My Duel with the Vatican.* New York: Greenwood Press, 1968.

L'Osservatore Romano (weekly). Vatican City.

Mackin, Theodore, SJ. *Divorce and Remarriage.* New York: Paulist Press, 1984.

Maguire, Daniel. "Moral Absolutes and the Magisterium," *Corpus Papers,* 1970.

Mann, Horace K. *Lives of the Popes in the Middle Ages.* Vol. 18. London: Kegan Paul, 1932.

Martos, Joseph. *Doors to the Sacred: A Historical Introduction to Sacraments in the Catholic Church.* Garden City, N.Y.: Doubleday, 1982.

Maxwell, John F. *Slavery and the Catholic Church: The History of Catholic Teaching Concerning the Moral Legitimacy of the Institution of Slavery.* Chichester, U.K.: Anti-Slavery Society, 1975.

McBrien, Richard P. "Two Views of the Church: The U.S. and the Vatican." In Chamberlain and Howell, pp. 81–102.

———. *Harper-Collins Encyclopedia of Catholicism.* 1994, 1995.

———. *Lives of the Popes.* San Francisco: Harper, 1997.

McCarthy, T. G. *The Catholic Tradition before and after Vatican II, 1878–1993.* Chicago: Loyola University Press, 1994.

McClory, Robert. *Turning Point.* New York: Crossroad, 1995.

———. *Power and the Papacy.* Liguori, Mo.: Liguori Publications, 1997.

McNamara, Jo Ann Kay. *Sisters in Arms.* Cambridge, Mass.: Harvard University Press, 1996.

McSorley, Richard. *New Testament Basis of Peacemaking.* Scottdale, Pa.: Herald Press, 1985.

Megivern, James. *Bible Interpretation.* Wilmington, N.C.: McGrath, 1978.

Messenger, Ernest. *Evolution and Theology: The Problem of Man's Origin.* New York: Macmillan, 1932.

Miller, J. Michael, ed. *The Encyclicals of John Paul II.* Huntingdon, Ind.: Our Sunday Visitor, 1996.

Minus, Paul M. *Catholic Rediscovery of Protestantism.* New York: Paulist Press, 1976.

Moll, Helmut, ed. *The Church and Women: A Compendium.* San Francisco: Ignatius Press, 1988.

Morals on the Book of Job [by Gregory I]. Vol. 2, part 4. Oxford: Parker, 1845.

Morris, Charles. *American Catholic.* New York: Random House, 1997.

Musto, Ronald. *The Catholic Peace Tradition.* Maryknoll, N.Y.: Orbis Books, 1986.

————, ed. *Catholic Peacemakers: A Documentary History.* Vol. 2: *From the Renaissance to the Twentieth Century.* New York: Garland Publishing, 1996.

National Conference of Catholic Bishops. *Justice in the World* (Second Synod of Bishops, 1967). Washington, D.C., 1971.

Neuner, J., SJ, and J. Dupuis, SJ. *The Christian Faith in the Doctrinal Documents of the Catholic Church.* Westminster, Md.: Christian Classics, 1975.

New Catholic Encyclopedia. New York: McGraw-Hill, 1967.

Noonan, John T. *The Scholastic Analysis of Usury.* Cambridge, Mass.: Harvard University Press, 1957.

————. "An Almost Absolute Value in History." In *The Morality of Abortion: Legal and Historical Perspectives,* J. T. Noonan, ed. Cambridge, Mass.: Harvard University Press, 1970, pp. 1–59.

————. *Power to Dissolve: Lawyers and Marriages in the Courts of the Roman Curia.* Cambridge, Mass.: Harvard University Press, 1972.

————, trans. *Gratian, Decretum. Pars 2, Causae 27–36.* N.p., 1982.

————. *Contraception.* Cambridge, Mass.: Harvard University Press, 1986.

O'Neill, David P. *Priestly Celibacy and Maturity.* New York: Sheed & Ward, 1965.

Origins: CNS Documentary Service (weekly). Catholic News Service, Washington, D.C.

Passelecq, Georges, and Bernard Suchecky. *The Hidden Encyclical of Pius XI.* New York: Harcourt Brace, 1997.

Paul VI, Pope. *On the Development of Peoples.* Washington, D.C.: U.S. Catholic Conference, 1967.

Pawlikowski, John T. "The Vatican and the Holocaust: Unresolved Issues." In Schweitzer and Perry, pp. 293–312.

Perry, Marvin, and Frederick M. Schweitzer, eds. *Jewish-Christian Encounters over the Centuries.* New York: Peter Lang, 1994.

Peters, Edward. *Inquisition*. Berkeley: University of California Press, 1988.
———, ed. *Heresy and Authority in Medieval Europe*. Philadelphia: University of Pennsylvania Press, 1980.

Pius XII. *Munificentissimus Deus*. Washington, D.C.: National Catholic Welfare Conference [1950].

Pope Speaks, The (bimonthly). Huntingdon, Ind.: Our Sunday Visitor.

Powell, James M., ed. *Innocent III: Vicar of Christ or Lord of the World?* Washington, D.C.: Catholic University Press, 1994, 2nd edition.

Priests for Equality. *The Inclusive New Testament*. Brentwood, Md.: Quixote Center, 1996.

Prince, Michele. *Mandatory Celibacy in the Catholic Church*. Pasadena: New Paradigm Books, 1992.

Pullen, Brian. *Sources for the History of Medieval Europe from the Mid-eighth to the Mid-thirteenth Century*. New York: Barnes & Noble, 1966.

Ranke-Heinemann, Ute. *Eunuchs for the Kingdom of Heaven: Women, Sexuality, and the Catholic Church*. New York: Doubleday, 1990.

Ratzinger, Joseph. "Reply to the Dubium." Rome: Vatican, October 28, 1995.

Riegner, Gerhart. "A Warning to the World: The Efforts of the World Jewish Congress to Mobilize Christian Churches against the Final Solution." In Perry and Schweitzer, p. 301.

Riga, Peter. "Pope Paul VI and Celibacy." In *Married Priests and Married Nuns*, J. F. Colaianni, ed. New York: McGraw Hill, 1965, pp. 69–104.

Riley-Smith, Louise and Jonathan. *The Crusades: Idea and Reality, 1095–1274*. London: E. Arnold, 1981.

Roberts, Alexander, and James Donaldson, eds. *The Ante-Nicene Fathers: Translations of the Writings of the Fathers Down to AD 325*. Grand Rapids, Mich.: Eerdmans, 1989.

Rossi, Mary Ann. "Priesthood, Precedent and Prejudice: On Recovering the Women Priests of Early Christianity." *Journal of Feminist Studies in Religion* (May 1991): 73–94.

Rudin, Josef. "A Catholic View of Conscience." In *Conscience*, C. G. Jung Institute, ed. Evanston, Ill.: Northwestern University Press, 1970.

Russell, Frederick H. *The Just War in the Middle Ages*. London: Cambridge University Press, 1975.

Schaff, Philip, ed. *A Select Library of the Nicene and Post-Nicene Fathers of the Christian Church*. Grand Rapids, Mich.: Eerdmans, 1980.

Schatz, Klaus. *Papal Primacy from Its Origins to the Present*. Collegeville, Minn.: Liturgical Press, 1996.

Schillebeeckx, E. *Celibacy*. New York: Sheed & Ward, 1968.

Schroeder, H. J., OP. *Canons and Decrees of the Council of Trent*. London: Herder, 1941.

Schweitzer, Frederick. "Medieval Perceptions of Jews and Judaism." In Perry and Schweitzer, pp. 131–68.

Shannon, Albert C. *The Popes and Heresy in the Thirteenth Century.* Villanova, Pa.: Augustinian Press, 1949.

Sipe, A. W. R. *A Secret World: Sexuality and the Search for Celibacy.* New York: Brunner/Mazel, 1990.

Smith, Janet. *Humanae Vitae: A Generation Later.* Washington, D.C.: Catholic University Press, 1991.

Somerville, Robert, in collaboration with Stephan Kuttner. *Pope Urban II, the Collectio Britannica, and the Council of Melfi (1089).* Oxford: Clarendon Press, 1996.

Steininger, Viktor. *Divorce: Arguments for a Change in the Church's Discipline.* London: Sheed & Ward, 1969.

Stow, Kenneth R. *Catholic Thought and Papal Jewry Policy 1555–1593.* New York: Jewish Theological Seminary of America, 1977.

Sullivan, Francis. *Creative Fidelity: Weighing and Interpreting the Documents of the Magisterium.* New York: Paulist Press, 1996.

Sweeney, James R., and Stanley Chodorow, eds. *Popes, Teachers, and Canon Law in the Middle Ages.* Ithaca, N.Y.: Cornell University Press, 1989.

Swidler, Leonard, and Herbert O'Brien. *A Catholic Bill of Rights.* New York: Sheed & Ward, 1988.

Swidler, Leonard, and Arlene Swidler, eds. *Women Priests: A Catholic Commentary on the Vatican Declaration.* New York: Paulist Press, 1977.

Swimme, Brian. *Hidden Heart of the Cosmos: Humanity and the New Story.* Maryknoll, N.Y.: Orbis Books, 1996.

Synan, Edward A. *The Popes and the Jews in the Middle Ages.* New York: Macmillan, 1965.

Tablet, The (weekly). London: Tablet Publishing Co.

Tanner, Norman P., SJ, ed. *Decrees of the Ecumenical Councils.* London and Washington, D.C.: Sheed & Ward and Georgetown University Press, 1990.

Tavard, George H. *Two Centuries of Ecumenism.* London: Burns & Oates, 1960.

———. "The Scholastic Doctrine." In Swidler and Swidler, pp. 99–106.

Tierney, Brian. "Origins of Papal Infallibility." In *Journal of Ecumenical Studies* 8 (1971).

———. *Origins of Papal Infallibility, 1150–1350.* Leiden: Brill, 1988.

Vacandard, Elphhge. *The Inquisition: A Critical and Historical Study of the Coercive Power of the Church.* New York: Longmans, 1926.

van der Meer, Haye. *Women Priests in the Catholic Church? A Theological-Historical Investigation.* Philadelphia: Temple University Press, 1973.

Vaux, Kenneth L. *Ethics and the Gulf War: Religion, Rhetoric and Righteousness.* Boulder, Colo.: Westview, 1992.

Weigel, George. *Tranquillitas Ordinis.* New York: Oxford University Press, 1987.

White, Andrew Dickson. *A History of the Warfare of Science with Theology.* New York: Appleton, 1897.

Wojtyla, Karol. *Love and Responsibility.* Trans. H. T. Willetts. New York: Farrar Straus Giroux, 1981.

Woods, William. *A Casebook of Witchcraft.* New York: Putnam, 1974.

Wrenn, Lawrence G., ed. *Divorce and Remarriage in the Catholic Church.* New York: Newman Press, 1973.

Young, Serinity, ed. *An Anthology of Sacred Texts about Women.* New York: Crossroad, 1993.

EDITORS AND CONTRIBUTORS

Editors

Maureen Fiedler, SL, is a Co-Director of the Quixote Center and the National Coordinator of Catholics Speak Out, a Center project that encourages Catholics to take adult responsibility for the church. She writes and speaks widely on church issues and is a frequent commentator on National Public Radio. She is a member of the Loretto Community.

Linda Rabben is an anthropologist who has published widely on human rights, development, and environmental issues. She is the author of *Unnatural Selection: The Yanomami, the Kayapó and the Onslaught of Civilisation,* a book on Brazilian indigenous peoples, published in 1998 by the University of Washington Press and Pluto Press (U.K.). Her nonprofit organization, Human Rights Umbrella, is a sponsored project of the Quixote Center.

Contributors

Sheila Briggs is Associate Professor in the School of Religion at the University of Southern California at Los Angeles.

Charles Curran is the Elizabeth Scurlock University Professor of Human Values at Southern Methodist University in Dallas, Tex.

Charles N. Davis of Arlington, Va., is a retired U.S. government intelligence analyst and an active layman contributing many writings to the work of the church.

Christine Gudorf is Professor of Religious Studies at Florida International University in Miami.

John Haught is the Landegger Distinguished Professor of Theology at Georgetown University in Washington, D.C.

Diana Hayes is Associate Professor of Theology at Georgetown University in Washington, D.C.

Maggie Hume of Washington, D.C., is a free-lance journalist and the author of *Contraception in Catholic Doctrine: Evolution of an Earthly Code.*

Alice Laffey, SSD, is Professor of Religious Studies at the College of the Holy Cross in Worcester, Mass.

Robert McClory is Professor of Journalism at Northwestern University in Evanston, Ill.

Richard McCormick, SJ, is the John A. O'Brien Professor Emeritus of Christian Ethics at the University of Notre Dame in Indiana.

Amata Miller, IHM, is Chief Financial Officer and Associate Professor of Economics at Marygrove College in Detroit.

James Orgren is Professor of Astronomy Emeritus at the State University of New York College at Buffalo.

Anthony Padovano is Professor of American Literature and Religious Studies at Ramapo College of New Jersey, President of CORPUS/USA, and Vice-President of the International Federation of Married Priests.

Rosemary Radford Ruether is Professor of Theology at Garrett-Evangelical Theological Seminary in Evanston, Ill.

William H. Slavick is Professor of American Literature (retired) at the University of Southern Maine in Portland and Coordinator of Pax Christi/Maine.

Kenneth Stow is Professor of Jewish History at the University of Haifa in Israel.

George Tavard is Professor Emeritus of Theology at Methodist Theological School in Delaware, Ohio.

About the Quixote Center

The Quixote Center is an international justice and peace center headquartered in Brentwood, Maryland, near Washington, D.C. The Center's projects include:

- *Catholics Speak Out*, which works to empower Catholics in all walks of life to speak out as adults on important issues facing the church. One purpose of this book is to serve as a resource for Catholics who accept such responsibility;

- *Priests for Equality*, which publishes the Scriptures and lectionaries in inclusive language;

- *The Quest for Peace*, which does extensive economic development work with the poor of Nicaragua;

- *Haiti Reborn*, which promotes literacy and grassroots democracy in Haiti;

- *Equal Justice/USA*, which works against the death penalty and injustices in the U.S. criminal justice system;

- *The Prison Radio Project*, which tries to give a human voice to prisoners by broadcasting their commentaries and interviews; and

- *Human Rights Umbrella*, which helps survivors of human rights abuses in Brazil and the U.S.

For more information on the Quixote Center, contact Quixote Center, P.O. Box 5206, Hyattsville, MD 20782-0206. Ph: 301-699-0042. Fax: 301-864-2182. Web Page: *www.quixote.org.* E-mail: *quixote@igc.org.*

INDEX

abortion, 149–50, 152, 153, 154
Aix, Council of, 198
Alexander II, 75
Alexander III, 82, 160–61, 164, 178, 204
Alexander IV, 69, 76, 103
Alexander VII, 83
Ambrose, 12, 114, 122, 194
annulments, 165–67
anti-Semitism, 66–80, 199
Aristotle, 203, 204
Arles, Council of, 69
artificial insemination, 143
Augustine
  on the canon, 41
  on contraception, 149, 152, 153
  on the Jewish people, 67
  as misinterpreting Paul on divorce, 163
  on punishing heretics, 51
  on religious freedom, 46
  on sexuality, 137
  on theological dissent, 101
  on war and peace, 186, 187, 194
  on women, 122, 133
Auvergne, Council of, 68

Balasuriya, Tissa, 3, 108, 212
Basel, Council of, 70
Bellarmine, Robert, 19
Benedict VIII, 129
Benedict XIV, 71, 77, 84, 200–201, 205
Benedict XV, 36–37, 61, 190
birth control. See contraception
Boff, Leonardo, 3, 184
Boniface I, 12
Boniface VIII, 14, 55, 76, 93, 117
Bourges, Synod of, 160

Calixtus II, 68
capitalism, 52, 198
Celestine I, 92
celibacy, 144–45, 176. See also married clergy

Chrysostom, John, 67, 114
Clement of Alexandria, 146, 153
Clement IV, 70, 76, 77
Clement V, 33, 41, 199, 204
Clement VI, 14, 70, 93
Clement XI, 34, 42
clergy. See married clergy
Code of Canon Law (1917)
  on divorce and remarriage, 161
  on ecumenism, 57
  on scriptural interpretation, 36
  on slavery, 86
  on usury, 201, 205
  on women in the church, 117
Code of Canon Law (1983)
  on democracy in the church, 96
  on ecumenism, 59
  on sexuality, 143
  on usury, 201, 205
Commission for Religious Relations with the Jews, 74
Compiègne, Council of, 160
conciliarism, 19, 97–98
Congregation for the Doctrine of the Faith
  on artificial insemination, 143
  ecumenism and, 63
  on homosexuality, 144
  on infallibility, 16, 17–18, 20
  on sexuality, 142–43, 144
  on theological dissent, 108
  on women in the church, 119–20
Congregation for Sacraments and Divine Worship, 119
Congregation of the Inquisition. See Inquisition
conscience, primacy of, 22–31
Constance, Council of, 11, 14, 19, 93
Constantine, 193–94
Constantinople, Second Council of, 13
Constantinople, Third Council of, 13
contraception, 141, 147, 149–58, 176
Copernican theory, 169–77
Crusades, 188–89, 194

239

Of Related Interest

William J. O'Malley, S.J., Mitch and Kathy Finley,
Kathleen Hughes, R.S.C.J., Barbara Quinn, R.S.C.J.,
and Timothy E. O'Connell

The People's Catechism
*Edited by Raymond A. Lucker, Patrick J. Brennan,
and Michael Leach*

"*The People's Catechism* is just that: for the people, drawn from human experience, revealing grace all along the human journey. Easy to read and identify with, written in modern idiom for real people, this book will be a gift to seekers and searchers and to those who wish to appreciate better the ancient truth in an engaging, readable style. A truly contemporary catechism worth the attention of catechists, pastors, and RCIA teams."
— WILLIAM J. BAUSCH, parish priest and
author of *The Total Parish Manual*

"What the editors and authors of *The People's Catechism* have done is given flesh to *The Catechism of the Catholic Church* and reflected on it in the light of their own experience, teaching, and the living out of faith in their own lives. I especially found helpful the many examples of lived faith as applied to the sound teaching of the *Catechism*. In my own case the *Catechism* will be even a richer source because of the reflections in *The People's Catechism*."
— MOST REV. JOHN R. ROACH,
Archbishop of St. Paul and Minneapolis

0-8245-1466-1
$14.95 paperback

Please support your local bookstore, or call 1-800-395-0690.
For a free catalog, please write us at
THE CROSSROAD PUBLISHING COMPANY
370 LEXINGTON AVENUE, NEW YORK, NY 10017

We hope you enjoyed Rome Has Spoken.
Thank you for reading it.

crossroad